G_s

HC

D0253284

Environmental Politics

CCU Library
8787 W. Alameda Ave.
Lakewood, CO 80226

Environmental Politics

PUBLIC COSTS, PRIVATE REWARDS

Edited by
Michael S. Greve and Fred L. Smith, Jr.

With a Foreword by James Q. Wilson

New York
Westport, Connecticut
London

Library of Congress Cataloging-in-Publication Data

Environmental politics : public costs, private rewards / edited by
   Michael S. Greve and Fred L. Smith, Jr. ; foreword by James Q.
   Wilson.
      p.   cm.
    Includes bibliographical references and index.
    ISBN 0-275-94237-6 (alk. paper). — ISBN 0-275-94238-4 (pbk.)
    1. Environmental policy—United States. 2. Environmental policy—
Economic aspects—United States. I. Greve, Michael S. II. Smith,
Fred L. (Fred Lee).
    HC110.E5E498796   1992
    363.7'056'0973—dc20   91-44009

British Library Cataloguing in Publication Data is available.

Copyright © 1992 by Michael S. Greve and Fred L. Smith, Jr.

All rights reserved. No portion of this book may be
reproduced, by any process or technique, without the
express written consent of the publisher.

Library of Congress Catalog Card Number: 91-44009
ISBN: 0-275-94237-6
ISBN: 0-275-94238-4 (pbk.)

First published in 1992

Praeger Publishers, One Madison Avenue, New York, NY 10010
An imprint of Greenwood Publishing Group, Inc.

Printed in the United States of America

∞™

The paper used in this book complies with the
Permanent Paper Standard issued by the National
Information Standards Organization (Z39.48-1984).

10 9 8 7 6 5 4 3 2

CONTENTS

TABLES AND FIGURES

FOREWORD

Like many Americans, I am an environmentalist. I want cleaner air (especially here in Los Angeles), less erosion, and more wetland preserves and wildlife habitats. I worry that each year fewer birds nest near my home and more hillsides are scarred by thoughtless developers. I am upset when the Santa Monica beach is periodically closed because of untreated sewage overflowing into the ocean. I plant trees; I contribute to the Nature Conservancy and the Audubon Society. I cheerfully vote for referenda that will increase my taxes earmarked for conserving open space and protecting mountain lions.

I commend this volume to the reader, not because I hate environmentalism and wish to see it derailed, but because true environmentalism has already been derailed by mindless or mischievous policies that claim, wrongly, to serve the environment. This book contains several compelling examples of why good intentions are not enough and how environmental slogans have turned into private gain.

It is easy to defeat the ideological or self-interested enemies of environmental protection; it is only necessary to expose these people and their motives, and public opinion will do the rest. It is far harder to defeat the pseudo-environmentalists. They claim to be serving the public when in fact they are serving political and organizational interests of their own. These interests range from anti-market and anti-capitalist ideologies through the desire to win reelection by brandishing empty environmental slogans to a pecuniary stake in saving jobs, thwarting competitors, and selling machinery. There is, of course, nothing wrong in principle with public policy being fashioned out of a struggle among self-interested parties, any more than there is anything wrong with products being sold as a result of bargaining among self-interested consumers and producers.

What *is* wrong is allowing Congress, the courts, and the bureaucracy to shape the terms of that struggle in such a way as to insure that the resultant policies will defeat the very purposes they announce. This happens when Congress sets unrealistic timetables to achieve goals or fails to determine priorities among competing goals or when it opts for the most costly rather than the least costly means to achieve those goals. It happens when bureaucrats embrace dubious science or slogans masquerading as science. Worst of all, it happens when environmental policies are drafted, administered, or interpreted so as to confer subsidies on groups by protecting their markets, their jobs, or their causes.

The contributors to this book give and analyze examples of all these forms of pseudo-environmentalism. Unfortunately, they don't give examples of real environmentalism—that is, of policies done right. That is a pity, for it may lead the unwary reader to suppose that these authors are only interested in mistakes. Some may be, but I think most, if not all, are not. What they are all interested in is casting a penetrating light into the pitfalls, especially those pitfalls produced by groups seeking to exploit the public's desire to protect its environment in a way that will confer private benefits in the name of public goods.

James Q. Wilson
Collins Professor of Management and Public Policy
University of California at Los Angeles

ACKNOWLEDGMENTS

The editors of this book earn their living not as academics but as policy advocates. Michael S. Greve is the Executive Director of the Center for Individual Rights (CIR), a public interest law firm. Fred L. Smith is the President of the Competitive Enterprise Institute (CEI), a nonprofit, nonpartisan policy research and advocacy organization. Although both groups concern themselves with environmental issues (among other matters), neither this book as a whole nor the editors' contributions are in any sense intended to reflect CIR's or CEI's "official" positions.

However, our respective organizations merit grateful mention because they provided us with free time to write and edit this book and with the logistic support that made this venture possible. We are particularly indebted to Karen Henry (CEI) and Jason James (CIR) for their editorial and organizational assistance.

The Gordon Center for Public Policy at Brandeis University provided financial assistance, which is gratefully acknowledged.

John T. Harney, our editor at Greenwood Publishing Group, showed great courage and a high risk tolerance by supporting this project when it was still in its infancy. He has earned our respect and gratitude.

Our wives and children spent too many nights without their husbands and fathers when this project was nearing completion. We thank them for their patience and encouragement.

1 INTRODUCTION: ENVIRONMENTAL POLITICS WITHOUT ROMANCE

Michael S. Greve

Environmental advocacy groups lobby and litigate for regulations that substantially increase the volume of toxic waste and against regulations that would reduce such waste.

Congress enacts a "clean fuels" policy that will cost car drivers billions of dollars. It does so with the full knowledge that the policy will do little or nothing to bring the nation's smog-filled cities into compliance with the Clean Air Act.

Twenty-four nations and the European Community sign an agreement to phase out the use of chemical substances suspected of depleting the ozone layer. Among the most aggressive supporters of the agreement are the chemical companies that produce those substances.

Environmental Politics: Public Costs, Private Rewards tells the details of these and other stories that confound the ordinary understanding of environmental politics and policy. Each chapter illustrates a single theme: the use and abuse of environmental regulation for political and economic objectives that have little or nothing to do with the environment.

TWO PERSPECTIVES ON ENVIRONMENTAL REGULATION

While public support for stringent environmental regulation is near an all-time high, economists and policy analysts have become increasingly disenchanted with the ways in which we have chosen to manage and control environmental risk. There is no longer any serious dispute among experts that the prevailing "command and control" style of environmental regulation is horribly expensive and inefficient and that more flexible, incentive-based regulation would produce vastly more beneficial results. It is almost equally uncontested that the government's risk selection is badly flawed. An extensive study commissioned by the Environmental Protection Agency (EPA) and published by the agency under the title *Reducing Risk* acknowledges that the agency's commitments of personnel and budgetary resources to regulatory programs stand in no proportion to the magnitude of the risks that are being regulated.[1] Regulated risks are often quite small, while substantially more significant risks remain unregulated.

By and large, the contributors agree with this critical assessment of environmental command and control regulation and its results (although, of course, they would disagree about the merits of particular environmental policies or regulatory instruments). However, it is not the purpose of this volume to document, yet again, the staggering costs and inefficiencies of environmental policy. *Environmental Politics: Public Costs, Private Rewards* is about the *sources* of inefficiency. It asks, what explains the present, counterproductive system of environmental regulation? To this complex question, the book gives a relatively simple and, concededly, partial answer: Far more often than is commonly realized, the purpose and effect of environmental policy is to serve narrow political and economic objectives, *not* environmental objectives.

This position is not widely shared; more to the point, it is heresy. Public debate, as well as much—though, as we shall see, not all—academic discourse about environmental policy is dominated by what one may call the unreconstructed public interest view. It holds that environmental regulation—along with health, safety, and other "social" regulation—is uniformly intended to protect *public* interests and *public* goods.

Political controversies over environmental policy appear, from this perspective, as epic battles between public-spirited environmental groups, who seek to obtain tough environmental regulation, and corporate special interests and their sponsors in Congress, who seek to weaken regulation. Of course, it is agreed, compromises must be made. For example, frantic efforts by Congress to strike compromises among regional and economic interests to ensure passage of the comprehensive revision of the Clean Air Act in 1990 were covered by the press in some detail. The national newspapers provided extensive coverage of interest group conflicts and compromises, such as the regional disputes over the acid rain provisions of the bill. But few journalists suspected that many organized interests would, in fact, gain from the passage of the Act, and virtually no one suggested that these expected gains might be the real rationale and driving force behind the legislation. The leading question with respect to the role of business, regional, or other interests was always, what interests will have to sacrifice how much to a tough Clean Air Act that was unquestionably intended to advance the public good?

The public interest view is similarly uncritical with respect to the motives and the behavior of the political actors and institutions that frame and implement environmental policy (notably, the Environmental Protection Agency and its congressional overlords). When it comes to the environment, politicians appear entitled to a presumption of innocence. Whether or not one wishes to grant political actors such a presumption as a general matter, its application to environmental policy seems strangely at odds with the cynicism that is routinely brought to bear on other government institutions, including those charged with procuring benefits that are every bit as public as environmental benefits. The Pentagon, for example, is often pictured as being more interested in maximizing its budget and servicing its contractors than in providing a cost-effective national defense, and the coveted seats on the Pentagon's congressional oversight committees are widely (and, with some justification) viewed as pork barrel assignments. However, when it comes to the environment, it is generally taken for granted that Congress struggles earnestly to protect public interests; the parochial special interests are on the other side of the great environmental divide. Similarly, it is taken for granted that the EPA's mandate is, solely, to protect the public. The only interesting question is whether the agency is always tough enough in protecting the public against corporate polluters.

In fairness, this description of the public interest view is a bit overdrawn; few will wish to subscribe to it in this simplistic form and without modifications. Still, the caricature just presented captures the basic elements of the dominant view of the purpose and reality of environmental policy. Any sample of pronouncements by members of Congress, environmental policy advocates, or, for that matter, news stories on environmental politics would illustrate the point.

Environmental Politics: Public Costs, Private Rewards presents seven case studies of environmental policies and practices that challenge and confound the public interest view. The essays cover a broad range of environmental programs and policies, from toxic waste regulation to clean air and clean water programs and international environmental agreements, as well as a few health and safety policies. The purpose of the exercise is not to develop a general theory of the political economy of environmental regulation: There is, at present, no adequate empirical basis for such an endeavor.[2] Rather, by examining the role of interest groups and regulators in a broad range of environmental policy disputes and from a variety of perspectives, this volume seeks to provide empirical raw material and food for thought for experts whose interests lie in a more theoretical direction. At the same time, we hope to achieve the more practical purpose of confounding those individuals—experts and interested laymen alike—who hold dear the preconceptions of the public interest view.

The chapters fall into three loosely arranged groups. The first three essays describe coalitions between environmental advocacy organizations and industry groups. Jonathan H. Adler describes the coalition between environmentalists and the farm bloc that supported the clean fuels requirements of the 1990 Clean Air Act Amendments. Christopher L. Culp chronicles the efforts of small farm groups and an environmental advocate to prevent the commercial use of a biotechnologically engineered bovine growth hormone. And Marc K. Landy and Mary Hague describe the close alliance between the environmental movement and the waste treatment industry and its successful efforts to sustain and expand Superfund, a regulatory program that was almost uniformly recognized as a catastrophic failure. All three essays cast doubt on the comfortable assumption that the battle lines between the public interest and so-called corporate polluters are clear and immutable.

The next two essays have a more institutional bent. They examine two peculiar regulatory instruments that can be found in almost every federal environmental statute. R. Shep Melnick's essay, previously published in the *Public Interest* and reprinted here with a brief update, explains why legislators, bureaucrats, and environmental advocates support statutory deadlines and targets that are known to be unattainable when they are written into environmental statutes. This author's essay argues that provisions authorizing the private enforcement of environmental law—so-called citizen suit provisions—serve no intelligible purpose other than to provide funding for environmental causes.

The final two case studies deal with the increasingly salient topic of international environmental regulation. Daniel F. McInnis examines the Montreal Protocol, a landmark multinational agreement to phase out certain chemical substances suspected of depleting the ozone layer, and explains why, at critical junctures, the producers of those substances supported the agreement. Finally, David Vogel describes the growing connections between international trade and environmental and consumer regulation as well as the public interest movement's emerging interest in international trade issues.

The critical tenor of this volume naturally suggests the question of how to protect the environment more effectively and efficiently. Although the design of reform proposals was not among the authors' assignments, a few of them have chosen to supply their ideas, including ideas that presuppose some confidence in the government's ability to regulate the environment in a genuinely public-spirited manner. Taken together, though, the essays suggest that the government's capacity to do so is exceedingly limited—certainly, far more limited than is commonly believed. This, in turn, suggests that environmental risks may be managed most effectively not by government but by private parties. Fred L. Smith's conclusion explores this still unconventional, but increasingly plausible, idea.

INTEREST AND IDEOLOGY IN ENVIRONMENTAL POLICY

At first impression, the contention that much environmental regulation is regulation of, by, and for special interests may seem highly questionable. Environmental regulation, and social regulation in general, have imposed tremendous costs on the regulated industries, usually without creating readily discernible benefits to concentrated interests.[3] Moreover, on its face, environmental regulation appears to be a determined effort to protect the public interest in clean water and clean air against polluters. Environmental statutes, some running hundreds of pages in length, tell the regulated industries and the EPA with great specificity what they must do and when and how they must do it. One would think—until reading R. Shep Melnick's contribution to this volume—that such detailed regulation minimizes the EPA's discretion, and, hence, the extent to which special interests can blunt the full force of the law by "capturing" the regulating agency. Against this background, one may be inclined to dismiss the episodes compiled in this volume as isolated, though perhaps intriguing, exceptions to generally tough-minded and public-spirited environmental regulation. One may then proceed to ascribe the failures of environmental policy to other factors—perhaps the inherent complexity of the subject matter, a disregard for sound science, the alarmist tendency of the media, which impedes a sober assessment of the relative environmental and health risks of particular substances or activities, or some combination of these and other factors.

The most plausible of these alternative explanations centers on the pervasive role of ideology in environmental policy.[4] Clearly, much environmental regulation is animated by a quasi-religious mind-set that combines an aversion to even minimal risks with a strong preference for government intervention in markets and a fierce hostility toward corporations.[5] This would account for some of the observed inefficiencies of environmental policies—for example, for the many statutory and regulatory standards that set tolerable risk levels at or near zero, thus mandating the expenditure of vast amounts of money and effort in a chase to eliminate very marginal risks.

Harvard professor Steven Kelman, one of the most articulate proponents of what one may call a reconstructed public interest view, has proffered a version of this approach in an attempt to explain why environmental policy has proven virtually immune to theoretical and empirical criticism by economists.[6] This immunity does need to be explained. Economists agree almost unanimously that the prevailing command and control style of environmental regulation is exceedingly blunt and inefficient. Typically, mandatory standards will be insufficient to meet environmental quality goals in high-pollution areas, while mandating wildly excessive investments in areas that could attain environmental quality very cheaply and easily or that have already done so. Moreover, the costs of pollution reduction differ drastically from plant to plant and from industry to industry. Technology-based standards invariably mandate the installation of expensive equipment even when the same environmental benefits could be attained through lower cost abatement measures at other facilities.

When economists agree, politicians should probably listen; and, as Kelman observes, environmental policymakers *are* generally familiar with the economists' basic insights. However, this awareness has not translated into practical policy. Regulatory experiments with more flexible and environmentally more beneficial controls have remained just that—experiments, and very limited ones at that.[7] To the obvious question of why this is so, Kelman responds that congressional staffers, bureaucrats, and environmentalists tend to oppose emission charges and similar incentive-based regulatory schemes for ideological reasons, such as the sincere and public-spirited belief that a regulatory system based on such charges—as opposed to a set of absolute, enforceable prohibitions— would imply an endorsement of the regulated activity, a "license to pollute."

Kelman's evidence, consisting of interviews with participants in environmental policy-making, does show that this view is widespread among environmental policymakers. However, it also shows that neither environmental advocacy groups nor congressional staffers but rather industry lobbyists are, as a group and by a considerable margin, most hostile to emission fees and most supportive of command and control regulation (although, as one might expect, they consider the existing standards absurdly demanding). Plainly, ideology cannot explain this result, and Kelman fails to provide any other satisfactory explanation.[8] Kelman's evidence, though, is consistent with, and may support, the view explored in this volume: The popularity of command and control regulation may have as much to do with the interests of the regulated and the regulators as it does with its perceived environmental benefits.

This suggestion is not novel. Public choice theorists have argued for some time that the prevalence of command and control regulation is very hard to explain without taking the interests of the regulated parties into account.[9] The basic argument is relatively straightforward: Emission charges and similar instruments favored by economists are invariably detrimental to the interests of producers. In essence, they tax a resource that the producer formerly used for free. Direct regulation in the form of environmental quality standards, on the other hand, may benefit segments of the regulated industries in various ways.[10] Most obviously, technology-based standards benefit the producers of that technology and prevent nonprice competition and the entry of rivals who might provide substitute goods or services. Somewhat less obviously, uniform standards usually impose widely varying costs on different industries or on members of one and the same industry. Firms with a favorable cost structure will be relatively better off; they may even reap indirect benefits in excess of their direct compliance costs. In addition, environmental quality controls usually restrict industry output, either directly (for example, by driving marginal firms from the market) or indirectly (by raising prices). The remaining firms in the industry may welcome such restrictions for the same reasons that prompt citrus growers or dairy farmers to seek production quotas and marketing orders.

It is fully consistent with the perspective—and it is hard to explain any other way—that regulated industries often support stringent regulations that they would be expected to resist. For example, in 1980 some car producers supported even stricter miles-per-gallon standards than Congress eventually adopted.[11] (For these producers, the relative benefits of regulation outweighed the direct compliance cost.) Similarly, the relative advantages that may be conferred by regulation help explain the strong support of labor unions for environmental regulation. For example, it has been argued quite persuasively that labor unions lent their support to stringent coal mine safety regulations, not for safety reasons, but in order to purge small, nonunionized mines from the industry.[12] Several essays in this volume describe other policies, from toxic waste regulations to the phase-out of ozone-depleting substances, that were actively supported by the regulated industries.

The efforts of economic interest groups to obtain advantages through environmental regulation often prompt them to join hands with environmental groups—a phenomenon for which economist Bruce Yandle has coined the apt phrase "bootleggers and Baptists."[13] Perhaps the classic example of such a coalition in the environmental context was described by Bruce A. Ackerman and William T. Hassler in their study entitled *Clean Coal, Dirty Air.*[14] Under the 1970 Clean Air Act, utilities were permitted to choose whatever means they considered most cost-effective in meeting regulatory requirements to limit sulfur dioxide emissions. When it transpired that many utilities would burn low-sulfur coal mined primarily in the West, eastern producers of high-sulfur coal united with environmentalists and lobbied for statutory language that would require utilities to attain *percentage* reductions of sulfur dioxide emissions, no matter what the sulfur content of the coal burned by the utility. This policy—which, in practice, mandated a particular control technology, so-called scrubbers—was adopted in the 1977 Clean Air Act Amendments. *Clean Coal, Dirty Air* has become the most notorious example of a bootlegger and baptist coalition because it was highly successful and because the resulting policy was so manifestly inefficient and, possibly, harmful to the environment. However, the coalition was not a mere curiosity, as is shown by several essays in this volume.

Ostensibly public-minded command and control requirements can bestow benefits not only on identifiable economic interests but also on those who lobby and litigate for stricter environmental regulation. The environmental movement's enthusiasm for command and control regulation has been widely regarded as being driven by a concern for public benefits, though perhaps this concern may sometimes be overzealous and even misguided. It is at least worth asking, though, whether the ideological concerns of advocacy organizations may comport with their more tangible interests. A self-enforcing regulatory system that mimicked market incentives would make advocacy groups superfluous, at least with respect to the enforcement process; a coercive and litigious regulatory system makes them essential. This may help explain why environmental groups have been so slow and reluctant to endorse more flexible regulatory schemes even when such schemes would demonstrably result in greater environmental gains.[15] The essays by Marc K. Landy and Mary Hague, R. Shep Melnick, and Michael S. Greve in this volume each describe environmental policies and programs that, despite their highly dubious environmental merits, are fiercely defended by environmental groups because they provide substantial organizational and financial benefits for those groups.

Similarly, political decision-makers may benefit from command and control regulation. By definition, such regulation is highly centralized (usually at the federal level); environmental risks are controlled far from their sources. This circumstance permits legislators and regulators to hide, shift, and spread the costs of regulation. For example, automobile exhaust (*mobile source emissions*, in the terms of the trade) could be *hard to* curbed by taxing car owners in proportion to miles driven and exhausts *collect.* produced. Such a system would take account of the fact that mobile source *would* emissions are a serious problem only in a few metropolitan areas: The *encourage* fee would be low in areas where mobile source emissions do not present a problem (Montana) and high in areas where such pollution is severe (Los Angeles). Existing regulations of mobile sources, in contrast, seek to curb emissions by means of technology-based standards that have to be attained by automobile manufacturers. These *tailpipe standards* are known to be wasteful: While they impose costs on car buyers in areas that would satisfy air quality standards even without expensive tailpipe controls, they are a cruel joke on the citizens of Denver or Los Angeles, where no known technological gadget would bring about the attainment of federal air quality standards. As Jonathan H. Adler's essay shows, the same is true of the clean fuels requirements of the 1990 Amendments, which were superimposed on the tailpipe standards. Both types of controls also increase the price of new cars, thus slowing the replacement of old cars, which account for an overwhelming portion of mobile source emissions.

However, technology standards have the enormous *political* advantage of "hiding" the costs of pollution control in car prices. Only a portion of those costs will be passed on to the ultimate consumers (and polluters)—who will rarely attribute price increases, should they notice them, to the Clean Air Act. Then, too, some car owners—among them, the millionaires of Beverly Hills—will be better off, relative to a system of emission fees (the regulation-induced price increase of cars will be lower than the emission taxes would be); those who will be worse off—among them, Montana dirt farmers—will not notice. Command and control regulation, in short, provides political advantages by facilitating the de facto wealth transfers and cross-subsidies that are part and parcel of every environmental statute.

The list of politically induced distortions and inefficiencies could easily be expanded. Stringent standards for existing pollution sources, for example, are often accompanied by even more stringent standards for new sources. It requires little ingenuity to discern that this strategy is environmentally harmful in that it inhibits the development of new, usually cleaner technology and prolongs the life span of heavily polluting facilities; and that it benefits existing producers, whose assets are made more valuable by the restriction on market entry. Nor does it appear farfetched to attribute this feature of environmental policy to the circumstance that existing facilities are backed by constituencies who vote, lobby, and pay campaign contributions, whereas the new ones are often unrepresented.

FROM GOOD INTENTIONS TO INTEREST GROUP TRANSFERS

The fact that environmental regulation produces private rewards—or *rents*, in the economists' jargon—does not mean that those rents are always its *intended* result or its sole purpose. The cases in which purported environmental rationales serve as a mere smokescreen for naked wealth transfers and political extortion are the extreme end of a spectrum. At the opposite extreme lie the cases in which regulation-induced rewards are the unintended by-product of environmental regulation.[16] In between lie all the possibilities of political compromise and interest group accommodation. The extent to which regulation is shaped by its strategic uses can ultimately be determined only on a case by case basis and by means of what economists like to call *casual empiricism*.

The cases examined in this volume are, by and large, closer to the end of the spectrum at which ostensible environmental rationales become a disguise for conferring benefits on favored constituencies. The policies under examination were shaped substantially—and some, predominantly—by their strategic use, either at the time of their original enactment or in the course of their implementation. Several essays in this volume describe environmental statutes that were put in place as a result of political entrepreneurship rather than interest group demand; bureaucrats, experts, and congressional committee chairmen and their staff, not interest groups, were the predominant forces in the original design of the Clean Air Act, Superfund, and the Resource Conservation and Recovery Act.[17] Once enacted, however, such programs are quickly overrun by interest groups, and by the time the original policy design is reconsidered, entrenched interests and their congressional patrons can no longer be dislodged.

One can trace this trend in the development of the Clean Air Act, the "granddaddy" and paradigm of modern environmental regulation. The 1970 Clean Air Act was passed in a great hurry and in an extremely emotional atmosphere. The first Earth Day had been staged with great fanfare, and the bill had become the subject of a bidding war between President Richard Nixon and senator and presidential aspirant Edmund Muskie, chairman of the Senate Public Works Committee and chief sponsor of the bill, both of whom were trying to position themselves as being pro-environment for the 1972 election. Powerful interests did have to be accommodated to allow the statute to pass. For example, certain American automobile manufacturers managed to extract a concession: Provisions dealing with automobile emission technology were written so as to prohibit, to all practical purposes, a type of air-cooled engine used by a foreign manufacturer (Volkswagen). (This accounts for the disappearance of the technology from the American market after 1974.) However, such accommodations were exceptions; in the hothouse atmosphere of 1970, the affected interests were, by and large, in no position to make strategic use of the opportunities provided by the bill.

This age of innocence (if such it was) has long since passed. The 1977 Clean Air Act Amendments incorporated the "clean coal, dirty air" deal between high-sulfur coal producers and environmentalists; they also ratified a creative judicial interpretation of New Source Performance Standards (the emission standards that apply to new stationary sources), which amounted to an enormous wealth transfer from small, non-unionized to large, unionized firms and from the Sun Belt to the Rust Belt.[18] And, while we may never know what deals went into the 600–plus pages of the 1990 Amendments to the Clean Air Act, the legislative process that preceded their enactment can only be described as a special interest feeding frenzy. The "clean fuels" policy discussed by Jonathan H. Adler was a pointless gimmick when it was first proposed by the Bush administration; it was a massive subsidy program for the ethanol industry when it was finally enacted. Even the acid rain controls of the Amendments, which allow for emission trading and have been widely hailed as innovative, market-oriented, and a break with the regulatory past, appear to have been undercut by a blatantly political allocation of initial entitlements.[19]

This admittedly cursory and impressionistic look at the Clean Air Act is confirmed by three essays in this volume. The contributions by R. Shep Melnick and by this author discuss, respectively, statutory deadlines and citizen suit provisions—two regulatory instruments that made their debut in the 1970 Clean Air Act but have since become part and parcel of every environmental statute, even as their substantive environmental merits have become increasingly suspect. And Marc K. Landy and Mary Hague's essay on Superfund provides a particularly dramatic illustration of an environmental program that has gone from a well-intentioned—

though flawed—policy design to a catastrophic failure that is sustained by entrenched interest groups.

These observations are not particularly surprising. The distributive effects of comprehensive environmental schemes, as well as the political dynamics they will unfold, are often difficult to predict at the outset. However, as regulatory regimes firm up, their costs and benefits become clearer and interest groups and legislators become more adept at using the existing tools for their own ends. New interest groups spring up in support of increased regulation; the waste management industry comes to mind, as do the legions of environmental lawyers and consultants with a manifest interest in centrally administered statutes that generate high transaction costs. As the differential impact of seemingly neutral controls becomes evident, the business community finds it harder and harder to maintain a united front; environmentalists find it easier to divide and conquer and to form tactical coalitions with industry groups and labor unions. Eventually, even firms with a principled commitment to earn profits in the market rather than in the bowels of Washington, D.C., discover that they cannot be good corporate citizens in a corrupt regime. "Playing the game," always a temptation, becomes a necessity.

The tendency of environmental statutes to become playing fields for interest groups and politicians has disturbing implications. As a practical matter, it means that environmental regulation becomes ever more rigid and immune to reform. Even as we learn from the failures of the past, and even as the need for reform becomes more urgent, we will be stuck with statutes and regulations that are no longer sustained by any plausible environmental rationale.

THE GREENING OF CORPORATE SOCIALISM

There is nothing new in principle about the strategic use of social regulation. Politicians and interest groups have long known that special interest regulation has a better chance of passage and survival if it is dressed up as health and safety regulation; only witness Germany's centuries-old beer purity law or, closer to home, state and federal statutes enacted for the purported—but transparently fraudulent—purpose of protecting "pure" milk and butter.[20] Modern environmental and health and safety regulation poses the same dangers. For example, Christopher L. Culp's essay shows that the move to ban bST, a biotechnological innovation that would greatly increase milk production, in many respects parallels the dairy industry's efforts a century ago to regulate margarine.

However, the formal similarities are, in the end, less remarkable than the differences in scale and context. The environmental regulatory apparatus that has been erected over the past two decades is vastly more comprehensive and ambitious than any health and safety regulations preceding it, and it makes all the difference in the world, both in terms of total economic impact and in terms of the potential for political manipulation, whether we protect dairy producers against "excessive competition" or whether we regulate business across the board, as environmental statutes typically do; whether we protect bakery workers from working excessive hours or whether we regulate each and every industry in an effort to produce clean air everywhere in the United States.

As the scope of environmental regulation increases, so does the potential for interest group transfers. Paradoxically, though, it is precisely its comprehensive reach and the ostensible effort to protect what is truly public that imbue environmental regulation with a moral pathos, a claim to legitimacy, and an immunity to criticism that more targeted and focused regulatory programs have long ago lost. The enormous potential of environmental regulation to reward private interests and its undisputed claim to serve the public interest thus reinforce each other; the regulatory process feeds on itself.

At the same time, the more traditional and direct tools of redistribution, rent seeking, and favoritism have been discredited. Economic regulation has receded in areas such as transportation, airline traffic, labor relations, and antitrust. Similarly, the 1986 tax reform, whatever its macroeconomic merits and consequences, was a large step toward a tax code that is more neutral vis-à-vis alternative uses of private resources. While these reforms were partly due to the increased exposure of the American market to the international economy, they were also based on the recognition that political resource allocation—regulation—rarely benefited the public. Environmental regulation, in contrast, still enjoys broad public legitimacy and support. As a consequence, some of the parties who have been robbed of more direct instruments of rent collection have eagerly seized on environmental policy as an opportunity to play with the same old broken toys—as long as they are painted green.

These concerns should dampen the current enthusiasm for international regulation of the global environment. A worldwide agreement to limit "greenhouse gases," which is now under discussion, could easily dwarf even the massive dislocations and distortions caused by the Clean Air Act; and surely, there is no shortage of parties who would gladly seize on an "environmental" agreement to secure advantages that they would otherwise be unable to obtain. Daniel F. McInnis's instructive essay shows that the Montreal Protocol, widely heralded as a landmark international agreement, was essentially a cartel arrangement among certain chemical producers. To be sure, if dire predictions of ozone depletion come true, the protocol may turn out to have been based on remarkable foresight, but the cartelization and protection of powerful industries may easily become the purpose of international environmental agreements, rather than merely a price that must be paid. The emergence of integrated world markets has tended to make national economies more competitive; structural barriers to the free movement of capital and labor are gradually receding. However, as David Vogel shows, the integration of the world economy also creates new pressures and opportunities for market controls in the name of environmental protection. Environmental concerns are one of the few "hooks" on which protectionist forces can hang their hats, and they have begun to do so with alarming frequency.

CONCLUSION

Some readers may be put off by the tireless emphasis on the political use of environmental regulation—if not by now, then after reading a few of the case studies compiled in this volume. Admittedly, it is a perfectly legitimate and serious objection to the present enterprise that the relentless criticism of environmental policy as selfish may further increase an already widespread public cynicism about government and that it threatens to undermine the broad public consensus that has heretofore sustained aggressive environmental protection.

However, the objection is ultimately not persuasive. What I have called the public interest view of environmental policy is so deeply ingrained that nothing short of sustained criticism would even begin to trigger a realistic debate about government's capacity to procure public environmental benefits. Even those who are rather sanguine about the purposes and results of environmental policy should welcome such a debate, for whatever the presumed costs of public cynicism may be, the undisputed reign of the public interest view poses the risk of serving as a shield for the arguably far more pervasive and destructive cynicism of politicians and interest groups who manipulate public environmental purposes for private reward.

To date, alas, there has been virtually no public or, for that matter, official recognition of the political use of environmental policies, even as those policies have increasingly come to be recognized as inefficient and misguided. *Reducing Risk*, the EPA-commissioned study mentioned earlier, attributes the failures of environmental regulation in large part to the EPA's reactive regulatory approach (termed "Space Invaders" regulation by EPA administrator William Reilly) and proposes to replace reactive regulation with better science and a comprehensive strategic planning process. Consistent with this orientation, the document criticizes the EPA's preoccupation with discrete human health risks and urges an increased attention to global ecological risks.

Reducing Risk is a welcome step toward a more rational public debate about risk. However, in light of the growing mismatch between environmental expectations and rhetoric, on the one hand, and the political purposes and effects of regulation on the other, one must worry about the EPA's apparent enthusiasm for comprehensive planning and global environmental protection.[21] Most *existing* environmental statutes are heavily centralized, planned control schemes, and the case studies collected in this volume tend to show that such schemes are quickly overrun by special interests and hopelessly politicized. In fact, precisely the most centralized and planned schemes appear to be the most used and abused.

In this light, one must at least entertain the thought that the observed inefficiencies and irrationalities of environmental regulation may be due not to a lack of centralized strategic planning and vision, but to an excess thereof. One must contemplate the possibility that no rational planning process will trump interest group politics. And one must question, for reasons stated here and at greater length in Fred L. Smith's conclusion, the fundamental assumption behind modern environmental regulation— namely, that centralized political control, and only such control, will effectively protect the environment. Particularly readers who do not share the perspective of this volume will benefit from Smith's plea to mobilize the energies and ingenuity of a free society for the protection of the environment: It shows that the seemingly demoralizing perspective of this book may, after all, contain an inspiring lesson.

NOTES

The title of this introduction is borrowed from James M. Buchanan, "Politics without Romance: A Sketch of Positive Public Choice Theory and Its Normative Implications," in Buchanan and Robert D. Tollison, eds., *The Theory of Public Choice-II* (Ann Arbor: University of Michigan Press, 1984), 11.

1. Science Advisory Board, Environmental Protection Agency, *Reducing Risk: Setting Priorities and Strategies for Environmental Protection* (Washington, D.C.: EPA, 1990).

2. Nor, for that matter, is there an adequate theoretical basis. In what appears to be the sole monograph on the subject, Bruce Yandle observed only two years ago: "By now enough books have been written on environmental law and policy, benefit-cost analysis of environmental regulation, and efficiency analysis of the environmental protection agency (EPA) to fill a long library shelf. But, as yet, no single book has been written that examines unrelentingly the political economy of environmental control" *The Political Limits of Environmental Regulation* (New York: Quorum Books, 1989), ix–x. The statement still appears to be accurate (with, of course, the exception of Yandle's book). There is, however, a growing body of excellent books and articles on aspects of the "political economy" of environmental regulation. In addition to the works cited throughout this Introduction see, for example, Elinor Ostrom, *Governing the Commons: The Evolution of Institutions for Collective Action* (Cambridge: Cambridge University Press, 1990); and Robert A. Leone, *Who Profits* (New York: Basic Books, 1986).

3. See, for example, George Priest, "The Structure and Operation of the Magnuson-Moss Warranty Act," in Kenneth Clarkson and Timothy Muris, eds., *The Federal Trade Commission Since 1970* (Cambridge: Cambridge University Press, 1981), 246–76; Richard Posner, "Theories of Economic Regulation," *Bell Journal of Economics* 5 (1974): 353 (pointing out that many consumer and environmental regulations "are not an obvious product of interest group pressures"); and Fred S. McChesney, "Regulation, Taxes, and Political Extortion," in Roger E. Meiners and Bruce Yandle, eds., *Regulation and the Reagan Era* (New York: Holmes and Meier, 1989), 224.

4. This is not to deny that factors other than ideology or political and economic interests—for example, "scare campaigns" and an attendant disregard for sound science—have a profound impact on environmental policy. However, efforts to explain the failures of environmental policy with reference to such factors tend to collapse either into an explanation based on interests and institutions—the perspective of this volume—or into "ideology." For example, the often and rightly maligned disregard for sound science in environmental policy-making does not explain very much, unless and until one explains *why* science is routinely ignored.

5. A very sophisticated version of this argument is Mary Douglas and Aaron Wildavsky, *Risk and Culture* (Berkeley, Calif.: University of California Press, 1982). See also David Vogel, *Fluctuating Fortunes* (New York: Basic Books, 1989), 93–99; Michael McCann, "Public Interest Liberalism and the Modern Regulatory State," *Polity* 21 (Winter 1988): 373–400; and Richard A. Harris and Sidney M. Milkis, *The Politics of Regulatory Change: A Tale of Two Agencies* (New York: Oxford University Press, 1989).

6. "Economists and the Environmental Muddle," *The Public Interest*, Summer 1981, 106–123.

7. See, for example, Robert Hahn and Gordon Hester, "Where Did All the Markets Go? An Analysis of EPA's Emission Trading Program," *Yale Journal on Regulation* 6 (1989): 109–53.

8. Kelman ascribes the phenomenon to the fact that industry trade associations have far fewer contacts with outside experts than do congressional staffers or advocacy groups. This will not do. It is inconceivable that the economists of large corporations or trade associations are unaware of rudimentary microeconomic principles and their application to environmental regulation.

9. See, for example, Michael T. Maloney and Robert E. McCormick, "A Positive Theory of Environmental Quality Regulation," *Journal of Law and Economics* 25 (April 1982): 99–124.

10. The basic argument was made by James Buchanan and Gordon Tullock, "Polluter's Profits and Political Response: Direct Costs Versus Taxes," *American Economic Review* 65 (1975): 139. The article produced a veritable flood of literature on the choice of regulatory instruments. See, for example, Maloney and McCormick, "A Positive Theory"; Donald N. Dewees, "Instrument Choice in Environmental Policy," *Economic Inquiry* (1983): 53–71; and Matthey McCubbins, "The Legislative Design of Regulatory Structure," *American Journal of Political Science* 29 (1985): 721.

11. Bruce Yandle, "A Cost-Benefit Analysis of the 1981–1984 MPG Standard," *Policy Analysis* 6 (Summer 1980): 291–304.

12. George R. Nuemann and Jon P. Nelson, "Safety Regulation and Firm Size: Effects of the Coal Mine Health and Safety Act of 1969," *Journal of Law and Economics* 183 (1982): 25.

13. Bruce Yandle, "Bootleggers and Baptists—The Education of a Regulatory Economist," *Regulation* 7 (May/June 1983): 12–16.

14. Bruce A. Ackerman and William T. Hassler, *Clean Coal, Dirty Air* (New Haven, Conn.: Yale University Press, 1981).

15. See Richard B. Stewart, "The Discontents of Legalism: Interest Group Relations in Administrative Regulation," *Wisconsin Law Review* (1985): 674–75 passim.

16. Roger Noll and Bruce M. Owen, *The Political Economy of Deregulation* (Washington, D.C.: American Enterprise Institute, 1983).

17. For the Clean Air Act, see below. For Superfund, see Marc K. Landy and Mary Hague's essay in this volume. For the Resource Conservation and Recovery Act, see Marc K. Landy, Marc J. Roberts, and Stephen R. Thomas, *The Environmental Protection Agency: Asking the Wrong Questions* (Oxford: Oxford University Press, 1989), 89–93.

18. Robert Crandall, *Controlling Industrial Pollution: The Economics and Politics of Clean Air* (Washington, D.C.: The Brookings Institution, 1983); and Ann P. Bartel and Lacy Glenn Thomas, "Predation through Regulation: The Wage and Profit Effects of the Occupational Safety and Health Administration and the Environmental Protection Agency," *Journal of Law and Economics* 30 (1987): 239–64.

19. Francis S. Blake, "Tilting the Marketplace," *Regulation* 13 (Summer 1990): 5.

20. See Geoffrey P. Miller, "The True Story of Carolene Products [*United States v. Carolene Products Corp.*, 58 S.Ct. 778] 1987," *Supreme Court Review* 1987 (1987): 397–428.

21. For a more extensive discussion and critique of *Reducing Risk*, see Michael S. Greve, "The EPA Rediscovers the Environment," *American Enterprise* 6, no.2 (Nov./Dec. 1991): 52–61.

2 CLEAN FUELS, DIRTY AIR

Jonathan H. Adler

On November 15, 1990, President George Bush signed into law the Clean Air Act Amendments of 1990, far and away the most sweeping and expensive clean air legislation in the nation's history. In many respects, the Amendments followed the well-traveled path of command and control regulation that was laid out by the original 1970 Clean Air Act and its 1977 Amendments. Once again, Congress tightened emissions standards for industrial plants and automobiles (*stationary* and *mobile* sources, in the terms of the trade). Once again, Congress established purportedly ironclad statutory deadlines by which cities have to attain the stringent ambient air quality standards mandated by the Act.

However, the 1990 Amendments also contained major policy innovations. Among the most significant of these is a comprehensive "alternative fuels" program. Whereas previous federal efforts to reduce automobile emissions had focused almost exclusively on automakers, who were forced to meet tough tailpipe emissions standards, the 1990 Amendments were the first major congressional attempt to reduce car emissions by means of setting standards for the contents and composition of motor fuels. The Amendments stipulate that motor fuels sold in the nine smoggiest cities will have to reduce toxic emissions and volatile organic compounds (VOCs) by 15 percent.[1] Beginning in 1992, gasoline sold in cities that fail to attain the federal standards for carbon monoxide and ozone will have to contain a minimum of 2 percent oxygen.

These and other, less comprehensive clean fuels provisions will cost an estimated $3 billion annually.[2] Consumers will be paying more money for fuel; oil refiners will be forced to spend billions of dollars altering and refining distribution methods. However, by any reasonable estimation, these expenditures will fail to produce an appreciable improvement of air quality. One must wonder, then, how the requirements found their way into the Amendments. A desire to substitute a symbolically appealing technological "fix" for more effective but politically less palatable approaches to the clean air problem is one part of the answer. The other part is the relentless legislative desire to confer economic benefits on powerful constituencies—even at the price of compromising environmental objectives.

THE QUEST FOR CLEAN AIR

The framework for modern air pollution control is the 1970 Clean Air Act. At the time the most comprehensive environmental law in the nation's history, the Act took sweeping steps to address the air pollution problems faced by many American communities. The Act set demanding ambient air quality standards for six "criteria" air pollutants (sulfur dioxide, carbon monoxide [CO], nitrogen dioxide [NOx], ozone, particulates [soot, dust, and so forth], and lead), and it established tight deadlines under which the standards had to be attained. Emission standards for stationary and mobile sources were the principal regulatory instrument through which the standards and deadlines were to be met.

The results of this regime were mixed. Pollution from many sources decreased dramatically, with emissions from automobiles registering particularly significant reductions. Today's cars emit 96 percent less hydrocarbons and carbon monoxide and 76 percent less nitrogen oxide than those built 20 years ago. Although the average passenger car today is driven longer and farther than an "uncontrolled" car in the 1960s, it will emit about 80 percent less hydrocarbons and 60 percent less nitrogen oxides during its lifetime.[3]

Largely as a result of these achievements, ambient levels of criteria air pollutants have declined sharply. Average carbon monoxide levels dropped from 11.96 parts per million (ppm) in 1975 to 6.88 ppm in 1987. During the same period, ozone levels decreased from 0.153 ppm to 0.129 ppm and total suspended particulates from 61.9 micrograms per cubic meter (ug/m³) to 49.4 ug/m³. Perhaps the most spectacular achievement was the decrease of lead concentrations by over 80 percent. And, while automobile use continued to increase, national emissions of VOCs from transportation sources decreased from 12.4 million metric tons in 1970 to 6.0 million in 1987.[4]

Even these gains, however, were insufficient to attain the ambient air quality standards of the Clean Air Act. The original attainment deadlines have been repeatedly extended, and ozone and smog problems are still acute in many urban areas, particularly the Northeast.[5] Eighty-one of the nation's largest cities still fail to attain air quality standards.

In 1989, the continued pattern of widespread nonattainment, a hot and smoggy 1988 summer, and long inaction at the clean air front during the Reagan years had combined to create a sense of crisis. Shortly after his inauguration, President Bush, who had waged an aggressive campaign promising to be the "environmental president," presented his strategy for reducing air pollution. Observing that "too many Americans continue to breathe dirty air," the president proclaimed that the new legislation would "make the 1990s the era for clean air."[6] The administration's proposal was ambitious, and it set the stage for aggressive congressional action. As House Energy Committee chairman John Dingell (D-Michigan) would later comment, "The President led, the public wanted [clean air legislation], and the House responded."[7]

With respect to mobile sources, the president's proposal followed earlier legislation in that, once again, it tightened tailpipe emission standards. In addition, however, the president's proposal contained a surprise element in the form of clean fuels mandates: The plan required the annual sale of 500,000 alternative-fueled cars in the nine most polluted cities by 1995 and 1 million such vehicles by 1997.

"CLEAN" FUELS?

At first sight, the quest for a clean fuel may seem attractive. Various alternative fuels, as well as reformulations of conventional gasoline, hold the promise of reducing harmful automobile emissions. For example, the addition of oxygen to gasoline—which can be achieved through various alternative or reformulated fuels—would result in a reduction of carbon monoxide emissions. Automobiles account for 70 percent of such emissions, which, at high levels of concentration, can lead to respiratory problems. Similarly, certain alternative fuels may reduce emissions of VOCs and NOx, which lead to the formation of ozone and thus contribute to urban smog.

Upon inspection, however, the case for clean fuels loses much of its attraction. The stated purpose of clean fuel requirements is to bring the most heavily polluted areas into attainment. Even under the most optimistic scenarios, though, clean fuels requirement cannot possibly do so. Los Angeles, for example, exceeds the CO standard by over 100 percent. Since each percentage point of reduction of ambient CO levels requires roughly a 2 percent reduction of automobile CO emissions, the gradual replacement of the existing automotive fleet with clean fuels vehicles can hardly be expected to bring Los Angeles into attainment.[8] Similarly, the ozone level reductions that are attainable through alternative fuels are less than spectacular; even clean fuels programs far more drastic and expensive than those eventually written into law would produce comparatively marginal environmental benefits.[9]

To be sure, many experts have argued that public health considerations do not require ambient air quality standards at the current level of stringency, and many more experts have seriously questioned the usefulness of determining attainment by measuring short-term peak concentrations rather than longer averages.[10] (Even Los Angeles, the city with the nation's dirtiest air, meets ozone standards more than 97 percent of the time.) However, apart from the fact that the Bush administration treated the standards as sacrosanct, and apart from the question of whether attainment in a technical sense is a good measure of effective clean air policy, the simple fact is that in contrast to what may have been the case in 1970, today's air pollution problems defy a standard-setting, command and control solution, whether the standards apply to tailpipes or fuels.

One reason for this is the law of diminishing marginal returns. Since automobile hydrocarbon emissions have already been reduced by 96 percent over their 1969 levels, further emission reductions are difficult to attain—and exceedingly expensive. The tailpipe standards of the 1990 Amendments will already increase the price of new vehicles by $100 to $600; the alternative fuel provisions will increase sticker prices even more.[11] This is not simply a matter of economic costs: Dramatically higher sticker prices discourage consumers from buying new cars and thus extend the life span of older cars—which account for an overwhelming portion of air pollution from mobile sources.[12] The Amendments could slow fleet turnover to such an extent as to offset the benefits that might be gained from running a portion of the automotive fleet on alternative fuels.

A clean fuels policy is marred by another fundamental difficulty: There is no such thing as a truly clean fuel. Any alternative fuels policy will involve tradeoffs between different emissions, all of which can have negative environmental effects.

The most widely touted clean fuel is ethanol, an alcohol fuel typically made from corn. Ethanol helps reduce carbon monoxide emissions by increasing the fuel's oxygen content. The widespread use of gasohol, a blend of 10 percent ethanol and 90 percent gasoline, could possibly reduce CO emissions by as much as 22 percent nationwide while reducing fuel mileage by only 2 percent.[13] Ethanol could also cause a slight reduction in lead emissions.

However, ethanol is hardly an environmentally sound fuel. In fact, it may be the most polluting of the so-called clean fuels. Ethanol is more volatile than gasoline, meaning that it evaporates more quickly. Relative to gasoline, ethanol could increase evaporative hydrocarbon emissions by as much as 50 percent and total VOC emissions by as much as 25 percent. The use of gasohol (as opposed to pure ethanol) would increase VOC emissions by as much as 20 percent and NOx emissions by about 8 to 15 percent.[14] Because VOCs are among the most common smog precursors, widespread ethanol use would increase urban smog.[15] Moreover, ethanol is water soluble and cannot be transported via pipeline; most gasohol is produced by adding ethanol to gasoline at locations near the point of retail sale. This process—known as splash blending—may exacerbate the problem of evaporative emissions. Finally, ethanol use would substantially increase the emission of other pollutants such as aldehydes, which are believed to be potent carcinogens.[16]

At the same time, ethanol is far more expensive than ordinary gasoline. Without subsidies, ethanol is likely to be over a full dollar more expensive than gasoline for the energy equivalent and gasohol, between 10 and 20 cents more expensive. In addition, the amount of grain required to replace a meaningful portion of current gasoline consumption would be sufficient to produce a staggering increase in food prices. The Congressional Research Service (CRS) has estimated that ethanol production to displace a mere 5 percent of current gasoline consumption would increase food prices by $13 billion per year, or over $2 per gallon of ethanol produced.[17]

Other clean fuels do not share all of ethanol's environmental drawbacks, but it is not clear if they provide significant environmental benefits over gasoline, either. For example, methanol, an alcohol fuel typically made from coal or natural gas, has the great advantage of reducing emissions of particulates and benzene by a very large margin.[18] One CRS study found that methanol use could reduce reactive hydrocarbon emissions anywhere from 34 to 83 percent, which could lead to a sizable decrease in smog formation.[19] However, neither CO nor NOx emissions are significantly reduced by replacing gasoline with methanol. Moreover, unfortunately, it is believed that methanol would increase emissions of formaldehyde 5 to 10 times over conventional gasoline.[20] Methanol is also 25 times more toxic than gasoline, leading the American Association of Poison Control Centers to assert that widespread methanol use could result in "an unacceptable increase in methanol-induced blindness, permanent neurologic disability, and death" nationwide.[21] Experts remain divided on the relative advantages of methanol and conventional gasoline. One research firm concluded that "methanol offers no clear advantage over gasoline in reducing vehicle emission levels."[22] The American Methanol Institute, on the other hand, believes that methanol can meet any rational emissions standard, including one that would require a decrease in aldehyde emissions.[23]

The case *against* methanol rests on its costs. Although methanol is not significantly more expensive per gallon than gasoline, it provides only 70 percent of the mileage per gallon, thus reducing vehicle range and increasing fuel costs. The American Petroleum Institute (API), for one, believes that methanol could not be economically competitive with gasoline unless oil prices reached $35 a barrel. Moreover, methanol is much more corrosive than gasoline. To compensate for methanol's increased corrosivity, automobiles are likely to be modified, increasing sticker prices by as much as $300. Also, methanol distribution costs could be prohibitively expensive. Although methanol advocates assert that methanol can be economically competitive on a "level playing field," the Office of Technology Assessment (OTA) concluded that of 11 pollution control methods examined, methanol was the most expensive, at as much as $30,000 per ton of VOC reduction.[24]

Other alternative fuels exist, but none of them are viable, given current technology. Compressed natural gas, or CNG, can reduce CO and VOC emissions by between 50 and 80 percent over ordinary gasoline, but it is prohibitively expensive for most applications. Due to the nature of the fuel, entire fuel systems need to be redesigned, and heavier fuel tanks are required to carry a less energy-efficient fuel. Although CNG may be economical for fleet vehicles, which are often purchased in sizable quantities and are typically fueled from a central point, it is economically infeasible for the general public. Electric cars will soon enter the automotive market in select areas such as California, where, under the new Clean Air Act, 2 percent of new cars are to be electric by 1998, increasing to 10 percent by 2003. However, the exorbitant cost of these so-called no emissions vehicles—an estimated additional $10,000 per vehicle—and their limited range make them an unlikely contender for nationwide use in the near future. Besides, the environmental benefits of electric cars are more questionable than is commonly assumed.[25]

THE BATTLE OVER CLEAN FUELS

When the Bush administration presented its clean air proposal, it was fully aware that all clean fuels, besides being considerably more expensive than ordinary gasoline, involved significant environmental trade-offs. Moreover, it was clear that clean fuels requirements could not possibly bring about attainment in the heavily polluted areas for which they were ostensibly designed. Finally, studies available at the time showed quite conclusively that a small fraction of the automobiles on the road were responsible for the vast preponderance of mobile source air pollution—which should have created doubts about any program that *retards* the turnover of the automobile fleet.[26] These considerations notwithstanding, the administration made the clean fuels strategy a key component of its clean air agenda.

It appears that the administration favored clean fuels not only for their perceived environmental benefits but also because of their potential to reduce the nation's dependence on foreign oil. Far more important, though, were considerations of public perception. For one thing, the administration wanted to present a tough clean air bill, yet one that was not merely "business as usual." In its effort to make good on the promise of an "environmental presidency," the administration was searching for distinctive, innovative approaches. One of these was a comprehensive acid rain program, announced by the administration with great fanfare as a solution to an urgent problem; the other was the alternative fuels policy, hailed by President Bush as a "bold new initiative to reconcile the automobile to the environment."[27] Alternative fuels had the crucial advantage of promising progress at the clean air front without imposing accountablity on the ultimate polluters—namely, car owners and drivers. As the *Wall Street Journal* put it, the administration hoped that "a switch to cleaner-burning alternative fuels . . . would help clean the air while allowing Americans to continue driving their cars."[28]

Once the administration had announced its clean fuels proposal, there was no longer a question that any legislation would contain *some* alternative to conventional gasoline. The environmental community promptly lined up in favor of stringent limits on vehicular emissions. Richard Ayres, chairman of the Clean Air Coalition (which comprises virtually all major environmental organizations), declared before the Senate Environment and Public Works Committee that "the reductions promised in the President's clean fuels proposal should serve as the minimum cleanup objective for an alternative fuels program."[29] The question was, *which* alternative fuel?[30]

The administration's stated objective was a "fuel-neutral" approach—meaning a bill that would grant no special preference to any one alternative fuel or reformulated gasoline. Its actual proposal, however, showed a pronounced bias for methanol over any type of reformulated or clean gas. Powerful executive officials—notably, the president's chief counsel, C. Boyden Gray—strongly favored the fuel. Methanol also had supporters in the EPA, especially in the Office of Mobile Sources and the Emission Control Technology Division.[31] Because that division conducts the EPA's research on vehicle emissions, its voice carried substantial weight.

The administration's asserted "fuel neutrality" quickly came under attack in Congress. Senator James Jeffords (R-Vermont) commented in his opening statements at one of the first committee hearings on the clean fuels requirements, "Whether or not a clean fuels program can be developed which is, indeed, fuel neutral remains to be seen."[32] This skepticism was warranted not only in light of the administration's evident pro-methanol bias but also because it is inherently difficult to design neutral fuel regulations. Any alternative fuels requirement must either mandate the fuel's composition or else set specific emission requirements. Since all fuels generate *some* emissions, any given emission requirement will tend to be a decision for some fuels and against others.

In the wake of the administration's proposal, industries and interest groups lined up to attempt to modify the proposed regulatory language so as to protect their interests. Of all the interest groups involved, the one with the most to lose was the oil industry: Alternative fuels requirements had the potential of displacing gasoline with a fuel for which the petroleum industry had little or no existing production capacity.

Since Congress' past clean air efforts had focused on tailpipe emissions and forced the automakers to produce cleaner-burning automobiles, it was natural to expect that the oil industry would attempt to place the burden of mobile source regulation on the automakers. While this strategy had proven successful, by and large, in previous rounds of clean air legislation, it seemed insufficient in 1989. For one thing, stricter tailpipe standards seemed far less plausible than they had in the past. The Motor Vehicle Manufacturers Association (MVMA), which represents General Motors, Chrysler, Ford, Volvo, and several truck manufacturers, argued with considerable justification that yet another round of tightening tailpipe standards would yield very marginal gains—and only at an extravagant price. Moreover, and more important, the President's proposal had created unprecedented momentum for clean fuels. In the past, automakers had successfully opposed regulations requiring the production of clean fuels vehicles on the grounds that, as long as the fuels were largely unavailable, demand for such vehicles would be nonexistent; oil companies had, with equal success, opposed clean fuels mandates as long as there was no demand due to the absence of vehicles that would run on such fuels. The administration's initiative in effect broke this stalemate.

In light of these circumstances, the oil industry concentrated on limiting the scope and impact of the proposed clean fuels regulations. The industry emphasized the extremely high costs of retrofitting refineries and developing an infrastructure for alternative fuels, and it stressed that no alternative fuel could be viewed as a panacea. At the same time, though, the oil industry made certain concessions in an effort to forestall federal clean fuels mandates. It consented to the use of alternative fuels and especially CNG in fleet vehicles, and it conceded that some areas (such as California) would set their own clean air and clean fuels standards. Finally, the oil companies recognized that Congress would, in any event, mandate some changes in the existing gasoline formula, such as reductions of fuel additives or fuel oxygenation in the winter to curb CO emissions. In short, the industry was prepared to accept a small cut in market share and a slight reformulation of gasoline to avert drastic moves toward a national conversion to alternative fuels.

Carmakers, for their part, relied, as they had in the past, on Congressman Dingell, the representative for Michigan's 16th District (Detroit) and powerful chairman of the House Committee on Energy and Commerce, which would mark up the president's Clean Air bill. Dingell had worked on the 1977 Clean Air Act Amendments to relax tailpipe standards; in 1989, as in 1977, he intended to protect the auto industry to the greatest extent possible. However, Dingell believed that infighting among key industries would pose a serious threat to the automakers and, for that matter, to other industries. Fearing that political opportunism would saddle a few unfortunate industries with most of the burden for cleaning the air, Dingell put individual industries on notice that they could hang together or hang separately, and pressured them into forming a united front. Partially as a result of Dingell's urgings, the Clean Air Working Group (CAWG) was formed. Led by William D. Fay, a veteran of the coal industry, CAWG united representatives from an impressive array of industry leaders and representatives: the Chemical Manufacturers Association, Du Pont, the Edison Electric Institute, Ford, General Motors, the National Association of Manufacturers, the National Coal Association, as well as the API and the MVMA.

The Working Group did prevent much of the industry infighting that often accompanies massive regulatory bills, and it may, in fact, have helped its members from hanging separately. Almost certainly, it also facilitated the accommodation of various industries through an assortment of clean fuels policies that were narrowly tailored to specific markets. For example, the natural gas industry—recognizing that the economies of scale made widespread CNG use an economically disastrous and politically infeasible policy for noncommercial vehicles—had concentrated on obtaining a CNG requirement for fleet vehicles. This effort was largely successful—in part because of a lack of resistance from the oil industry, and in part because fleet operators were, in turn, granted exemptions from regulatory requirements so as to facilitate their compliance with the CNG requirements.[33] In addition, the cities of Los Angeles and New York energetically promoted national measures to address their local air pollution problems. The California alternative fuels pilot program, which contains limited mandates for the sale of "clean-fueled vehicles" and the appropriate motor fuels beginning in 1996, resulted from these efforts, as did a provision allowing other states to opt into this program. (As of July 1991, New York, New Jersey, and the six New England states had pledged to adopt the California standards. Additional states, including Pennsylvania, Maryland, and Texas, were also considering such a move.)

On the alternative fuels side, the crucial battle raged between methanol and ethanol. The methanol industry, represented by the American Methanol Institute (AMI), had the advantage of being able to build on the administration's bias toward its product. However, in terms of size, resources, and political capital, the industry was no match for the ethanol lobby. Ethanol interests were represented by the Renewable Fuels Association (RFA), by the Clean Fuels Development Coalition (representing various smaller producers of ethanol and other potential alternative fuels and fuel additives), and by the National Corn Growers' Association. In addition, ethanol could count on the influence of the Archer Daniels Midland Company (ADM), the largest domestic producer of ethanol. Although ADM did not engage in any direct lobbying in the clean air debate, it followed its general policy of "using various trade associations as mouthpieces while keeping itself seemingly above the fray."[34] For example, ADM is very influential in the Renewable Fuels Association and the National Corn Growers Association. It may even be fair to say that RFA *is* ADM's lobbyist.[35]

The methanol and ethanol industries were not only different in size, they also pursued very different political strategies both before and during the battle over the Clean Air Act Amendments of 1990. The ethanol industry, and ADM in particular, have consistently pursued government subsidies and mandates as a means of creating a market for their product. ADM chief executive officer (CEO) Dwayne Andreas himself has described his company as "totally immersed in these government programs."[36] Ethanol, in particular, is largely dependent on agricultural subsidies and gas tax exemptions on both the state and federal levels. In the debate over the Clean Air Act, the ethanol lobby's objective was again to obtain regulations that would tilt the playing field toward ethanol.

The methanol industry, on the other hand, had made its political debut in California where, in the 1980s, Governor George Deukmejian's administration had begun to promote alternative fuels—without, however, providing government subsidies. California regulations permitted the use of any fuel, as long as the fuel-vehicle combination met stringent emission standards. As a result, methanol came into (albeit very limited) use in California, primarily in flexible-fuel vehicles. This experience led the methanol industry to focus on promoting its product by stressing its competitiveness. Throughout the debate over the Clean Air Act Amendments, the industry's pitch was that methanol could compete against any other alternative fuel—or, for that matter, against gasoline—on a level playing field.

Ironically, the dynamics of the legislative process may have favored the approach of the ethanol industry. Supported by corn growers throughout the Midwest, ethanol had a constituency that was experienced at clamoring for government subsidies. For farm state legislators, supporting ethanol was an easy means of building political capital. The methanol lobby, on the other hand, found that the demand for a level playing field attracted neither a sufficiently strong constituency support nor the attention of legislators. "If you didn't ask for something," one consultant to the methanol industry recalls, "you wouldn't be taken seriously. No one wanted to hear that there was a cleaner-burning fuel that could compete economically without government assistance. There is not a strong political interest unless someone is receiving a subsidy."[37]

In light of the alternative fuels industries' aggressive lobbying, the oil industry came to realize that its strategy of making minor concessions in order to avert across-the-board alternative fuels mandates might be insufficient to stop the juggernaut that had been set in motion by Bush's proposal. On January 11, 1990, the Senate Committee on the Environment and Public Works held long hearings on the subject of alternative fuels. While most witnesses addressed the pros and cons of alternative fuels, George Babikian, president of Arco Products Co., talked about the vast opportunities offered by *reformulated gas*. Previous fuel modifications—for example, lead removal—had always resulted in other problems, such as the need to add benzene to maintain octane levels. Babikian now told the committee that reformulated gasoline could be designed to meet virtually any emissions standard, albeit at slightly higher cost:

Gasoline can be reformulated to meet equitable fuel-neutral standards for today's cars, as well as for automobiles of the future. . . . All fuels that have the potential to clean up the air should be allowed to compete, and the fuel that can compete at the most effective cost is the fuel that ought to survive. . . . I'm convinced that we can play in that ball park.[38]

On that note, Babikian announced that within two years Arco would introduce a new fuel, EC-X, that could be used in all gasoline-powered vehicles.

The implications of Babikian's testimony were clear: In contrast to alternative fuels, which would require expensive vehicle modifications, reformulated gasoline could be used in all existing conventional automobiles. In addition, reformulated gasoline—but not alcohol fuels—would "hit the whole fleet right away, and so the impact is sooner, bigger."[39] As API's vice-president observed following Arco's testimony, "If [stricter tailpipe standards and reformulated gas] are sufficient to reach attainment, then there would be no purpose to an alternative fuels program."[40] The promise of a clean gas strengthened the oil industry's hand and cemented its coalition with the auto industry, which preferred not to begin production of more expensive alternative fuels vehicles. The alternative fuels debate shifted dramatically; reformulated gasoline suddenly represented a serious threat to alternative fuels.

The environmental movement saw reformulated gasoline as an opportunity: If reformulated gasoline could dramatically reduce the emissions of existing vehicles, it should be made to meet the most stringent "neutral" requirements possible. The ethanol lobby, on the other hand, wanted to preserve its ability to keep its product in the market as a fuel additive. Toward this end, the industry had to ensure that regulations would *not* be "fuel-neutral." Accordingly, the ethanol industry strongly opposed facially neutral emission ceilings and sought to obtain regulations that would mandate fuel *content*. Such regulations could provide a market for ethanol and ethanol blends—and, preferably, exclude all other alternative fuels.

On this score, both the administration proposal, as introduced and modified in the House of Representatives as H.R. 3030, and the Senate bill, S. 1630, met the ethanol industry's needs, at least in part: Both bills contained fuel content requirements. The most important of these were provisions mandating that fuels sold in certain regions meet minimum levels of oxygen, on the theory that higher levels of oxygen can reduce car emissions of CO and, potentially, of smog precursors. As noted above, adding ethanol is one way of raising oxygen content.

Both the Senate and the House bills would eventually contain an alternative fuels program consisting of three components: a so-called reformulated gasoline program for the worst ozone nonattainment areas (that is, the nation's 9 smoggiest cities), an "oxygenated fuels" program for 44 cities that fall well short of attaining CO standards, typically during the winter months, and a pilot program for California that would more ambitiously promote actual alternative fuels. The areas required to participate in one or more of the programs account for the overwhelming portion of total U.S. fuel consumption. Table 2.1 below lists the details of the alternative fuels provisions of the House and the Senate bills and of the Amendments as they were eventually enacted.

The debate over alternative fuels was dominated by wrangling over the precise level of oxygen requirements. The ethanol industry's objective was to obtain as high an oxygen mandate as possible for both CO and ozone nonattainment areas, for the simple reason that no reformulated or alternative gasoline can reach the oxygenation levels that can be achieved by blending ethanol with gasoline. A blend of 90 percent gasoline and 10 percent ethanol has an oxygen content of about 3.5 percent. In contrast, Methyl Tertiary Butyl Ether (MTBE), a methanol derivative fuel oxygenate produced primarily by oil companies, cannot attain an oxygen level of more than 2.7 percent. Thus, an oxygen requirement above that level amounts to a de facto ethanol mandate.

S. 1630, which was approved by the Senate Committee on Environment and Public Works by a vote of 19–1, required that gasoline sold in CO nonattainment areas contain at least 3.1 percent oxygen during the winter months. The committee made little effort to disguise that this was a de facto ethanol mandate: "In the absence of other avenues through which to encourage domestically produced ethanol to enter the fuel stream, this [3.1 percent oxygen requirement] is necessary."[41] The discussion of the provision in the committee report consisted largely of an attempt to show that the revenues lost to ethanol's gas tax exemption were made up by concurrent savings in farm subsidies.[42]

At the Senate Environment Committee's January 17 hearings, the oil industry and methanol lobbyists attacked the 3.1 percent oxygen mandate as a gift to the ethanol industry. Arco's Babikian complained that "The 3.1 percent requirement virtually gives an ethanol mandate."[43] Methanol advocates pointed out that "the overall benefits of oxygen are not linear. . . . [T]he greatest benefit occurs at the level of 2 percent [oxygen

Table 2.1
1990 Clean Air Act Amendments: "Clean Fuels" Provisions

	SENATE BILL (S. 1630)	HOUSE BILL (H.R. 3030)	CONFERENCE AGREEMENT
OXYGENATION OF FUELS			
CO NONATTAINMENT			
Areas	44 in CO Nonattainment	44 Areas (More Broadly Defined)	As in H.R. 3030
Period	Oct. 1 – March 31 Beginning Oct. 1991	To be Defined by EPA Beginning Oct. 1992	To be Defined by EPA; Minimum of Four Months, Beginning Nov. 1992
Oxygen Content (%)	3.1	2.7 (can be raised by EPA to 3.1)	As in H.R. 3030
Credits	To be Given to Those Who Sell Above 3.1%	Similar	To be Defined by EPA
	Trading Regulations to be Defined by EPA	Guidelines to be Drafted by EPA	As in S. 1630
	Trades Limited to Same CO Area	No Restriction	Similar to S. 1630
Waiver	At EPA's Discretion if Requirements Would Interfere With Other Attainment Efforts	No Waiver	As in S. 1630
REFORMULATED GAS FOR OZONE NONATTAINMENT AREAS			
Areas	9 Cities in "Extreme or "Severe" Nonattainment	9 Cities Plus Any Future Area With "Severe" or "Extreme" Ozone Problem	As in S. 1630
Deadlines	Two Phases (1992/1996)	To be Phased in 1992–2000	Two Phases (1995/2000)
Emission Standards	15% VOC Reduction During High Ozone Season	15% VOC Reduction Beg. in 1994 20% in 1997 25% in 2000	15% Reduction Until 2000 25% Thereafter
	No Net NOx Increase (as Determined by EPA)	Similar	As in S. 1630
Benzene Content	Maximum 1.0%	Maximum 0.8%	As in S. 1630
Aromatic HC's	Max. 30% in 1992 Max. 28% in 1994 Max. 25% in 1996	Similar	Max. 25%
Minimum Oxygen Contant	2.0% in 1992 2.5% in 1993 2.7% in 1994	Similar	2.0%
Waiver of Oxygen Content Requirements	EPA May Waive Requirement if They Would Compromise Other Attainment Efforts	No Waiver	As in S. 1630
CLEAN FUELS VEHICLES	Nine–City Program	California Pilot Program	As in H.R. 3030

content]. . . . . [A]ny [requirement] above 2.7 percent is unjustified. It would simply operate as another hidden subsidy for uneconomic ethanol."[44] Despite these objections, the 3.1 percent mandate for CO nonattainment areas was retained in the bill.

Senate leaders and administration representatives met in February to negotiate a compromise that would narrow the differences between S. 1630 and the administration proposal on all major issues, including alternative fuels. The version of the bill that emerged from these negotiations was a compromise between the original White House proposal and the Senate committee bill, which the administration deemed too costly for reasons unrelated to the alternative fuels provisions. The compromise contained, along with a program for the gradual replacement of the federal vehicle fleet with alternative fuels vehicles, a two-phase program for ozone nonattainment areas in addition to the CO provisions that existed in the committee bill. This program established requirements, effective in 1995, that would likely be met by reformulated gas, and more stringent second-phase requirements that most likely would force a mix of clean fuels vehicles (such as electric cars) and more advanced (and more expensive) reformulated gas, beginning in 1999.

Senate leaders pledged that they would support the compromise, described by Senate Minority Leader Robert Dole (R-Kansas) as "the single most important piece of legislation we'll deal with this year," against any and all amendments that would either weaken it or prompt a presidential veto.[45] Senator John H. Chafee (R-Rhode Island), ranking Republican on the Environment Committee, observed that he and other environmentalist senators would be "in the awkward position of voting against" environmental provisions that they would otherwise have supported.[46] Still, the last week of March saw several attempts to amend S. 1630. Amendments were proposed to toughen antipollution requirements and to waive vehicle emission requirements that increased American dependence on minerals imported from South Africa. These and other proposed amendments were defeated, as was an amendment sponsored by Senators Tim Wirth (D-Colorado) and Pete Wilson (R-California) that would have imposed stringent emissions requirements for alternative fuels vehicles in all ozone nonattainment areas. The standards of this amendment—labeled by the Sierra Club the "Key Environmental Vote of 1990"—were so severe that, according to API, the first-phase requirements could only be met by CNG or methanol in an extremely modified vehicle, and the second-phase requirements were likely to necessitate the use of electric vehicles. Majority leader George Mitchell's (D-Maine) motion to table the amendment passed by only a six-vote margin, despite the outspoken support of the Senate leadership which was concerned with the possible passage of a "deal-breaker" amendment.

Only one substantial amendment concerning alternative fuels passed, and it did so despite the fact that it could raise total consumer costs by several billion dollars and was not supported by the administration. The amendment, proposed by Senator Tom Daschle (D-South Dakota), set blending parameters for reformulated gasoline to be used in all vehicles in the nation's nine smoggiest cities (that is, the extreme and severe ozone nonattainment areas). The parameters included a year-round oxygen requirement of 2.7 percent by 1994 in those areas, *in addition to* the 3.1 mandate for CO nonattainment areas already in the bill. Supporters of the amendment defeated a motion to table by a vote of 30–69. The Daschle Amendment was then accepted by a voice vote.

The Daschle Amendment was supported by a few senators who hoped to break the Senate-administration deal and prompt a veto. This was not an unreasonable expectation: Concurrently with the Senate's consideration of the Daschle Amendment, the House Energy Committee rejected an almost identical provision by a narrow 21–22 vote, in large part because of strenuous opposition by the Bush administration and the oil industry, which contended that "the guidelines would raise costs to consumers by $100 billion, adding anywhere from 5 cents to 25 cents a gallon to the price of reformulated gasoline."[47]

The second group of supporters of the Daschle Amendment were environmentalists. Of course, they also had supported the Wirth-Wilson Amendment—which failed. In contrast to Wirth-Wilson, however, the Daschle amendment was virtually an ethanol mandate for ozone non-attainment areas. While gasoline blended with MTBE can reach the 2.7 percent oxygen requirement, it cannot do so *consistently*. Since the Daschle Amendment required an *average* minimum of 2.7 percent, it effectively eliminated MTBE as a fuel additive without the purchase of so-called oxygen credits from ethanol producers. As a result, the bill gained the support of the farm bloc led by Senate Minority Leader Dole, "who saw an opportunity to open new markets for ethanol [; consequently;] the amendment was passed despite being labeled veto bait by the White House."[48]

The ethanol-environmental coalition showed similar strength in the House. In late 1989, the House Energy Subcommittee on Health and the Environment, chaired by Congressman Henry Waxman (D-California) had somewhat weakened the alternative fuels provisions of H.R. 3030 (the Bush proposal) in an attempt to reduce the bill's bias in favor of methanol. The following spring, Congressman Bill Richardson (D-New

Mexico) sought to restore alternative fuels provisions in the full committee that would be even more stringent than those pushed by Daschle in the Senate. Richardson's proposal to mandate reformulated gasoline with oxygen requirements in over 30 ozone nonattainment cities failed by one vote in the Energy Committee, principally because of Committee Chairman Dingell's opposition. But the Richardson proposal faced more promising prospects on the House floor, where Dingell possessed less leverage than he did in his committee. When the committee reported the bill to the full House in May, sometime Dingell allies Edward Madigan (R-Illinois) and Terry Bruce (D-Illinois), who were the farm bloc's "point men" on the Energy Committee, decided to defect "with farm bloc allies to the environmentalists after Dingell refused to carve out a big role for gasoline substitutes made from corn."[49] The ethanol-environmental coalition had the force to carry the day, as it had in the Senate. Fearing the prospect of losing a floor fight that might have produced a provision as bad as or worse than the Daschle Amendment, Dingell decided to compromise with Richardson and Waxman and reformulated gas provisions were inserted into the committee amendments to the bill. These provisions mandated oxygen requirements for reformulated gas similar to those of the Senate bill: 2.7 percent for CO nonattainment areas in the winter months, and 2 percent, rising to 2.7 percent in 1994, for ozone nonattainment areas year-round.[50]

However, the House bill was, in certain respects, even more biased in favor of ethanol than the Senate bill. As noted, above a certain threshold—commonly believed to be around 2.1 percent oxygen content—fuel oxygenation can *increase* the level of NOx and smog formation. Thus, the widespread use of oxygenated fuels for CO nonattainment could impede the attainment of ambient standards for ozone, an issue of great concern to the environmental community and to cities in nonattainment for both ozone and CO, such as Los Angeles and San Diego. Moreover, oxygenated fuels can also *increase* emissions of hydrocarbons and air toxics.

To address these concerns, the Senate bill contained a "no net NOx increase provision": notwithstanding the nominal fuel oxygenation requirements contained in the bill, the oxygen content of fuels sold in ozone nonattainment areas would have to be raised only to the level at which net NOx emissions would increase. The EPA was authorized to define that level. Further, the Senate bill contained a "waiver" providing the EPA with the authority to reduce oxygenation requirements for both CO and ozone nonattainment areas if compliance with the full statutory standards would hamper other attainment efforts. Both the no NOx increase provision and the waiver were detrimental to ethanol interests: an unfavorable finding by the EPA with respect to ethanol's contribution to NOx emissions, hydrocarbon (HC) evaporative emissions, or toxic emissions could render statutory ethanol mandates illusory. While the House bill contained a similar no NOx provision at the insistence of Congressman Waxman, the "waiver" provision contained in S. 1630 was noticeably absent. Thus, the House bill strongly favored ethanol, even at the price of potentially compromising other attainment efforts.

Although the House and Senate bills passed by impressive margins, the differences between the bills had to be reconciled. The joint Senate-House conference agreed on requirements of 2.0 percent minimum oxygen content in ozone nonattainment areas year-round and 2.7 percent minimum oxygen content for CO nonattainment areas during the winter months. In addition, the bill featured both the "no NOx increase" provision and the waivers of the Senate bill.

Appearances notwithstanding, the reductions of minimum oxygen requirements and the inclusion of "no NOx increase" and waiver provisions constituted only a mild setback for ethanol interests. The bill emerged from the conference with a so-called "oxygen credits-trading program" for CO and ozone nonattainment areas which was in the original Senate bill (S. 1630) and was maintained as part of the agreement that reduced the required oxygen content from 3.1 percent as passed in S. 1630 to 2.7 percent as adopted in H.R. 3030. Under this program, producers of gasoline with an above-minimum oxygen content can acquire oxygen credits and sell them to retailers of gasoline with less oxygen. In practice, ethanol producers, who alone can raise oxygen content above 2.7 percent, would be the only beneficiaries of this program.

The bill was passed by both chambers and signed into law by President Bush on November 15, 1990. With respect to alternative fuels, though, the enactment marked more of a beginning than an end. Despite the ethanol industry's best efforts to obtain fuel requirements tantamount to an ethanol mandate, in the end, Congress blinked and stopped short of making a conclusive decision for or against any particular alternative fuel. The requirements for ozone nonattainment areas permit the use of a variety of alternative fuels or, for that matter, reformulated gasoline. The 2.7 percent oxygen content requirement for fuels sold in CO nonattainment areas during the winter months is, to all intents and purposes, an ethanol mandate; but the EPA can either raise the standard to 3.1 percent or allow state authorities to *reduce* it if it finds that compliance with the full standard would hamper other attainment efforts.

Similarly, the definition of "no net NOx increase" oxygenation levels, which has a profound impact on the use of particular types of alternative and reformulated fuels, was left to the EPA, as was the definition of trading parameters for the oxygen credit program. The EPA was now confronted with the difficult task of finding a politically acceptable solution.

ETHANOL'S LAST STAND

The EPA's primary concerns were to determine what does or does not qualify as a "clean fuel" or "reformulated gas," to draft regulations for the oxygen credit-trading program, and to define a "no NOx increase" level. The agency decided to address these issues not through an ordinary rule-making proceeding—the result of which would surely be challenged in court and entangled in years of litigation—but through a less formal process known as regulatory negotiation, or *regneg*. EPA officials, interested industries, representatives of the states, and the environmental community met in a series of negotiations for the purpose of drafting mutually agreeable regulations, and they signed an Agreement in Principle to abide by and uphold the regulations.

The regnegs, like the preceding legislative debate, revolved around the precise oxygen content requirements. After the conference negotiations between the House and Senate, concerns had again arisen over the potential for mandated formulas containing oxygen to increase NOx. One of the central mandates of regneg was to define a so-called simple model for certification of reformulated gasoline that does not cause a net NOx increase. This simple model would remain in effect until May 1997 when the EPA is due to complete research to construct a "complex model."

Environmental advocates and the state air regulators sought to ensure that fuel sold in CO nonattainment areas would not contribute to ozone formation. The ethanol industry, on the other hand, was concerned with maintaining its advantages—principally, by maximizing its ability to acquire oxygen trade credits that could be sold to fuel producers who fail to meet the standards. Ethanol supporters pushed for a maximum allowable oxygen content of 3.5 percent in the simple model.

As noted, a level of 2.1 percent oxygen content is generally considered safe for NOx purposes, and the regneg participants set the maximum oxygen content for gasoline sold in ozone nonattainment areas at that level. However, since comprehensive studies had shown that MTBE would result in no net NOx increase even at its maximum level of 2.7 percent, the EPA proposed that the simple model define the "no NOx increase" oxygen level at 2.7 for MTBE and 2.1 for other additives. This did not sit well with the ethanol lobby, which had not fought for a high ozone nonattainment oxygen standard merely to hand over a comparative advantage to the producers of MTBE, an additive approximately 23 percent less expensive to produce than ethanol. Thus, ethanol representatives proposed that until further tests were conducted, all additives should be held to the limit of 2.1 percent. However, the EPA, environmentalists, and state air officials harbored grave concerns over ethanol's potential to increase NOx concentrations; state regulators even demanded the authority to prevent implementation of the credit trading program where it might compromise other clean air efforts. Ignoring the ethanol industry's threat to walk out of the regnegs over the issue, the regneg participants left the maximum oxygen levels at 2.7 percent for MTBE and 2.1 percent for non-MTBE oxygenates.

In response, the ethanol industry staged an end run around the regneg process. Whereas the regneg participants had heretofore eschewed the use of political leverage to influence the negotiations, the ethanol industry now solicited a letter from Dole, Daschle, and 25 other senators—primarily from farm states—to EPA Administrator William Reilly. The senators charged that the proposed simple model would jeopardize future clean air efforts by marginalizing fuel additives or formulations about which little is known (i.e., ethanol). The senators further complained that giving state regulators authority over credit trading programs would violate congressional intent, inasmuch as "the credits trading program is essential to encouraging the use of fuels with a higher oxygen content in the marketplace."[51]

The pressure was effective. In August 1991, EPA assistant administrator William G. Rosenberg presented ethanol representatives with a compromise. The supplemental rule-making proposal now under consideration presumes that oxygen contents up to 3.5 percent will *not* cause an increase in NOx emissions, except during the summer months of ozone nonattainment. This compromise is highly advantageous to ethanol producers, and to ADM in particular. ADM produces ethanol only during the winter; during the summer, its plants are used for corn syrup production. Under the announced compromise, ADM will be able to produce and sell high-oxygen ethanol during the winter, accrue oxygen credits, and sell them during the summer, thus ensuring a year-round revenue stream. Whether the compromise is equally beneficial to the environment is much less clear: Any fuel with a 3.5 percent oxygen content will almost certainly cause an increase in NOx emissions.[52]

CONCLUSION

Under the 1990 Clean Air Act Amendments, gasoline sold in ozone nonattainment areas must have a Reid Vapor Pressure (RVP, the standard measure of fuel volatility) of nine pounds per square inch (psi).[53] The reason for this requirement is that "evaporative hydrocarbon emissions . . . are now the most significant source of vehicle hydrocarbon emissions during the summer, when ozone formation is at its peak."[54] However, ethanol is far more volatile than gasoline. Accordingly, the Amendments *relax* the volatility requirement for fuels containing 10 percent ethanol.[55] The Senate Committee on Environment and Public Works helpfully explained that without this exemption, the costs of producing ethanol-blended fuel that could meet RVP standards "would likely result in the termination of the availability of ethanol in the market place."[56]

The RVP exemption illustrates that legislators were prepared to go to extraordinary lengths in creating a market for ethanol, regardless of the environmental results. However, it is not the only such illustration. The oxygen standards, the credit-trading program, the definition of "no NOx increase" in the EPA's simple model—all were driven exclusively by political considerations. The result was a regulatory regime of mind-boggling complexity, a web of standards, mandates, requirements, and timetables that is incomprehensible to all but a handful of bureaucrats and to the representatives of the interests that are being regulated or served. Attached to this comprehensive management plan, for the sole benefit of certain industry interests, is an oxygen credit-trading program, which is proudly presented as evidence of regulatory flexibility and incentive-based regulation.

There is something faintly comical about this triumph of symbolism and subsidies over substance. Legislators identify the precise level of oxygen mandates sufficient to purchase the votes of the farm bloc—and manage to pretend that decisions over a few tenths of a percentage point of oxygen content are decisions for or against clean air. They mandate the use of natural gas in fleet vehicles and, in turn, exempt those vehicles from idling requirements and grant them permission to use High Occupancy Vehicle lanes, still pretending that the legislation has something to do with clean air. Finally, legislators vote on a 600–plus-page package of mandates, requirements, timetables, and deadlines, most of them more convoluted even than the clean fuels program—and pretend that they have carefully considered the environmental ramifications of a minimum oxygen requirement of 2.0 percent for gasoline sold in ozone nonattainment areas during the summer months, barring a net NOx increase.

But while the cynics snicker—and ethanol producers laugh all the way to the bank—the American public faces the less amusing prospect of paying $3 billion per year for so-called clean fuels without a discernible environmental benefit. This is particularly unfortunate because the Bush administration had a unique opportunity to reform clean air regulation, including the regulation of mobile source emissions, in a manner that would have produced more clean air at much lower cost than was possible under the convoluted command and control regime of the old Clean Air Act. In contrast to the authors of the original Act, the Bush administration had the benefit of two decades worth of experience with federal clean air legislation and was in a position to know what would work and what would not work. It knew that an overwhelming portion of air pollution from mobile sources was produced by relatively few automobiles. It knew that uniform, nationwide emission and technology standards were a singularly inefficient way of cleaning the air. And it knew that a further tightening of technology standards would produce, at best, marginal environmental benefits while imposing staggering economic costs.

In contrast to the Reagan administration, the Bush administration had sufficient credibility on environmental issues to propose effective and relatively inexpensive approaches to mobile source regulation without being immediately accused of weakening environmental regulation. A scheme to speed fleet turnover and to get old, heavily polluting "clunkers" off the roads or at least out of metropolitan areas would have been one approach. A somewhat more ambitious approach would have incorporated emission fees. Various fee systems had been proposed by economists, and the technologies to implement an unobtrusive system existed. During the clean air debate, they were even demonstrated in front of the Rayburn Senate Office Building.[57] If clean fuels are as clean as their supporters maintain, they would have benefited from an emission fee system: The cleaner the car, the smaller the fee for driving it.

However, such proposals would have met with political opposition, and they would have required the administration to tell the American people the truth about air pollution—that perfectly clean air everywhere is a political chimera, that even the amount of clean air that is realistically attainable does not come without costs, and that mobile source pollution has much more to do with our personal habits than with inadequate technology or greedy "corporate polluters." Instead of facing these obstacles, the administration made do with the existing, convoluted and inefficient regulatory scheme, tightened it at the margin, and superimposed upon it a superficially attractive technological fix. Once the clean fuels mandates had been introduced, environmental considerations receded into the background and constituency service became the overriding concern.

It is not without irony that the clean fuels program—one of the Bush administration's distinctive contributions to clean air regulation—mutated into an ethanol subsidy largely for reasons related to the administration's *other* distinctive contribution—the acid rain program. Touted even more fervently as innovative by the administration than the clean fuels program, the acid rain program was even more misguided and bereft of scientific support. The National Acid Precipitation Assessment Program (NAPAP), a 10-year, $500 million study commissioned by Congress, concluded in 1990 that "there is no evidence of widespread forest damage from current ambient levels of acidic rain in the United States" and continued to criticize all previous assessments of the harm caused by acid rain to public health and to the environment as grossly overstated.[58] However, at this point, the president and the EPA had already decided that the nation needed an acid rain program. Congress simply ignored the NAPAP study and adopted an acid rain program similar to the one proposed by the president.[59] The program will cost an estimated $3 to $7 billion and put more than 200,000 jobs at risk. Most of these costs will fall on midwestern and farm states.[60] It was in large part for this reason that farm state representatives demanded compensation—and received it in the form of an ethanol program.

The fact that this program is exceedingly expensive and pointless from an environmental perspective is perhaps not the worst of it. In promising, once again, that technology will solve the intractable problems of air pollution, the clean fuels program is part of a charade that has long precluded a sensible public debate about air pollution.

NOTES

1. The nine areas are Los Angeles, New York, Chicago, Houston, Milwaukee, Baltimore, Muskegon (Mich), Philadelphia/Trenton, and San Diego.

2. "Cost vs. Benefits: Analysis Gets Soft," *Wall Street Journal*, 4 April 1990, p. A15.

3. Statement of William G. Rosenberg (Assistant Administrator, Air and Radiation, U.S. EPA), Hearings before the Subcommittee on Energy and Power of the Committee on Energy and Commerce, U.S. House of Representatives, 18–19 October 1989, No. 101–120 (Washington, D.C.: GPO, 1990), 227.

4. The Council on Environmental Quality, *Environmental Quality: Twentieth Annual Report* (Washington, D.C.: CEQ, 1990), Tables 41, 42.

5. See R. Shep Melnick's comments in Chapter 5 of this volume.

6. Text of remarks by the president on the Clean Air Act announcement, June 12, 1989 (Office of the Press Secretary, The White House), 1–2.

7. Quoted in Margaret E. Kriz, "Politics at the Pump," *National Journal* (2 June 1990), 1329.

8. David E. Gushee, *Emissions Impact of Oxygenated (Alcohol/Gasoline) Fuels*, Congressional Research Service, 20 May 1987, 6.

9. One study found that "a switch to M85 [85 percent methanol, 15 percent gasoline] cars in Los Angeles beginning in 1990 could reduce peak ozone levels in a 3-day smog attack in the year 2000 by 8 percent. A switch to M100 [100 percent methanol] could reduce the peak levels 16%." "Gasoline: The Unclean Fuel?" *Science*, 13 October 1989, 201.

10. See, for example, National Research Council, *Rethinking the Ozone Problem in Urban and Regional Air Pollution* (Washington, D.C.: National Academy Press, 1991), Chapter 2; Alan J. Krupnick and Paul J. Portney, "Controlling Urban Air Pollution: A Benefit-Cost Assessment," *Science*, 26 April 1991, 522–28 and 9 August 1991, 606–09; Kent Jeffreys, "Rethinking the Clean Air Act Amendments," Policy Backgrounder No. 107, National Center for Policy Analysis, 16 October 1990; and Peter Spencer, "Clearing the Air on Urban Smog," *Consumers' Research*, March 1990, 12–14.

11. "Clean Air Accord Is Reached in Congress that May Cost Industry $25 Billion a Year," *Wall Street Journal*, 23 October 1990.

12. This trend has already been observable since the passage of the previous clean air legislation. According to the *Wall Street Journal*, for the average American the average number of weeks of work required to purchase the average priced new car increased over 35 percent between 1979 and 1989. "Even Detroit Concedes Sticker Shock," *Wall Street Journal*, 8 August 1991.

13. Robert C. Anderson, Thomas Lareau, and Roger Wollstadt, *The Economics of Gasoline Ethanol Blends*, Research Study No. 45 (Washington, D.C.: American Petroleum Institute, November 1988), 28.

14. Anderson, Lareau, and Wollstadt, *Gasoline Ethanol Blends*; and Thomas C. Austin and Christopher S. Weaver, *The Air Pollution Consequences of Using Ethanol-Gasoline Blends in Ozone Non-Attainment Areas*, (Sacramento, Calif.: Sierra Research, Inc.), 8 May 1990.

15. According to Thomas Austin and Christopher Weaver at Sierra Research, nationwide use of such gasohol fuel would increase ozone formation by 6 percent, and a study conducted by the Air Pollution Control Division of the Colorado Department of Health concluded that the year-round use of 10 percent ethanol-blended gasoline in Denver would increase ozone formation by as much as 13 percent in the mile-high city. Austin and Weaver, *Air Pollution Consequences*, 2; and Anthony Woodlief, *The Clean Fuels Myth and the Market Alternative: Mobile Source Emissions Charges* (Washington, D.C.: Competitive Enterprise Institute, 1989), 4.

16. The EPA estimates that ethanol would increase formaldehyde emissions by 50 percent and acetaldehyde emissions by 100 percent over ordinary gasoline. Cited in Austin and Weaver, *Air Pollution Consequences*, 15–16. Ethanol has even been credited by the Environmental Defense Fund (EDF) with a 25 percent increase in the emissions of greenhouse gases, as so much fuel needs to be expended to harvest and process corn for ethanol production. Diane C. Fisher, *Reducing Greenhouse Gas Emissions with Alternative Transportation Fuels* (EDF, April 1991).

17.. CRS study cited in Anderson, Lareau, and Wollstadt, *Gasoline Ethanol Blends*, 48.

18. Charles L. Gray, Jr., and Jeffrey A. Alson, "The Case for Methanol," *Scientific American* 261 (November 1989): 111.

19. This range covers both methanol-dedicated vehicles and flexible-fuel vehicles that would be capable of running on both methanol and gasoline. David Gushee, *Alternative Fuels for Motor Vehicles: Some Environmental Issues*, Congressional Research Service, 20 September 1988, 11.

20. Estimates from Thomas Austin, senior partner, Sierra Research, Inc., briefing of American Petroleum Institute, 30 August 1989 (Washington, D.C.: API) and James S. Cannon, *Drive for Clean Air* (New York: INFORM, Inc., 1989), 49.

21. Extrapolating data from U.S. poison centers, AAPCC concluded that widespread methanol use could lead to 195 additional deaths per year, largely due to accidental ingestion in the course of attempted siphoning. Toby Lovitz and William O. Robertson, "The Health Hazards of Methanol Use," *Consumers' Research*, March 1990, 17.

22. Thomas C. Austin, Robert G. Dulla, Gary S. Rubenstein, and Christopher S. Weaver, *Potential Emissions and Air Quality Effects of Alternative Fuels—Final Report*, No. SR89-03-04, 28 March 1989 (Sacramento, Calif.: Sierra Research, Inc.), 1.

23. Statement of Ray Lewis (President, American Methanol Institute), Hearings Before the Subcommittee on Environmental Protection of the Committee on Environment and Public Works, U.S. Senate, 11 January 1990, No. 101–584 (Washington, D.C.: GPO, 1990), 79.

24. The other methods included such measures as on-board vehicle fuel emission controls, enhanced inspection and maintenance programs, and volatility limitations. U.S. Office of Technology Assessment, U.S. Congress, *Summary: Catching Our Breath: Next Steps for Reducing Urban Ozone*, (Washington, D.C.: Office of Technology Assessment, 1989), 15.

25. "The environmental and social impact of a clean-fuel program runs far beyond the fuel itself. Electricity might be the cleanest possible fuel in the Los Angeles basin, but environmental damage would result from constructing power plants outside the basin to supply it." William F. Pedersen, Jr., "Running On Empty: Auto Emissions Plans Short on Specifics," *Legal Times*, 4 December 1989, 32.

26. As of July 1988, pre-1983 vehicles still accounted for 54 percent of American automobile registrations, yet these vehicles were credited with 84 percent of the HC and CO emissions and 72 percent of the NOx emissions. Clean Air Act Amendments of 1989, *Report of the Committee on Environment and Public Works*, Senate Report No. 101–228 (Washington, D.C.: GPO, 1989), Chart 6 (Minority Views of Senator Symms). Even Charles Gray, the head of EPA's Motor Vehicle Emissions Laboratory and one of the administration's principal methanol advocates, acknowledged that the primary pollution problem from mobile sources is the failure of automobile emissions control systems over time. "Gasoline: The Unclean Fuel?" *Science*, 13 October 1989, 199.

27. Text of remarks by the president on the Clean Air Act Announcement, June 12, 1989, 3.

28. "Bush Proposes Revision of Clean-Air Law That Would Cut Acid Rain 50 Percent by 2000," *Wall Street Journal*, 13 June 1989, p. A3.

29. Statement of Richard Ayres, Senate Hearing No. 101–584, 67.

30. As the National Wildlife Federation's William Klinefelter commented, "There is no silver bullet here. That's why everyone is jockeying for their best position." Kriz, "Politics at the Pump," 1331.

31. James MacKenzie of the World Resources Institute described the EPA as "100 percent in favor of methanol—if not institutionally, at least on the staff level." Senate Hearing No. 101–584, 57.

32. Statement of Senator James Jeffords, Senate Hearing No. 101–584, 6.

33. The Amendments contain exemptions for fleet vehicles from various traffic regulations, such as the use of High Occupancy Vehicle (HOV) lanes and idling restrictions.

34. "Grain King's Business Is a Daily Grind for Profit," *Insight*, 19 February 1990, 13.

35. ADM accounts for approximately one-third of the dues RFA collects from its members, and it pays RFA so-called "production assessments" that raise its share of the RFA's budget to between 70 and 80 percent.

36. "Grain King's Business," 11.

37. Personal interview with author, 21 August 1991. Name withheld by request.

38. Statement of George Babikian (President, ARCO Products Co.), Senate Hearing No. 101–584, 68, 80–81.

39. Statement of Richard Klimisch (Executive Director, General Motors Environmental Activities Staff), Senate Hearing No. 101–584, 57.

40. Statement of Michael Canes (Vice President, American Petroleum Institute), Senate Hearing No. 101–584, 71.

41. *Clean Air Act Amendments of 1989*, Senate Report No. 101–228, 449 (minority views of Senator Steve Symms).

42. Even if this assertion is true, the tax exemption still acts as a subsidy and deprives the federal Highway Trust Fund of money that would otherwise go to the maintenance of roads.

43. Statement of George Babikian, Hearing No. 101–584, 69.

44. Statement of Ray Lewis, Senate Hearing No. 101–584, 76.

45. "Senate-White House Deal Breaks Clean Air Logjam," *CQ*, 3 March 1990, 652.

46. "Senate-White House Deal," 654.

47. "Showdown on Clean Air Bill: Senate Says 'No' to Byrd," *CQ*, 31 March 1990, 986.

48. Kriz, "Politics at the Pump," 1329.

49. "Power Check on Air Bill Crusader," *Washington Post*, 13 October 1990, p. A1.

50. The House bill also called for a 25 percent reduction of VOCs by the year 2000, in addition to a 15 percent reduction by 1994 required in the Senate bill. These provisions are significantly more "fuel-neutral" than formula requirements, such as mandatory oxygen content.

51. Letter from Senators Daschle, Dole, et al. to William K. Reilly, dated 31 July 1991. On file with the author.

52. Austin and Weaver, *Air Pollution Consequences*, pp. 2–4, Table 2.

53. Public Law 101–549 (15 November 1990), 104 Stat. 2489.

54. *Clean Air Act Amendments of 1989*, Senate Report No. 101–228, 95.

55. Public Law 101–549, 2490.

56. *Clean Air Act Amendments of 1989*, Senate Report No. 101–228, 110.

57. Rick Henderson, "Going Mobile," *Reason* (August/September 1990), 33.

58. NAPAP Report, quoted by Senator John Glenn, *Congressional Record*, 27 March 1990, S. 3254.

59. The report received only a one-hour hearing in the Senate and was never presented to the House. Senator Glenn lamented that "we spend over $500 million on the most definitive study of acid precipitation that has ever been done in the history of the world and then we do not want to listen to what [the experts] say." *Congressional Record*, 27 March 1990, S. 3254.

60. Robert Hahn and Wilbur Seteger, "Analysis of Clean Air Bill S. 1630," (Washington, D.C.: Clean Air Working Group, February 1990); and Temple, Barker and Sloane, Inc. *Economic Impact of Acid Rain Control Legislation: How Could Industry Be Affected? A Case Study Analysis* (Washington, D.C.: Temple, Barker and Sloane, 1985).

3 SACRED COWS: THE BOVINE SOMATOTROPIN CONTROVERSY

Christopher L. Culp

In April 1990, the Wisconsin and Minnesota legislatures imposed temporary bans on the use or sale of bovine somatotropin (bST), or bovine growth hormone (bGH), a biotechnological innovation that could increase the production of milk per cow in the United States by as much as 25 percent. These bans are the most visible political results to date of an anti-bST crusade, which is being carried on by an odd coalition between, on the one hand, public interest advocates opposed to any kind of biotechnology and, on the other hand, segments of the dairy industry. Ostensibly, this campaign, which has now spanned more than six years, is based largely on health and safety concerns. The bST opponents claim that bST may be unsafe for human consumption and that it might dilute the "pure" image of U.S. milk that consumers demand. However, these concerns are utterly without foundation. An examination of the bST controversy shows that the push for anti-bST regulations is an effort, not to advance public interest, but rather to protect a small group of inefficient farmers from the market forces of competition.

THE CAMPAIGN AGAINST bST

Synthetic bovine somatotropin is an imitation of the pituitary hormone that stimulates lactation in cows. A means of enhancing a natural metabolic process, bST supplements the growth hormone that is produced by the cow on its own. There are virtually no biochemical or aesthetic differences between milk from cows treated with synthetic bST and cows relying only on natural hormone production.

Synthetic bST is not a new substance. As early as 1937, endocrinologists surmised that a bovine pituitary extract could enhance milk production. The first clear benefits from the modern analogue of those substances became apparent in 1973, when synthetic bST was originally produced. Since then, the four manufacturers of bST—Monsanto, Eli Lilly and Company, American Cyanamid Company, and the Upjohn Company—have spent over $500 million on research and development of the substance. In 1985, the benefits of synthetic bST were demonstrated more conclusively when researchers at Cornell University found it to be as effective at stimulating lactation as the substance produced naturally by cows. Estimates of how much milk production should rise upon the adoption of bST vary widely: Most estimates suggest an increase in milk production of about 10 percent per cow, but some indicate that up to a 25 percent increase is possible.[1] Producers expect the demand for bST, once it is approved, to be substantial. Some estimates suggest that the worldwide demand could range from $500 million to $1 billion per annum.[2]

In 1985, the Food and Drug Administration (FDA) determined that milk and meat from cows that had been treated with bST was safe for human consumption and permitted dairy products from test cows treated with bST to be sold on the market. However, the agency soon ran into resistance from Jeremy Rifkin, president of a small nonprofit organization called the Foundation for Economic Trends (FET). It is fair to say that Rifkin and his organization are substantially more critical of modern technology and more resolutely anticapitalist than so-called establishment environmental organizations such as the Environmental Defense Fund or the Sierra Club. As early as 1977, Rifkin had staked out a position against biotechnology and genetic engineering. In several books and articles published in subsequent years, Rifkin expressed concern over the potentially devastating consequences of genetic engineering, such as accidental releases, and he argued that no social institution—least of all, scientists and corporations—could safely be entrusted to control the course of biotechnology.

In 1985, Rifkin contacted the Wisconsin Family Farm Defense Fund, a farmers' organization that had begun to lobby against bST out of concern over the adverse economic consequences a widespread use of the product might have on small farms. Rifkin offered his assistance and suggested that the campaign against bST should be fought not only on economic but also on public health grounds.

In 1986, Rifkin joined forces with the Humane Society to petition the FDA to prepare an environmental impact statement on bST before approving it for commercial sale. The petitioners expressed concern over the negative impact bST might have on the health of cows. However, perhaps sensing that the health-related arguments alone would fail to garner sufficient support for an anti-bST campaign, Rifkin and the Humane Society also emphasized the possibility that lower milk prices and increased production could put financial pressure on small dairy farmers—a consideration that was not among the FDA's traditional concerns.

In 1989, though, the anti-bST forces were provided with scientific ammunition of sorts. Dr. Samuel Epstein, of the University of Illinois Medical Center in Chicago, published several articles purporting to show that milk and meat from bST-treated cows might be unsafe for human consumption.[3] In 1990, anti-bST forces received further support when former FDA veterinarian Richard J. Burroughs, who had been involved in the initial FDA review of bST, asserted that his former employer had not thoroughly researched the potential dangers of bST to humans and cows.

However, the evidence supporting the bST opponents' position on the safety of bST was, and is, extremely weak. Epstein's study has been subjected to extensive criticism; both the FDA and the four bST manufacturers have persuasively rebutted virtually every one of Epstein's claims. Henry Miller, a physician and special assistant to the FDA commissioner on biotechnology, has characterized Epstein's report as "a gross distortion of scientific facts."[4] Opponents to bST respond that the manufacturers' evidence is inherently suspect and that the FDA is overly solicitous of industry interests and insufficiently rigorous in examining bST's potential health effects. Whatever one may think of the former claim, the latter surely lacks plausibility in light of the FDA's generally very—even, many would say, excessively—cautious and time-consuming drug approval process.[5]

Moreover, the industry and the FDA are hardly alone in their assessment of bST. An overwhelming body of evidence, much of it published in respected, peer-reviewed scientific journals such as the *Journal of the American Medical Association*, shows that milk and meat from bST-treated cows is perfectly safe for human consumption. (The FDA's own study, which also shows bST to be safe, was subjected to extensive peer review.[6]) Over 130 articles in print attest to the lack of any ascertainable health effects on humans from using products from bST cows; over 1,000 studies involving over 10,000 dairy cows have been conducted on bST to date, all of which have led to similar conclusions. Most recently, a panel convened by the National Institutes of Health determined that products from bST-treated cows are safe for human consumption. In short, arguments to the effect that bST is unsafe or that there is a paucity of scientific evidence do not withstand scrutiny. The Office of Technology Assessment (OTA) has observed, appropriately, that the claims made by Rifkin, Epstein, and a few other bST opponents "imply a worldwide conspiracy involving at least 1,000 animal scientists in academia, government, and industry and hundreds of dairy farmers involved in the bST experiments. The possibility of such a conspiracy seems remote."[7]

For all their implausibility, charges that bST might be unsafe have helped to bring about state and federal actions that have retarded the adoption of bST. Burrough's allegations, for example, prompted Sen. Patrick Leahy (D-Vermont), chairman of the Senate Agriculture Committee, to commission a General Accounting Office study of the FDA's review of bST. Similarly, Congressman Peter Smith (R-Vermont) has proposed a national moratorium on the sale and use of bST for three years to allow time for further research.

Jeremy Rifkin and the Foundation for Economic Trends have been the catalyst behind much of the anti-bST campaign. However, they alone could not have mounted an effective challenge. It was only when (and because) small farmers, often organized at the state level, joined the coalition of forces opposing the approval of bST—and moved the locus of opposition to bST away from the public interest sector of Washington to the agricultural sector at the state level—that the anti-bST forces gained measurable political victories.

As we shall see, political opposition to bST eventually led to moratoria on bST sales and use in Wisconsin and Minnesota, as well as attempts to pass similar legislation elsewhere. Initially, though, the anti-bST coalition attempted to convince the FDA to embargo the sale of products from bST test herds, citing both public health and economic reasons. This campaign was joined by national farm groups such as the National Farmers Union (NFU) and the National Save the Family Farm Coalition, a self-described "coalition of 47 grassroots farm and rural groups" that seeks to provide "economic justice for family farmers, vitality in our rural communities, and stewardship of our natural resources."[8]

When the efforts to persuade the FDA to stop the sale of dairy from bST test herds proved unavailing, the coalition changed its strategy and, in August 1989, petitioned several major food chains to stop carrying bST test products. Five companies replied to this request, noting that they did not buy dairy products from test herds. (These companies—Safeway, Kroger, Stop and Shop, Vons, and Supermarket General—still do not sell products from bST test herds.) While the anti-bST coalition portrayed this response as a victory, the stores had actually refused to buy products from test herds as early as 1985, largely due to demand considerations and without any prompting by the anti-bST coalition. Dannon, Yoplait, Kraft, Borden, Haagen Dazs, and other companies also refuse to use bST-treated products. The nation's largest dairy cooperative, Associated Milk Producers, Inc., has also refused to accept bST test milk from any of its 21,000 members.

Rifkin and his organization continued their battle at the federal level against bST by filing a suit in federal court against the National Dairy Promotion and Research Board for violating their congressional mandate to remain "product neutral" by endorsing bST. The suit also requested the FDA to order the four bST manufacturers to halt their political lobbying in favor of the innovation. However, by this time—June 1991—the focus of effective opposition had already shifted to the state level.

In April 1990, Wisconsin Governor Tommy Thompson signed into law a moratorium on bST in that state that was effective until June 1, 1991. This action triggered a similar ban in neighboring Minnesota, where only a few days earlier Governor Rudy Perpich had signed into law a moratorium to last 13 months after any similar law was passed in Wisconsin. (Legislation aimed at banning, regulating, or mandating further study of bST was also proposed in Vermont, Massachusetts, Michigan, New Hampshire, New York, and Virginia, but all those measures failed.) In May 1991, the Minnesota House of Representatives passed legislation extending the moratorium on bST until June 1992, contingent on similar action in Wisconsin. As of August 1991, the Wisconsin legislature was still considering a bill to extend the moratorium there for two more years.

The economic effects of these moratoria seem negligible, since the FDA is not likely to approve bST for commercial sale until 1992 anyway. Nonetheless, anti-bST activists were well advised to spend time and effort to attain these measures. First, the state moratoria signal "public" opposition to bST. Wisconsin State Representative Barbara Gronemus, a key opponent of bST, observed that "a temporary bGH moratorium [is] a definite positive first step in assuring the family farmer and the consuming public that their majority sentiments against bGH have been heard."[9] A good argument can be made that it was due only to the success of the anti-bST campaigns in the states that Rifkin and his allies were able to sustain their campaign in Washington, D.C. Second, bST critics can reasonably hope that state restrictions on bST could pave the way for further, and possibly stronger, state restrictions later; witness the recently proposed extensions of the moratoria. Third, and perhaps most important, bST opponents may be able to gain support for tighter regulation of the new technology at the national level by building constituencies and by demonstrating a political power base at the state level. For example, John Kinsman, a Wisconsin dairy farmer and an outspoken critic of bST, informed the Wisconsin legislature that "[U.S.] Congressman Peter Smith is introducing a moratorium bill in Congress. In meetings with other congressmen, they have indicated they will strongly support Smith's bill. They further state that they and others in Congress have expected the Wisconsin legislature to take the lead in passing moratorium and labeling legislation."[10] The proposed Wisconsin labeling bill to which Kinsman alluded would have required any products that had possibly been produced from bST test herds to be labeled accordingly. Although the bill was killed in committee, similar legislation may well resurface in the future.

THE ECONOMIC EFFECTS OF bST

A persistent theme of the bST opposition is the effect of the widespread use of the substance on the dairy industry: bST, opponents argue, will increase milk production, depress milk prices, and result in diminished farm income and, hence, the failure of marginal "family" farms.[11] The continued existence of such farms is considered socially desirable by bST opponents, regardless of efficiency considerations. In promoting this argument, the anti-bST coalition has been assisted by Ben & Jerry's Homemade, Inc., a Vermont-based ice-cream manufacturing company that promotes its high-quality, high-priced products through creative and public displays of "political correctness." (Ben & Jerry's products themselves deliver a social message; they are marketed under names such as "Rainforest Crunch" and "Peace Pops.") The adverse impact of bST on small farms, Ben & Jerry's has pronounced, "goes to the heart of what kind of farm community we want in this country."[12]

The likely economic effects of the widespread use of bST are not quite as clear and predictable as the anti-bST coalition makes them out to be. Still, in contrast to the bST opponents' claims concerning its health effects, the contention that bST will have an adverse impact on small— and relatively inefficient—farms appears, by and large, correct.

Effects on Milk Prices and Production

For several reasons, the economic effects of a broad-scale use of bST are difficult to predict. Consumer reactions to the widespread use of bST are difficult to anticipate, yet they may have profound effects on both the adoption rate of bST and its economic effects. Government actions at all levels—state, federal, and international—must also be expected to affect the economics of bST. State moratoria such as the ones passed and proposed again in Wisconsin and Minnesota would create an unavoidable "adoption lag" for these regions. At the federal level, changes in the dairy support price system—which, as is briefly discussed below, may occur in response to the adoption of bST and its effects—may, in turn, have an impact on the profitability of bST. Internationally, the adoption of bST by foreign countries—a possibility that could become far more likely in the event that the European Economic Community decides to lift its moratorium on bST—could dramatically affect the incentives of U.S. farmers to adopt bST. (A unilateral failure to use bST, would almost ensure the despoliation of the U.S. dairy industry, barring complete protectionism.)

Moreover, while the general effects of bST on cow productivity are known, some important questions remain to be answered. For example, the effectiveness of bST may depend on climatological conditions. (Some research suggests that bST has a smaller effect on lactation in hot and humid regions of the country.) More important, it is, as yet, unclear whether bST will provide a constant increase in milk production per cow or whether the production response will be proportional to the cow's output. If a constant production response is assumed, bST is either feasible for all cows or for none. By contrast, if bST produces a proportional response, it may be more feasible for use on cows with a higher productivity. Also, higher producing cows will require more feed, and shocks causing a dramatic increase in feed prices (such as the drought of 1988) could affect the profitability of bST and, hence, its effect on the dairy industry and on particular farms.

However, despite all this uncertainty, several important points of consensus emerge from the available evidence. Foremost, the all-milk price will fall after the introduction of bovine somatotropin.[13] The United States Department of Agriculture (USDA) estimates that by 1995, bST will reduce the all-milk price by 55 cents vis-à-vis a "non-bST scenario," which predicts a slight rise in the all-milk price from its present level. Another study by the National Milk Producers Federation (NMPF) predicts a decline in the bST all-milk price of between 10 and 50 cents by 1995.

This reduction in the price of milk will have profound effects on dairy farm profitability. While bST offers cost savings to farmers, some farmers will lose more income from the reduction in milk prices than they will save from the reduction in costs. The economic effects of the widespread use of bST upon any given farm will depend on factors such as farm size, productivity, and geographical location. Broadly speaking, bST will likely accelerate and exacerbate trends that are already underway in dairy industry.

First, bST would increase the production of milk in the United States. A USDA model suggests that U.S. milk production could grow from 149 billion pounds in 1990 to 161 billion pounds in 1996.[14] Similar conclusions were reached by the NMPF and by other independent researchers. However, milk production likely will increase in any event; the USDA model predicts an increase in milk production to 152 billion pounds by 1996 even without bST. Use of bST would merely reinforce an uptrend in milk production that has been well defined since at least 1969.[15]

Second, the widespread use of bST is likely to reduce the number of cows in the United States. As with milk production, though, the decline is projected to be very close to the trend rate. The USDA model predicts a reduction in the number of cows by 900,000 from 1990 to 1996, with or without bST. The NMPF study suggests that bST will have a moderate effect on the number of cows: Without bST, its model predicts a decline in cow numbers of 700,000 by 1995 compared to a 1.1 million cow decline if bST is available. (It is also of note that the USDA model predicts the greatest decline in cow numbers in the Upper Midwest and the Northeast dairy-producing regions—with or without bST.)

Large versus Small Farms

A third and, for present purposes, more significant effect of bST adoption is that it will likely reduce the number of farms in the United States. Again, a trend toward specialization and fewer but larger dairy farms has been underway for many years, but bST could exacerbate it.

Virtually all major research on bST suggests that its successful adoption will require proficient dairy management. To achieve the maximum possible response from bST, farmers must adopt careful planning with respect to meeting the increased feed requirements of their animals and administering bST treatments. Then, too, it appears that bST will fail to generate productivity gains if cows are subjected to stresses associated with improper management and feeding practices. In short, poor management may result in a near-zero response to bST. Even if bST results in some short-run productivity gains for poorly managed farms, long-term productivity losses could result, possibly to a level below the original productivity of the cow.

Much of the available research suggests that small farms are more likely than large ones to exhibit poor and inefficient management practices. Herd size tends to be positively correlated with production per cow, and production per cow within a dairy-producing region is widely regarded as a good proxy for management ability. In other words, larger farms within each region may find it more profitable to adopt bST. In addition, some evidence suggests that herd size and farm profitability within a region are positively correlated. Larger farms within each region are, thus, more likely to adopt bST for financial reasons. This point is significant because most evidence indicates that adopters of bST will find it profitable, while nonadopters who do not find bST profitable will lose because of the decline in all-milk prices.[16,17] Finally, farm size influences not only the *extent* but also the *rate* of adoption. Large, financially strong dairies tend to be the most innovative, and hence will be the major early adopters of bST. Since early adopters will be the primary benefactors of the new technology, late adopters—smaller farms with low per-cow productivity—will be those to disappear after the approval of bST.[18]

In sum, large, efficient farms will likely be the major beneficiaries if bST is adopted. Smaller farms may well be better off if bST remains commercially unavailable. This, of course, explains why small farm groups have opposed the innovation.

Regional Effects

There is some evidence that bST may exacerbate the competitive disadvantage of dairy farms in the Upper Midwest and the Northeast vis-à-vis farms in the West and Southwest. If so, bST would again reinforce a preexisting trend: While the number of farms in the United States has been falling since 1969, dairy production has been rising in the Pacific and Southwestern states relative to the rest of the U.S. dairy sector. This is because the costs of production in the Upper Midwest are much higher than in the West and because the average size of farms in the West is much larger than in other parts of the country, particularly the Upper Midwest.[19]

In addition, production per cow tends to be higher in the West than in the Upper Midwest and the Northeast. To the extent that larger herds indicate better management and economies of scale in the dairy sector, Western farms may be at a slight competitive advantage vis-à-vis Midwestern and Northeastern farms.[20] Adoption of bST may exacerbate this trend; as noted, larger farms are more likely to adopt bST profitably than small farms. Moreover, the economic payoffs from bST adoption, net of bST's cost, likely will be much lower in the Upper Midwest and Northeast than in the Southwest.

In addition, the quality of soil resources may play an important role. Farms with a higher quality of soil are more likely to be able to meet the higher nutritional requirements of bST-treated cows. While the older dairy regions, such as the Upper Midwest and the Northeast, may have some economic advantage from growing their own feed, they have only marginal soil resources. Farms in these regions may not be able to sustain the increase in feed production necessary to meet increased feed requirements. Regions such as the Pacific and Southwest typically purchase their feed inputs, but these purchases of high-quality forage are made at a relatively low cost.[21]

USDA analyses of the structure of U.S. dairy production come to a different conclusion. They assume that all farms, regardless of size, will adopt bST at the same rate. Thus, smaller farms with lower output per cow have a higher rate of return to bST than under alternative models, given a constant increase in milk production per cow. The USDA thus concludes that the "fewer but larger" trend will continue *within* all dairy production regions, with or without bST, but that shifts in production *between* regions may not occur at all.[22] This prediction is lent credence by additional factors. The assumption that differences in production per cow indicate different levels of management quality may hold within a dairy region but not across dairy regions that are characterized by many different traits, such as quality of forage and climate.[23] Moreover, even if the rate of bST adoption is higher by larger farms in more efficient regions (implying a shift in production toward those regions), the production areas with higher relative efficiency and larger sized farms are also those regions where the effects of bST may be muted by climatological factors.[24] In other words, any shift in production toward regions such as the Southwest that is induced by efficiency considerations may be offset by the bigger production response from bST that is possible in cooler regions such as the Upper Midwest.

The probable regional effects of bST are considerably less certain and clear-cut, then, than its differential impact on small versus large farms. Still, if the prediction of a faster adoption of bST by larger farms between regions is correct, then production may shift to regions in which productive efficiency is higher and production costs are lower. Wisconsin and Minnesota comprise a relatively inefficient region of dairy production, and the Northeast is roughly as inefficient as the Upper Midwest in many respects. The enactment or consideration of anti-bST legislation in these regions is consistent with the hypothesis that these farmers demand anti-bST legislation to shelter their inefficient farming practices from market forces.

This is not to say, though, that the enactment of the anti-bST legislation in Minnesota and Wisconsin will, in fact, have a beneficial impact on all farmers in those states. The moratoria impose an artificial adoption lag on all farms in that region. Due largely to shipping regulations, milk produced in the Upper Midwest is largely sold in that region, thus insulating regional producers to some extent against competitive pressures. Nonetheless, the moratoria could place farmers in the region at a competitive disadvantage: While increased milk production in other regions could lead to lower milk prices, farms in the Upper Midwest would be denied the potential cost savings of bST—unless, of course, the moratoria can forestall the adoption of bST everywhere.

bST's Impact on the Farm Support Systems

Some critics of bST have expressed concern that increased milk production is likely to increase the outlays of the U.S. dairy support program, under which the Commodity Credit Corporation (CCC) is required to purchase surplus dairy products at a predetermined price. As noted, bST will likely increase milk production while also reducing the price of milk. Since it is highly unlikely that the sharp price reduction will produce an offsetting increase in commercial demand, the increased production will entail a substantial growth of CCC purchases and, at the current price support floor, of CCC outlays.[25] Indeed, the USDA estimates that after 1993, bST will increase CCC purchases by roughly 8 billion pounds.

Quite clearly, bST opponents are concerned with this scenario not because of the costs taxpayers might incur, but because the dairy support system might come under increased strain and public scrutiny if it were to become too expensive. This happened in the early 1980s, when milk production boomed. Expenditures on federal dairy purchases rose from $250 million in 1979 to a staggering $2.5 billion in 1983, when the CCC purchased an equivalent of 12.1 percent of all milk marketed. These strains on the federal support system prompted the institution of the Dairy Termination Program, under which farmers were paid to export or slaughter their herds and leave dairying for five years; they further led to the adoption of a *supply/demand adjuster*, which automatically reduced price supports once surpluses were projected to exceed certain levels. At the farm level, the supply/demand adjuster translated into lower support prices for farmers. Use of bST may well produce similar effects: A larger volume of CCC purchases will likely create pressure to reduce the burden on the CCC, perhaps by cutting the support price. Consequently, bST's other effects, such as the decline in the number of farms, may be exacerbated as greater numbers of farms lose the substantial windfalls provided by government subsidy programs.

It is less clear how much of a role the fear of a threat to the dairy support system has played in the opposition to bST. At first sight, a desire to protect the support system fails to explain why the bST opposition has been concentrated in Minnesota and Wisconsin. The Upper Midwest is actually one of the regions that benefits *least* from federal dairy supports: Milk support prices are determined by the Minnesota-Wisconsin price plus a transportation differential, thus ensuring that the subsidy received by farmers in the Upper Midwest is the lowest. In fact, one study has found that the abolition of a classified price system would shift production *toward* the Upper Midwest, possibly providing benefits that might offset for the farmers in that region the adverse effects of bST's adoption.[26]

If protecting dairy subsidies were the only incentive behind the anti-bST movement in the farm sector, opposition to bST should be concentrated in regions (such as Appalachia) where prohibitions on shipping reconstituted milk and milk marketing order laws generate artificial rents that would not exist in a competitive market. The absence of significant political opposition to bST in these regions suggests that concern over the integrity of the dairy support system is not, or at least not exclusively, the cause of resistance to bST.

Nonetheless, the support system mitigates the economic losses that nonadopters of bST may experience. If the system were jeopardized, or if the response of the system to bST is expected to lead to significantly lower milk prices, potential nonadopters *everywhere* would oppose bST on the grounds that prices would fall further, reducing farm income. The fact that nonadopters may be most widespread in the Upper Midwest and the Northeast, along with the fact that fixed, subsidized prices provide a degree of protection to higher production cost regions by blunting the adverse effects of price declines, may explain some of the opposition to bST in those regions.

LESSONS OF THE bST CONTROVERSY

Most dairy farmers will find themselves better off once bST is available. This is the reason why only a small segment of the farm sector actively opposes bST and part of the reason why only a few states have adopted or seriously tried to adopt anti-bST legislation. However, as noted, good management practices are requisite to the successful adoption of bST. Because farms with a higher productivity per cow, a larger herd size, good financial health, and access to low-cost, high-quality feeds likely will find bST most attractive, bST may reinforce a trend toward productive efficiency that is already underway in the dairy sector. Even smaller farms with high production costs might benefit from bST. In order to do so, though, these farms will have to improve their management practices and increase their productive efficiency. Acceptance of bST will therefore increase the already existing competitive pressures on relatively inefficient farms.

In order to protect themselves against these pressures, small dairy farmers in the Upper Midwest have joined hands with a public interest advocate in Washington, D.C., who opposes biotechnology on ideological grounds. This coalition has managed to block the approval of bST and to retard its implementation, despite the fact that the beneficiaries of bST far outnumber the potential losers. In addition to most dairy farmers, consumers will almost certainly gain from the adoption of the innovation, since it will result in lower milk prices. (However, the reduction in milk prices that will be passed on to the consumer at the retail level is difficult to quantify.) As dairy production becomes more efficient, intermediate and "forward" industries such as dairy processors could gain additional business and benefit from lower input prices. A recent USDA study estimated that the sum of forward industry rents and consumer surplus resulting from the adoption of bST would be $3.8 billion over a 10-year period.[27] Other researchers estimate that such gains could precipitate a onetime boost in the nonfarm economy of approximately $106 million in Wisconsin alone.[28]

However, bST's potential beneficiaries are a disparate group with little in common. With the exception of bST manufacturers, they have little economic incentive to expend real resources to lobby for the innovation; despite the total gain, the per capita gain in each group is likely to be quite small. Hence, the anti-bST coalition has so far managed to forestall bST's approval. More regulation may well be in stock. Most likely in the short run are requirements that products from bST-treated cows be labeled accordingly. Labeling requirements would permit inefficient farmers to preserve some of their windfalls, largely because of the negative impression conveyed to consumers by the presence of any mandatory labels: Since labels are usually associated with products that are considered bad or risky, they could well reduce the demand for bST product vis-à-vis unlabeled, "pure" milk products, despite the lack of any significant chemical difference between the two.

This story, of course, is familiar in its broad outlines. It is quite common for small, special interest groups to demand regulation and to prevail over broader but much more diffuse interests. Similarly, the coalition between farm interests and public interest advocates—joined by an ice-cream maker with a social conscience—resembles the "bootlegger and Baptist" coalitions described in other essays in this volume.

Even in its more specific aspects, the bST controversy is depressingly familiar. Notably, the tendency of special interests in the dairy sector to go to the state legislatures before attempting federal action is a recurrent theme in dairy regulation. For example, in its struggle to halt the introduction of nonperishable "filled milk" in the first decades of the century, the dairy industry attempted, with some success, to attain discriminatory legislation at the state level before seeking congressional protection.

The states acted as "laboratories" . . . in the sense that they provided an ideal testing ground for special interest measures. State legislation gave the dairy industry an opportunity to develop its case against filled milk, to assess the feasibility, enforceability, and constitutionality of different legislative approaches before attempting to develop a national campaign.[29]

The same pattern of political action was observable in the dairy industry's quest for antimargarine statutes nearly 50 years earlier. When margarine was developed as a low-cost substitute for butter, the dairy industry fought to suppress it. The industry feared that if butter and margarine were otherwise indistinguishable, consumers would buy the lower cost product. By forcing imitation butter to be so identified in stores, the industry was able to force product differentiation and reduce the demand for oleomargarine vis-à-vis butter. Due to a lack of enforcement and a strong consumer preference for margarine, labeling legislation eventually failed to provide effective protection for dairy interests. It did not, however, abate the demand for producer protection in that industry. Soon after the failure of labeling legislation became apparent, several states enacted legislation that prohibited the sale of margarine altogether. When state prohibitory legislation also proved insufficient to prevent margarine from competing with butter—because not all states prohibited the sale of margarine and margarine was transportable—legislation was eventually proposed at the federal level. The result was the Margarine Tax Act of 1886—one of "the first instances of federal legislation in which one domestic industry sought to enlist the government's coercive power to stamp out competition from another domestic industry."[30] (Wisconsin, which is now in the forefront of the anti-bST movement, did not repeal its butter protection laws until 1967, by which time such protection was only a faint memory in most other states.) To be sure, the butter industry sought to protect itself from competition by another industry whereas in the case of bST, farmers who perceive the costs of bST to outweigh its benefits are seeking protection from competitors within the *same* industry. In other respects, however, the similarities between the political struggles are striking. The movement from margarine labeling legislation to prohibitory legislation to a national tax suggests that a similar path may be in store for bST: The state moratoria could lead to labeling legislation, which could, in turn, lead to eventual bans on bST.

There is simply no rationale for such regulation on public health grounds or, for that matter, efficiency grounds. Opponents to bST have argued that regulatory intervention is needed because bST may impose costs on all dairy producers in the form of reduced consumer demand for dairy products. According to this argument, bST is "unnatural" and will despoil the wholesome image of milk in the United States. However, if the adoption of bST were to result in a dramatic reduction of the demand for dairy products, one would expect farmers simply not to adopt it. Of course, if products containing bST cannot be distinguished by consumers, farmers would have a strong individual incentive to use it, but it would then be in the *purchasers'* interests to determine whether milk supplied by farmers contains bST and, depending on consumer demand, to guarantee that products sold to consumers are "bST-free."

The refusal of several grocery stores to market products from bST-treated cows after the FDA approved it in 1985 indicates that dairy purchasers are in a perfect position to make such a determination. The Food Marketing Institute, a lobbying group for supermarkets, commented on the decision of several stores not to market bST products: "We follow consumer attitudes. Consumer acceptance is king. . . . Our members have no desire to offer what isn't going to sell."[31] Ben & Jerry's is free and able to ensure that its products are bST free and to market them accordingly; in fact, it does so already. In short, the market is perfectly capable of determining the usefulness of bST. There is no market failure; the claim that bST will spoil the wholesome image of milk is just a thin disguise for the protection of small group of inefficient farmers at the expense of consumers, intermediary industries, forward industries, bST producers, and more efficient dairy producers.

There is nothing inherently wrong with an argument that we *should* protect family farms, even at the price of sacrificing possible efficiency gains. One may or may not share this position, one may dispute whether bST regulation is an effective means of accomplishing this purpose, and one may haggle over the extent to which society as a whole should sacrifice efficiency gains to aid special interests. However, the opponents of bST plainly do not desire a debate on these terms. On the one hand, the bootleggers, sensing that the naked economic argument would not win in the political arena, dress up special interest legislation with health claims that border on the fraudulent. On the other hand, and more disconcertingly, a determined ideological opponent of biotechnology has managed to leverage special interest concerns into a single-minded crusade against bST and biotechnological products in general.

Bootleggers and Baptists are very unevenly represented in the anti-bST campaign; unlike establishment environmental groups such as the Sierra Club or the Natural Resources Defense Council, Jeremy Rifkin and the Foundation for Economic Trends are too marginal to serve as equal partners for business interests. The political dynamics of the campaign reflect this fact: While Rifkin can claim responsibility for initiating much of the anti-bST movement, that movement did not begin to make headway until the dairy industry became an active participant and took the political fight against bST to the states.

However, the ease with which Rifkin has managed to piggyback on narrow economic interests is an ominous signal for the entire biotechnology industry. Bovine somatotropin is the flagship of agricultural biotechnology; the fact that the manufacturers have spent over $500 million to date on the development of bST indicates that they expect the product to generate substantial profits. Use of bST offers very significant benefits, and it has been proven to be completely risk free by an overwhelming body of evidence. If even *this* product cannot be approved and marketed without great difficulties, delays, and costs, the future of biotechnology may be in doubt.

NOTES

1. See, for example, G. H. Schmidt, "Economics of Using Bovine Somatotropin in Dairy Cows and Potential Impact on U.S. Dairy Industry," *Journal of Dairy Science* 72 (1989): 737–45.

2. "Wisconsin Bars Gene-Engineered Drug," *New York Times*, 28 April 1990.

3. See, for example, Samuel S. Epstein, "BST: The Public Health Hazards," *The Ecologist* 19 (September/October 1989), 191–95. Epstein also suggested that the economic consequences of the hormone need to be considered more carefully.

4. Marjorie Sun, "Market Sours on Milk Hormone," *Science* 246 (17 November 1989): 876–77.

5. See Sam Peltzman, "An Evaluation of Consumer Protection Legislation: The 1962 Drug Amendments," *Journal of Political Economy* 81 (October 1973): 1049–91.

6. In August 1990, the FDA broke with tradition and, for the first time ever, published its "confidential" safety studies of bST in the peer-reviewed journal, *Science*, which gave bST a favorable safety assessment. For the FDA's report, see Judith C. Juskevitch and C. Greg Guyer, "Bovine Growth Hormone: Human Food Safety Evaluation," *Science* 249 (24 August 1990): 875–84. See also William H. Daughaday and David M. Barbano, "Bovine Somatotropin Supplementation of Dairy Cows," *Journal of the American Medical Association* 264 (22/29 August 1990), 1003–1005. Gerald Guest, director of the FDA's Center for Veterinary Medicine, commented on the reason for the unusual disclosure: "People were casting doubt on our review. There was a credibility question that we felt needed a response." "FDA Opens Secret Files in Drug's Defense," *New York Times*, 24 August 1990, p. A18.

7. Office of Technology Assessment, Congress of the United States, *U.S. Dairy Industry at a Crossroad: Biotechnology and Policy Choices*, Special Report OTA-F-470 (Washington, D.C.: Government Printing Office, May 1991).

8. Press Statement, National Save the Family Farm Coalition, 12 October 1988, Washington, D.C, on file with the author.

9. "BGH Compromise Satisfies Very Few," *Milwaukee Journal*, 28 April 1990, A22.

10. John Kinsman, testimony before the Wisconsin Agriculture Committees regarding a moratorium on the Bovine Growth Hormone (n.d.), on file with the author.

11. "Technology that Threatens the Family Farm," *Boston Globe*, 10 October 1989, p. A11.

12. "Store Bars Milk Produced by Drug," *New York Times*, 24 August 1989, p. I18.

13. The all-milk price is a weighted average of the fluid-grade and the manufacturing-grade milk prices. It is usually about $1 above the support price paid for manufacturing-grade milk.

14. This model, along with others, uses 1990 as a base prediction year because it assumed that bST would have been approved by now.

15. Milk production in the United States has expanded almost continuously over the past two decades. Until 1971, milk production was under 120 billion pounds; since 1985, annual production has exceeded 140 billion pounds.

16. Many analyses assume the market price of bST will be trivial. This may be a reasonable assumption. For example, the USDA assumes that the return to using bST will be twice the cost of using it. Relying on industry cost estimates, the USDA assumes a market price of bST to be 24 cents per cow per day. Other studies also suggest that the price of bST will be too low to affect adoption rates. However, the future costs of bST, including its marketing costs, may influence pricing decisions by the four manufacturers.

17. For example, the NMPF model predicts that the average annual cash income per cow from 1991 to 1995 will be $188 without bST and $151 with bST. Farm cash income for bST adopters is estimated to average $205 over this period, while nonadopters will experience a decline to $129 per cow. The USDA's research generally supports the NMPF results.

18. Fred Kuchler and John McClelland, *Issues Raised by New Agricultural Technologies: Livestock Growth Hormones*, Agricultural Economic Report No. 608 (Washington, D.C.: U.S. Department of Agriculture, Economic Research Service, April 1989). However, an analysis by Ronald D. Knutson, Robert D. Yonkers, and James W. Richardson suggests that late adopters of bST are not seriously penalized unless the price of milk declines within the first year after the introduction of bST. "Dairy Farm Income as Affected by bST: Regional Characteristics" (Paper presented before the National Invitational Workshop on bST, St. Louis, Missouri, September 1987). Another study by the same authors also suggests that the elimination of adoption lags does not explain fully the OTA results. Rather, the primary reason for the increased stress on small farms in the Upper Midwest (with or without adoption lags) is the extremely high relative cost of production exhibited by such farms in that region. Knutson, Yonkers, and Richardson, "The Impact of Biotechnology and Information Revolutions on the Dairy Industry," in Joseph J. Molnar and Henry Kunnvcan, eds., *Biotechnology and the New Agricultural Revolution* (Boulder, Colo.: Westview Press, 1989).

19. The costs of production are much lower in the West largely because of the highly subsidized water system there. In the unlikely event that water subsidies were curtailed in the West, the Upper Midwest would likely regain some of its productive advantage.

20. Even if the Upper Midwest does retain its market share of dairy production, a trend toward larger and more efficient farms within that region is almost unavoidable, as larger Midwestern farms typically have lower costs of production than smaller farms in that region. Office of Technology Assessment, *U.S. Dairy Industry*.

21. This point may be irrelevant if the widespread adoption of bST leads to large reductions in the numbers of cows such that the increase in feed demand is more than offset by the decrease in dairy livestock.

22. Richard F. Fallert, Tom McGuckin, Carolyn Betts, and Gary Bruner, *BST and the Dairy Industry: A National, Regional, and Farm-Level Analysis*, Agricultural Economics Report 579 (Washington, D.C.: USDA Economic Research Service, 1987).

23. Bruce W. Marion and Robert L. Wills, "A Prospective Assessment of the Impacts of Bovine Somatotropin: A Case Study of Wisconsin," *American Journal of Agricultural Economics* 72 (May 1990): 326–36.

24. Fallert et al., *BST and the Dairy Industry*.

25. The demand for milk is, in the economists' parlance, highly price-inelastic.

26. Jork Sellschopp and Robert J. Kalter, *Bovine Somatotropin: Its Impact on the Spatial Distribution of the U.S. Dairy Industry*, Agricultural Economics Research 89–14 (Ithaca, N.Y.: Department of Agricultural Economics, Cornell University Agricultural Experiment Station, September 1989).

27. Kuchler and McClelland, *Issues Raised*.

28. Fallert et al., *BST and the Dairy Industry*.

29. Geoffrey P. Miller, "The True Story of Carolene Products," *Supreme Court Review* 1987 (1987): 425.

30. Geoffrey P. Miller, "Public Choice at the Dawn of the Special Interest State: The Story of Butter and Margarine," *California Bar Review* 77 (1989): 83–131; quote at 126–27.

31. Reginald W. Rhein, *BST: A Safe, More Plentiful Milk Supply* (New York: American Council on Science and Health, 1990), 8.

4   THE COALITION FOR WASTE: PRIVATE INTERESTS AND SUPERFUND

Marc K. Landy and Mary Hague

The Comprehensive Environmental Response, Compensation and Liability Act (CERCLA), better known as Superfund, was passed in 1980
in the wake of widely publicized concerns over toxic spills and waste
problems at Love Canal, Valley of the Drums, and other sites.[1] Superfund
was heralded as a vital environmental program that would protect the
public health from the imminent and serious dangers of abandoned waste
dumps and would do so at small cost to the taxpayer.

After more than a decade of operation, disillusion has set in.
Superfund has produced an enormous legal morass that constitutes a
substantial drain on public and private resources; yet it has yielded very
little in the way of environmental improvement.[2] While estimates of
sites in need of cleanup have risen to thousands, fewer than 70 have
been fully cleaned.[3]

In the early years of Superfund, the lack of progress at the cleanup
front could plausibly be attributed to start-up difficulties and management
problems—in particular, the EPA's scandalous behavior during Anne
Gorsuch Burford's reign in the early Reagan years. It has been clear for
some time, however, that these explanations for Superfund's failure are
inadequate. The statute is based on premises that, however well inten-
tioned they may have been at the outset, have proven fatally flawed and,
in fact, positively harmful to the environment, the economy, and the
public's understanding of the difficult issues at stake.

Yet, despite near-universal disenchantment with Superfund's results,
the central elements of the statute continue to enjoy tremendous political
support. In fact, they have proven immune to reforms that would
promise speedier and less expensive cleanup. Congress substantially

revised Superfund in 1986, when it was already painfully obvious that the purposes of the statute had been lost in a maze of litigation. Unfortunately, the 1986 revisions not only failed to remedy Superfund's defects; for reasons discussed below, they exacerbated existing problems in several ways.

This immunity to reform stems from Superfund's flawed premises. Although environmentally, as well as economically and socially, counterproductive, these premises have yielded a policy design that provides substantial benefits both to government and to private parties. Initially crafted through bureaucratic initiative, this design has proven so beneficial to private interests that they now comprise a solid phalanx of support for the statute.

THE TWO PREMISES OF SUPERFUND

Superfund's policy design is based on two central premises. The first premise, "Shovels First," holds that in light of the dire and imminent risks posed by abandoned waste sites, priority will be accorded to prompt and speedy cleanup. The second premise, "Polluters Pay," states that the cleanup of Superfund sites will be paid for by the parties who polluted them.[4]

These two premises combined to create what, in 1980, was a genuine policy innovation—a massive public works program funded primarily by private parties whose contributions would be obtained by resort to tort law. Despite estimates that cleaning up thousands of existing sites would cost perhaps as much as $100 billion, the EPA asked for, and received, only $1.2 billion in federal funding. Even this part of the program incorporated the Polluters Pay principle, albeit in an attenuated form: The $1.2 billion would come not from general revenue but from a tax on chemical feedstocks.[5] The burden would thus be borne by chemical corporations who, even if they were not liable in a strict sense, were thought to bear a special moral responsibility for the improper treatment, storage, and disposal of their products. The overwhelming portion of the requisite funds, it was assumed, would be paid for by the responsible parties. It was expected that this scheme would provide ample revenues for the task at hand without straining public resources. However, probably to the EPA's surprise, the liability scheme proved so controversial and cumbersome that it not only failed to produce the required revenue but also, and more fatefully, undermined both the Polluters Pay and the Shovels First principles.

Liability under Superfund is, in the lawyers' language, strict, joint and several, and retroactive. This regime incorporates two crucial changes in modern tort law which Peter Huber aptly dubbed "the socialized offense" and the "socialized defense."[6] The socialized offense blurs the distinction, previously well established in nuisance law, between low- and high-probability risk. This maneuver greatly expands the universe of individuals who can claim to be victims. Individual plaintiffs must no longer prove that they have been harmed by a particular defendant. Instead, a whole range of activities—chemical manufacturing, nuclear power generation, and hazardous waste generation, transport, and storage, among many others—are considered inherently hazardous, and anyone with an affliction that could conceivably be related to exposure to such activities has grounds to sue.

The socialized defense is primarily a means of providing the funds that are required under the greatly expanded compensation requirements imposed by the socialized offense. Legal responsibility for harm is diffused so as to ensure that somewhere along the "family tree" of causation, a relative or relatives can be located who are able to afford to pay sufficient compensation. Superfund exploits this concept to the fullest.[7] Among those who can be held liable for damage at a site are prior owners, users, bankers, insurers, and waste generators and transporters. Since liability is strict and retroactive, few defenses are available to potentially responsible parties (PRPs, in EPA jargon.) A generator of waste can be held liable even if no direct link is established between the specific waste contributed to the site and the harm that occurs; it is sufficient to show that the waste was at the site and that harm can plausibly be said to have been caused by the site. Nor is it a defense against liability to show that a landfill complied with all legal requirements of the time and that its practices were consistent with the scientific knowledge then extant, if current scientific understanding indicates otherwise. Moreover, since liability is joint and several, any liable party can be held responsible for the entire cleanup settlement, regardless of how small his portion of responsibility may have been. Superfund requires this extraordinarily inclusive notion of responsibility because it extends the notion of who has been offended beyond a broad class of plaintiffs to include the entire public, as represented by the government.

However, the broadening of the socialized defense undercuts the original rationale for relying on liability mechanisms to fund the program—namely, that the polluters should pay: Superfund's liability scheme virtually ensures that the parties' actual contributions will stand in no discernible relation to their relative responsibility.[8] Superfund's supporters have not owned up to this contradiction because they believe that broad and comprehensive liability provides the only means of extracting sufficient resources via liability.

Similarly, the socialized defense has led to the tacit abandonment of the Shovels First principle. The potentially enormous costs confronting a firm caught within Superfund's liability net provide a powerful incentive to use every conceivable delaying tactic, either in the hope of finding some legal tool for wriggling free or for the purpose of dragging PRPs not identified by the EPA into settlements. As a result, apparently innocuous institutions such as schools, restaurants, and even the Elks Club have been caught in Superfund's liability net. In an effort to clean up a site near Utica, New York, the EPA sued two companies—a cosmetics producer and a manufacturer of metal components—who, in turn, sued over 600, mostly small, businesses and 41 towns and school districts. Among the defendants who settled the case—rather than battle large corporations over liability percentages—was the owner of a pizzeria.[9] Because of these dynamics, and because the EPA cannot secure sufficient cleanup funds through means other than liability, the shovels often remain in the tool shed while the EPA pursues PRPs along the slow and tortuous path of litigation.

Finally, the Shovels First and Polluters Pay premises combine to create perverse incentives that, in the end, hamper cleanup efforts. The most difficult conceptual and practical problem of site cleanup is the determination of "how clean is clean." The answer to this question—and, hence, the desirable extent of cleanup at a given site—cannot be determined simply on scientific grounds. In principle, one would want to clean until the site can be called perfectly "safe." However, environmental health risk is relative; there is no scientifically identifiable point at which an "unsafe" site becomes "safe." No matter how much cleanup has been performed at a site, it can always be argued that more cleanup would reduce the risk even further.

If local communities were required to contribute to cleanup spending, residents would have a reason to inquire what palpable good an expensive restoration process would be likely to achieve and whether most of the benefits could not obtained at substantially lower cost. Their answer to the question, "How clean is clean?" would be informed by their understanding of the sacrifices they have to make to obtain a given degree of cleanliness. However, under Superfund, cleanup spending is a free good for affected communities. Superfund's premises stipulate that abandoned waste sites pose severe health hazards, *and* that cleanup will be paid for by others. As a result, communities that have such sites have no reason to want to control cleanup spending. To the contrary: They have every reason to insist on the most extensive and expensive cleanup.

The pressure on the EPA to implement "Cadillac solutions" actually increases the risk posed by abandoned waste sites to the population as a whole. Rather than being able to spread its limited resources over many sites, thereby eliminating the genuine dangers they might pose, the agency finds itself spending more and more money at a small number of sites so as to reduce what have already become small risks to ever-more infinitesimal levels.

THE ORIGIN OF SUPERFUND

Superfund has proven to be a terrible burden to the EPA. Few sites have actually been cleaned up, and the liability regime has not been able to provide the large sums expected of it. The program is widely viewed to be a failure, and the EPA is routinely blamed for this.

Most embarrassingly, the initial fears that abandoned waste sites constituted a "ticking time bomb" and a manifest threat to public health have not been borne out. The studies done at Love Canal that did indicate serious health risk were later discredited, and the much more scientifically respectable studies conducted subsequently failed to show any significant risk beyond the heightened mental health problems stemming from the hysteria engendered by the incident.[10] Studies elsewhere have been similarly inconclusive. EPA's own internal assessments of program priorities admit that the toxic waste site problem is overrated and that too much of the agency's resources are spent on it.[11]

Nonetheless, despite its clear awareness of these problems, the EPA has been unwilling to launch a major public relations and lobbying effort to revise the faulty premises that impede reform. The reasons have nothing to do with Superfund's perceived environmental benefits and everything to do with the EPA's institutional interests.

Shovels First and Polluters Pay were conceived of and championed by EPA. The agency was particularly eager to gain authority over hazardous waste cleanup because this new responsibility would aid it in its efforts to reposition itself as a public health agency. In the late 1970s, the EPA no longer wanted to be viewed as a "bugs and bunnies" outfit that only protected swamps and forests. In an era of difficult economic conditions, the EPA could no longer count on sustained public support for ecological activities that appeared to provide individual citizens with few tangible benefits. In order to secure a stable political base, the agency had to be perceived as being at the center of efforts to ward off threats to the public health, the most notable being the threat of cancer.[12]

This shift in strategy bore fruit quickly. It enabled EPA to acquire new resources at a time of strict budgetary austerity. Whereas the overall 1979 budget for environment and natural resources increased by less than 1 percent (from $12.1 to $12.2 billion), EPA was able to increase its operating budget by 25 percent. One-third of this increase was earmarked for programs devoted to controlling pollutants posing a public health risk. In order to demonstrate that abandoned waste sites posed the sort of public health threats that fit the agency's mission, EPA Administrator Douglas Costle appointed a task force, headed by Deputy Administrator Barbara Blum, with instructions to use the Resource Conservation and Recovery Act (RCRA) and the Safe Drinking Water Act to bring as many cases as possible to the Justice Department.[13] The agency also launched a nationwide effort to discover new sites. Blum ordered regional officials to produce a list of sites in their region and to rank the 10 worst—a request that inspired deep resentment among regional officials, who knew that long after the headlines had faded, they would be faced with the task of calming the fears of angry residents and local officials.[14]

Despite this dissension in the ranks, the effort was a success. Throughout the course of the legislative debate, EPA released lists of new sites in many different locales. The agency warned that hundreds of Love Canals existed across the country.[15] Later, when the bill appeared to be endangered by opposition from the House Ways and Means Committee, EPA worked with favorably disposed congressional staffers to compile a list of sites in each committee member's district. Even Ronald Reagan's election in November 1980 could not stop the momentum created by the "ticking time bomb" image. The bill was passed by the lame-duck Congress called into session after the election and signed into law by President Jimmy Carter in December 1980.[16]

Congress reauthorized Superfund in 1986, when its weaknesses were already much in evidence. However, the EPA failed then, and it has failed to this day, to admit that the original policy design is seriously flawed and to advocate serious Superfund reform. While causing serious embarrassment, Superfund also provides the agency with vast resources and authority. Furthermore, its dubious environmental merits notwithstanding, the program has acquired a powerful political constituency.

This constituency, which is composed essentially of the environmental movement and the waste treatment industry, first made its presence felt during the 1986 reauthorization. Under Anne Gorsuch's leadership, the

EPA had gained such a reputation for ineptitude and infidelity to its legislative mandates that it could not play a meaningful role in the legislative process. The agency's abdication enabled Superfund's constituents and their congressional allies to dominate the program's reformulation. Because their priority was to expand and strengthen the program, not to reconsider its premises, the chance for reform was lost.

THE COALITION FOR WASTE

By 1986, Superfund's liability regime had already drained all meaning from the initial premise of Polluters Pay. Clearly, it would be fairer and more efficient to simply pay for cleanup from public funds. By requiring Congress to set a budget for Superfund, representatives would be forced to compare the value of this program to all the other programs that they want to fund. Furthermore, the establishment of a budgetary cap would have provided Superfund's implementors with a powerful weapon with which to resist demands for "Cadillac" cleanup: Money spent on a particular site would reduce the money available to spend elsewhere.

However, Congress did not even seriously consider the simple expedient of putting Superfund on-budget. Instead of making Superfund cheaper and simpler, Congress did precisely the opposite. It provided greater resources, created even more unrealistic program objectives, and made Superfund officials more vulnerable to public pressure.

Acknowledging that the liability regime would fail to provide sufficient revenue, Congress chose to supplement it with a vast expansion in the size of the fund, from $1.2 to $9 billion. The fee on chemical feedstocks was retained and then expanded to cover imported substances as well. New fees were placed on crude oil and gasoline, with the latter reserved to establish a new underground petroleum tank cleanup fund. Moreover, in a major departure from the funds' previous taxing principles, a broad based tax of $12 per $10,000 was levied on corporate income. However, this tax was designed to yield only $2.75 billion of the $9 billion total. The fund continued to be viewed as a supplement to, rather than a replacement for, the sums to be collected from potentially responsible parties.

The issue of "How clean is clean?" which the original Act had ignored, was addressed by requiring that Superfund sites be restored to the level of the air, water, and soil quality standards specified in various existing environmental laws. None of these standards had been written with the problem of abandoned hazardous waste sites in mind. This provision simply did not take into account the extraordinary expense that would be involved in trying to restore horribly degraded locations to the high level of quality required by the existing standards.

Finally, the 1986 Amendments vastly expanded public participation. As amended, the statute required that the public have an opportunity to participate in the selection of cleanup remedies and that technical assistance grants be made available to citizen groups to enable them to hire their own experts to interpret risk and engineering data. It also established a citizen suit provision enabling anyone to bring suit against the government for failure to perform adequate cleanup.

Although changes were made in the settlement procedures with an eye to encouraging voluntary settlement, these revisions did not alter the strict and expansive view of liability at the heart of the "socialized defense." Nor were they to prove very successful either at speeding cleanup or at raising greater revenue. Whatever new incentives to cooperate they created were countervailed by the even stronger incentives for noncooperation created by the environmental standards requirement. If the standards to be met by cleanup were foreordained, very little room remained for bargaining with PRPs about how much cleanup they would be expected to finance.

Environmentalists and the 1986 Superfund Debate

In contrast to their marginal role in the original Superfund debate, environmental organizations lobbied energetically for the 1986 revision. By this time, environmental organizations had come to recognize Superfund's pivotal role in promoting their interests. They eagerly supported new provisions that are, arguably, environmentally deleterious but that serve the movement's broader political agenda.

First, environmentalists opposed the imposition of a "waste-end" tax then under discussion as a means of funding the program. The feedstock and general business taxes that compose the fund are neutral from the perspective of inducing improved hazardous waste treatment. A tax on the volume of waste requiring disposal would provide an incentive to produce less waste. Although environmentalists do not dispute the environmental benefits of such an incentive, they argue that it would threaten the revenue-producing capacity of the fund: Less waste would mean less revenue and, therefore, less money for cleanup.[17] This argument is correct as far as it goes. Still, it is striking that environmentalists, who in other circumstances trumpet source reduction as the most desirable form of pollution control, are willing to sacrifice an opportunity to encourage it for the much less clear-cut benefit of spending more money on abandoned sites.

Second, environmentalists vociferously supported the requirement that Superfund sites be cleaned up to the levels required by existing environmental statutes. They rejected the use of a cost-benefit approach that would compare the benefits to be obtained by various levels of cleanup at a site to the cost of attaining those results. To obtain these high levels of cleanup, they also insist that the agency reject the relatively cheap alternative of containment in favor of the more expensive one of treatment.[18] Containment can often mean little more than capping the site, in other words, leaving the noxious materials in place but preventing them from spreading onto neighboring properties or leaching into water supplies. Treatment involves the use of chemical or biochemical agents to make the material less hazardous.[19] Environmentalists refer to this approach as *permanent treatment*, contrasting it with the impermanence of *containment*. Depending on the circumstances, treatment is either done on-site or off-site, the latter requiring expansive and potentially hazardous removal and transport of the waste.

Treatment, particularly if done on site, does have real environmental benefits, just as a defanged snake is less dangerous than a caged one. However, in light of the limited availability of Superfund monies, coupled with the very great number of sites, the insistence on permanent treatment and attainment of quality standards derived from other environmental statutes entails that only a small number of sites will be cleaned.

To understand why environmentalists would be willing to sacrifice environmental benefits that could readily be attained, one must recognize that their goals are not limited to environmental quality. As Michael McCann, Sidney Milkis, Richard Harris, and others have explained, environmentalists are part a broader political reform movement.[20] Milkis and Harris have described the intellectual and political evolution of this movement, which they term the "Public Lobby." Their interviews with Public Lobby activists show that:

When contemporary public lobbyists describe their activities and motivations they do so in the language of the New Left. The New Left provided both a source and a model for the Public Lobby, most of whom came to political maturity during its heyday in the 1960's.[21]

Public Lobbyists form a self-consciously coherent group that has proved immune to the generally rightward drift of most of their generation. In addition to an antiestablishmentarian style, the Public Lobby derives from the New Left a commitment to participatory democracy and a distrust of corporate America. In Michael McCann's formulation of Public Lobby ideology, distrust verges over into antipathy:

The core of [the Public Lobby's] ideology is a critical assumption about the structure of power in contemporary American public life, namely that business corporations dominate both government and the marketplace at great costs to our social welfare and democratic principles.[22]

Two quotes by Public Lobby activists attest to the centrality of participatory democracy in their political worldview. In the words of Daniel Becker, legislative counsel for Environmental Action (EA):

One of the most significant achievements brought about by public interest groups has been the development of the grassroots. EA is concerned with how to get people involved in the movement and to learn how to help themselves, equipping local citizens to protect their interests against corporate power.[23]

Similarly, Kathleen Sheekey, director of legislation for Common Cause, has stated: "The common thread among all concerned groups is activism. . . . What we are trying to do is develop citizens as lobbyists, to bring citizens into the decision-making process. Our work is much less advocacy than education."[24]

Although, for the most part, Washington environmental organizations lack a genuine grass-roots base, they see their task as redesigning the structure of national policy so as to facilitate citizen participation. They can justly claim credit for helping to create many of the procedural reforms that do exactly that. National environmental groups also recognize the political benefits to be gained when local organizations, using many of the channels they have created, become politically powerful enough to help elect to Congress individuals who share the Public Lobby point of view.

Whatever its limits as an environmental program, Superfund functions superbly to promote the Public Lobby's broader political agenda. Of all environmental programs, only the environmental impact statement requirements of the National Environmental Protection Act (NEPA) and, perhaps, the Endangered Species Act are as provocative of public participation and adversarial encounter. Superfund provokes community uproar by proclaiming that health hazards exist within its midst. It encourages political mobilization because its generous cleanup monies are only available to those communities that are able to get their site named to the federal list of approved sites. And it feeds antibusiness sentiment by proclaiming that cleanup will be paid for by the polluters or by their virtual surrogate, the chemical industry.

From the standpoint of encouraging citizen participation, it is utterly irrelevant whether progress is being made at the cleanup front. In fact, site cleanup is nowhere near as useful as disappointed expectations of site cleanup.[25] The citizen participation provisions of the 1986 reauthorization provide new opportunities for the movement to make use of administrative hearings and the courts to fan the flame of discontent. Community technical assistance grants provide funds that enable communities to hire experts to dispute agency claims that adequate cleanup has been performed. Most valuable of all in this regard, however, is the permanent treatment requirement, for, as long as strict standards are accompanied by "free" money, regardless of whether it is reaped from responsible parties or the federal fund, the very unattainability of those standards provides an invaluable organizing tool. Unattainable and unattained standards provide citizen activists and organizers with the ammunition they need to maintain a steady barrage of criticism of the EPA for failing to attain them and serve as a continual reminder to the affected community that it is being slighted.[26]

Because Superfund is so valuable politically, it must be protected fiscally. It is for this reason that the environmental establishment fought against the waste-end tax and for the feedstock fee. Although the fee does not promote source reduction, it is off-budget, easy to collect, and capable of providing the steady stream of revenue that a comprehensive Superfund program requires, particularly in view of the failure of the liability regime to serve as an adequate revenue-generating device.

The Environmental Movement's Allies

Besides the environmental community, the chief beneficiaries of Superfund have been the legal community and the hazardous waste treatment industry. No firm figures are available on how much money is spent for legal fees in Superfund disputes. However, the American Insurance Association commissioned a study by a consulting firm that, drawing on recorded litigation costs, estimated that the cleanup of 1,800 sites would consume a whopping $8 billion in litigation expenditures, 79 percent of which would be incurred by private parties.[27] Superfund liability is, along with bankruptcy, the most important source of new business for major law firms. One estimate puts the number of lawyers who are actively engaged in Superfund litigation at 20,000.[28] As long as the Polluters Pay premise remains untouched, Superfund will continue to produce a steady stream of revenue for corporate law firms.

The hazardous waste treatment industry has been similarly blessed. By any measure, hazardous waste treatment is a growth industry. Companies in this sector are growing at very high rates; one company grew into a 160-person firm in four years.[29] Most of this growth is attributable to stringent environmental regulations, and to Superfund in particular. A leading industry trade journal observed in 1987, "There is little doubt that the infusion of new EPA funding and changing regulations will keep the hazardous waste management action at near fever pitch during the next several years, at least."[30] A brochure for a 1989 industry convention urged prospective attendants to "win your share of the billions in profits ahead."[31]

The waste treatment industry's lobbying organization is the Hazardous Waste Treatment Council (HWTC). The council does not represent all Superfund contractors. As its name indicates, it primarily represents those who perform treatment, as opposed to containment or disposal. The HWTC broke off from the existing contractors' organization because that body also represented landfills which, the treatment industry argues, do not represent a permanent solution to the cleanup problem.[32]

For obvious reasons of economic interest, the HWTC has consistently lobbied for policies that would ensure a long-term, continual proliferation of Superfund sites, and it has sought to ensure that the most expensive forms of cleanup be employed at those sites. During the debates over the 1986 Superfund Amendments, for example, the HWTC lobbied fiercely—and successfully—for the abolition of a so-called postclosure liability trust fund that had been part of the original statute. The trust fund immunized landfill operators from liability for problems that might occur at their sites after they were officially approved as closed. It was felt that without such a provision, the open-ended liability exposure would prevent even highly qualified potential operators from agreeing to run federally approved landfill facilities. Doing away with the fund placed liability back on the shoulders of landfill operators and therefore created pressure for gold-plated, "Cadillac" treatment rather than disposal.

The HWTC's policy positions coincide with those of the environmental movement. As we have seen, the environmental movement has consistently supported an expansion of the fund; so has the waste treatment industry. Environmentalists strongly support so-called permanent treatment, as opposed to containment; so does the HWTC.

The HWTC participated in two influential joint research efforts with a broad coalition of environmental groups, including the Environmental Defense Fund, the National Audubon Society, the Sierra Club, the Natural Resources Defense Council (NRDC), and the U.S. Public Interest Research Group. The results of the first effort were published in 1988 under the title *Right Train, Wrong Track: Failed Leadership in the Superfund Program*. The report—a review of EPA records of decision concerning Superfund sites in 1987—criticized the agency for its alleged failure to implement Superfund and charged that the EPA was repeating past mistakes in using containment remedies as the most common approach to Superfund sites.[33] According to the report, the EPA was still making decisions in order to "minimize short-term expenses . . . rather than treating the waste to permanently eliminate the hazard."[34] The agency was also accused of inflating "the cost of treatment in justifying containment remedies and . . . using inaccurate, outdated information to establish the cost of treatment" and of selecting "bogus 'treatment' technologies even where it ha[d] data to show that those technologies will be ineffective on the waste materials of concern."[35]

In 1990, the same coalition between the HWTC and establishment environmental groups reviewed the EPA's 1988 records of decision and published the results under the title *Tracking Superfund*. This report acknowledged some improvement in EPA compliance with the 1986 Superfund Amendments but complained that containment was still being used more frequently than permanent treatment actions. As the HWTC's executive director stated in a separate statement, "If Congress made one thing clear in [the 1986 Amendments], it was that remedial actions which merely contain the waste or to stabilize the site are nothing more than a 'Superfund shellgame.' "[36]

More disturbingly, the environmental movement and the waste treatment industry have tried to block efforts to promote the reduction of sources of hazardous waste generation. In the debates over the 1986 Amendments, both the environmental movement and the HWTC opposed the proposed waste-end tax that would, in the long run, have reduced hazardous waste. Similarly, the HWTC and individual waste treatment companies have filed several lawsuits challenging EPA regulations issued under the Resource Conservation and Recovery Act that would have encouraged or at least permitted the recycling or treatment and disposal of certain substances used in industrial production, such as oil and metals. More recycling, of course, would mean less hazardous waste, and the treatment industry would rather have less of the former and more of the latter. A former EPA counsel observed about Waste Management, Inc., the nation's largest waste disposal company, "They're interested in having a lot of waste designated as hazardous so they can get rid of it."[37] The lawsuits found environmental groups on the waste industry's side.[38]

The cooperation between the environmental movement and the waste treatment industry on Superfund issues is, in some respects, similar to the coalitions between advocacy groups and industry described elsewhere in this volume. However, in other important respects, it is very different. For one thing, the coalition between the environmental movement and the HWTC is not tactical; it is much more in the nature of a permanent, symbiotic alliance. This is by no means a natural phenomenon. Waste treatment companies, after all, handle toxic waste, and are more prone to violate environmental standards than companies in less risky lines of business. Considering the environmental movement's stake in portraying violations of toxic waste regulations as particularly egregious and unconscionable, one might expect relations between the movement and the industry to be rather acrimonious. This, in fact, used to be the case, and some environmental groups still portray waste management companies as villains.[39] However, for the most part, conflict has been replaced with close cooperation, which has come about largely as a result of the industry's initiatives. In 1985, the nation's largest environmental company, Waste Management, Inc., made a strategic decision "to build bridges with the environmental groups that hector EPA to toughen its enforcement standards."[40] To this end, Waste Management hired attorneys and lobbyists with impeccable environmentalist credentials such as James Banks, formerly an attorney with the Natural Resources Defense Council and now Waste Management's general counsel. In addition, the company made grants amounting to hundreds of thousands of dollars to environmental organizations, including $135,000 to the National Audubon Society "to support lobbying for more stringent regulation of industrial wastes" and $117,500 to the National Wildlife Federation to be used, in part, "to investigate the potential for strengthening pollution control laws in Latin America."[41]

A second respect in which the coalition between environmental groups and the waste treatment industry differs from ad hoc, tactical coalitions between environmentalists and industry groups is, arguably, its sheer destructiveness. For the coalition partners, the benefits are obvious: By including the HWTC, environmentalists can refute the claim of being "antibusiness" and show that businessmen find their positions to be practical and commercially viable. Waste treatment companies, on the other hand, benefit from the environmental movement's ability to foster public hysteria over exceedingly marginal risks as well as from its undisputed public credibility, some of which rubs off on its allies. (It is the environmentalists' support that makes waste treatment companies look different from the—otherwise comparable—"gold-plating" defense contractor.) However, the policies this unholy alliance has advanced are detrimental to the very goals it purports to pursue. The waste treatment industry and the environmental movement have decided, each for their own reasons, that the expenditure of vast amounts of money on the abatement of exceedingly marginal risks is a public necessity. They have further decided that more hazardous waste is good for the environment.

IS REFORM IMPOSSIBLE?

Superfund's faulty premises block improvement of the program and provide a cloak for private gain at public expense. Environmentalists benefit from the powerful boost the law gives to community organizing efforts by instilling fear and resentment about abandoned waste sites. The hazardous waste treatment industry benefits from the law's bias in favor of "Cadillac" cleanup solutions. Lawyers and consultants benefit from the huge amount of business created by Superfund's extraordinarily complex liability scheme.

On the other hand, there is no natural constituency—other than the public at large—for reforming the statute. Although Superfund liability represents a major cost to the business sector as a whole, that sector has been handicapped in efforts to reform it because different provisions of the regime have very different impacts on different segments of the business community. Once a firm has been identified as a PRP, it is in its interest to drag as many other firms, banks, and insurers as possible into the liability net. Thus, while strict, retroactive, and joint and several liability imposes immense and unpredictable costs on the private sector as a whole, it may also, in a given circumstance, enable a particular firm to spread the pain of cleanup payments. Therefore, up to now at least, the business sector has not been able to achieve the unity required to launch a major assault on the liability regime.

The closest business has come to overcoming this fractionalization and to forging a broad coalition for reform is a proposal by the American International Group (AIG), the largest underwriter of commercial and industrial insurance in the United States, to circumscribe the liability regime as a whole and to fund site cleanup by means of a broadly based tax on business. AIG proposes that the use of liability to raise funds for Superfund be abandoned, and that cleanup be paid for instead by a fund financed by a fee on all commercial and industrial insurance premiums, with a mechanism to cover self-insured companies as well. Strict and joint and several liability would continue to apply to all current and future waste disposal to ensure that generators, transporters, and disposers would have incentives to handle waste responsibly.[42]

Although this proposal directly challenges the Polluter Pays premise, it makes no effort to refute Shovels First. Rather, it is couched as an effort to speed the cleanup which has been unduly hampered by the delays that the efforts to recoup from PRPs inevitably impose. AIG's literature uncritically cites information from the General Accounting Office (GAO) and the Office of Technology Assessment (OTA) attesting to the broad scope and seriousness of the abandoned site problem.

This selective criticism of the law is dictated by prudence. To attack the premise of "ticking time bombs" is to invite the wrath of all those in Congress, the media, and the environmental movement who have championed the idea of a hazardous waste health crisis. By confining its reform efforts to the Polluters Pay premise, the industry hopes to avoid setting off a political avalanche that would bury its most important objective, which is to diminish its liability exposure.

By saving the billions of dollars in losses that society incurs in the effort to establish liability for old sites, the AIG proposal offers important public benefits. However, by failing to insist on a careful evaluation of the actual danger to society posed by abandoned sites in general and the specific risks posed by individual sites, the AIG scheme might actually increase society's overinvestment in toxic waste management. On the one hand, the proposed tax would not fall on individuals and thus perpetuate the misconception that cleanup is free. On the other hand, the proposed tax would eliminate the last remaining source of resistance to boundless Superfund spending. For all its inefficiency, the liability scheme at least created one constituency—the PRPs—that favored less cleanup. If the liability scheme is abolished without being replaced with a mechanism to force an assessment of costs and benefits, the political momentum will go even further in the direction of expanding the program.

Superfund can be reformed only through the same sort of political entrepreneurship that produced the current, fatefully flawed regime. For several reasons, the EPA may now be in a position to tackle this task. In terms of public relations, Superfund has probably ceased to be an asset for the EPA; as noted, the agency is routinely blamed for the snaillike pace of cleanup. Moreover, the EPA knows that the public health benefits procured by Superfund are negligible and that the vast amounts of public and private resources currently invested in the program could be spent far more productively elsewhere. The agency even appears to be prepared to explain this to the public, and it is politically in a position to do so.[43] Over the past several years, the agency has regained a substantial amount of the credibility it had lost in the early Reagan years. At the same time, some of the public hysteria over "ticking time bombs" has subsided; the media and the public are gradually becoming aware that trace amounts of contaminants do not always constitute mortal risks and that government actions such as the spectacular 1983 evacuation of Times Beach, Missouri—where a substance containing dioxin had been sprayed on the roads—were based on wildly inflated risk estimates.[44]

To be sure, none of this guarantees that the EPA will exploit the existing political opening and throw its weight behind fundamental reform. Superfund constitutes a very substantial portion of the EPA's budget; powerful constituencies will resist any reform efforts, and legislators will be reluctant to reexamine Superfund, if only for fear of being denounced as antienvironment. In light of these circumstances, the EPA must be expected to tinker at the margins.

Marginal changes, however, will not do. Superfund needs radical design changes—above all, top-down budgeting. Instead of allowing each individual site cleanup decision to be made on its "merits," a fixed amount should be budgeted for site cleanup as a whole. Unlike air and water, whose movements do not respect state boundaries, sites do not move. Therefore, site cleanup decisions need not, and ought not, be made nationally. The annual budget for site cleanup should be allocated to individual states on the basis of a preestablished formula, and the states should be left alone to decide how best to cope with the cleanup problems they face.[45]

Like the AIG proposal, this scheme would end the use of the liability regime as a device for funding cleanup. However, instead of further inflating the program, it would place site cleanup on-budget and force it to compete openly with all other public programs for the revenue generated by the federal tax system. By doing away with the perception that Superfund is free, this change in policy architecture promises to rein in Superfund's expansive political dynamic. Members of Congress would have to measure the political utility of allocating money for site cleanup as compared to other competing claims on the budget. State officials could no longer successfully lobby for more money to clean up particular sites and thereby avoid making difficult decisions about how much should be spent where. Local officials would have to make difficult choices about whether high levels of cleanup were really worth spending scarce municipal funds to supplement the share they receive from the state. This recognition of scarcity would provide officials at all levels with a strong defense against the claims of environmentalists and the treatment industry for so-called permanent treatment and for the attainment of any and all environmental standards, no matter how inappropriate.

Top-down budgeting would not only enforce the exercise of political responsibility, it would likely aid civic education as well. The current Superfund regime has an Alice in Wonderland quality: The self-appointed guardians of the environment and an industry that is in a position to remedy environmental problems agitate for more toxic waste and against policies that would permit the reduction of genuine risks. Shovels First means lawyers first and shovels late or never, and the only form of public participation environmental advocacy groups seek to foster is the shrill clamor for someone else's money, which is very far removed from responsible citizen participation in a difficult decision-making process. Only if elected officials are made to face the reality of limited resources will they have an incentive to tell the public the truth and to explain that abandoned sites are not, by and large, ticking time bombs, but rather just another chronic nuisance created by the same industrial civilization that produces so many benefits as well.

NOTES

1. For an analysis of Superfund's origins and formulation, see "Passing Superfund" in Marc K. Landy, Marc J. Roberts, and Stephen R. Thomas, *The Environmental Protection Agency: Asking the Wrong Questions* (New York: Oxford University Press, 1990).

2. On the subject of Superfund implementation and policy analysis, see Thomas Church, Robert Nakamura, and Philip J. Cooper, *Implementing Superfund* (Washington, D.C.: Clean Sites Inc., 1991); Center for Hazardous Waste Management, *Coalition on Superfund Research Report* (Chicago, Ill.: Institute of Technology, Research Institute, September 1990); Office of Technology Assessment (OTA), Congress of the United States, *Coming Clean*, OTA-ITE-433 (Washington, D.C.: U.S. Government Printing Office, October 1989); and Office of Technology Assessment, *Superfund Strategy* (Washington, D.C.: U.S. Congress, OTA, 1985) OTA-ITE-252 (April 1985).

3. Numbers vary depending upon the source of information. In 1985, EPA estimated that there would be about 2,000 sites on the National Priorities

List, while OTS was estimating at least 10,000. See OTA, *Superfund Strategy*, 3. In 1989 EPA had 12,000 sites on its National Priorities List, while the estimate of total sites had risen to 30,000. See Center for Hazardous Waste Management, *Coalition on Superfund Research Report*, Executive Summary, v. For the number of fully cleaned sites, see *National Legal Times*, February 18, 1991, 39.

4. Steven Cohen, "Defusing the Toxic Time Bomb," in Norman Vig and Michael Kraft, eds., *Environmental Policy in the 1980's: Reagan's New Agenda* (Washington, D.C.: CQ Press, 1984), 283.

5. Landy, Roberts, and Thomas, *Wrong Questions*, 144.

6. Peter W. Huber, *Liability: The Legal Revolution and its Consequences* (New York: Basic Books, 1988), 65–82.

7. Ibid.

8. John Lyons, "Deep Pockets and CERCLA: Should Superfund Liability Be Abolished?" *Stanford Environmental Law Journal* 6 (1986–1987): 271.

9. "Industries and Towns Clash about Who Pays to Get Rid of Poisons," *New York Times*, 18 July 1991, p. A14. See also "Pollution Ploy: Big Corporations Hit by Superfund Cases Find Way to Share Bill," *Wall Street Journal*, 2 April 1991, p. 1; and "In the Clutches of the Superfund Mess," *New York Times*, 16 June 1991, p. F1.

10. See Landy, Roberts, and Thomas, *Wrong Questions*, 167; see also "Love Canal: False Alarms Caused by Botched Study," *Science* 212 (19 June 1981): 1404–07.

11. U.S. EPA, *Unfinished Business: A Comparative Assessment of Environmental Problems* (Washington, D.C.: U.S. EPA, Office of Policy Analysis, February 1987), I28–I34.

12. Landy, Roberts, and Thomas, *Wrong Questions*, 39–42.

13. Ibid., 141.

14. Ibid., 142.

15. Ibid.

16. Ibid., 133.

17. Linda Greer, Environmental Defense Fund, "The Waste-End Tax: An Idea before Its Time," *Environmental Forum*, December 1983, 18.

18. See Environmental Defense Fund, Hazardous Waste Treatment Council, Audubon Society, National Wildlife Federation, Natural Resources Defense Council, Sierra Club, and U.S. Public Interest Research Group, *Right Train Wrong Track* (Washington, D.C.: Environmental Defense Fund, 1988).

19. See "Cleanup Technologies" in OTA, *Superfund Strategy*, Ch. 6.

20. Michael McCann, "Public Interest Liberalism and the Modern Regulatory State," *Polity* 21 (Winter 1988): 373–400, and Richard A. Harris and Sidney M. Milkis, *The Politics of Regulatory Change: A Tale of Two Agencies* (New York: Oxford University Press, 1989).

21. Harris and Milkis, *The Politics of Regulatory Change*, 74.

22. McCann, "Public Interest Liberalism," 381.

23. Harris and Milkis, *The Politics of Regulatory Change*, 77.

24. Ibid., 77–78.

25. See, for example, Peter Montague, "What We Must Do—A Grass-Roots Offensive against Toxics in the 90's," *The WorkBook* 14 (July/September 1989): 90.

26. R. Shep Melnick, "Pollution Deadlines and the Coalition for Failure," *The Public Interest* 75 (Spring 1984): 123.

27. Maurice R. Greenberg, "Financing the Clean-Up of Hazardous Waste: The National Environmental Trust Fund," American International Group, 2 March 1989, 41.

28. "Setting Sights on Superfund," *National Law Journal*, 18 February 1991, 36 (citing estimate by the Environmental Law Institute).

29. Ibid.

30. *Chemical Week*, 19 August 1987, 53.

31. Office of Technology Assessment, *Assessing Contractor Use in Superfund*, (Washington, D.C.: U.S. Congress, OTA, January 1989), 42, n. 65.

32. Hazardous Waste Treatment Council, *The Hazardous Waste Treatment Council: Goals and Accomplishments* (Washington, D.C.: Hazardous Waste Treatment Council, 5 September 1990), 1.

33. Environmental Defense Fund et al. *Right Train Wrong Track* (Washington, D.C.: Environmental Defense Fund), 1988; and Environmental Defense Fund, Hazardous Waste Treatment Council, Friends of the Earth, Audubon Society, Natural Resources Defense Council, and Sierra Club, *Tracking Superfund* (Washington, D.C.: Environmental Defense Fund, 1990).

34. Environmental Defense Fund et al., *Right Train Wrong Track*, 4.

35. Ibid.

36. Richard Fortuna, letter to the editor, *Environmental Forum*, May/June 1988, 5.

37. Peter Carbonara, "The Greening of Waste Management," *The American Lawyer*, December 1990, 44.

38. See, for example, *Hazardous Waste Treatment Council v. U.S.E.P.A.*, 861 F. 2d 270 (D.C. Cir. 1988). The Natural Resources Defense Council was a coplaintiff in the case.

39. William Gifford, "When Environmentalists Are Good for Business," *Legal Times*, 7 May 1990, 27.

40. Carbonara, "The Greening of Waste Management," 44.

41. Gifford, "When Environmentalists Are Good," 26.

42. American International Group, "Putting Cleanup First: The National Environmental Trust Fund," *Environmental Issues Forum* (Washington, D.C.: American International Group, 1991).

43. Earlier this year, the EPA published a review of its policies and priorities, which was conducted by the agency's Science Advisory Board, under the title *Reducing Risk: Setting Priorities and Strategies for Environmental Protection* (Washington, D.C.: U.S. EPA, 1990). The report, which has been favorably received by the agency's leadership, criticizes the EPA's

preoccupation with sometimes minuscule public health risks and urges it to pay increased attention to ecological problems such as global warming.

44. See "U.S. Officials Say Dangers of Dioxin Were Exaggerated," *New York Times*, 15 August 1991, p. A1.

45. Determining the level of such a budget and deciding how to share it among the states would not be easy, but it is no more difficult than the myriad other budgetary decisions that the Congress is called on to make. Congress could base Superfund revenue sharing either on the state population or on the percentage of total recognized sites for each state.

5 POLLUTION DEADLINES AND THE COALITION FOR FAILURE

R. Shep Melnick

ROLE REVERSAL

At first the activity on the floor of the House of Representatives seemed ordinary enough. Representative Henry Waxman (D-California), chairman of the subcommittee with jurisdiction over the Clean Air Act and one of Congress' staunchest supporters of rigorous environmental regulation, was engaged in yet another battle with his formidable committee chairman, Representative John Dingell (D-Michigan), known to some as "Tailpipe Johnny" for his annual efforts to relax auto emission standards. But this time something had gone awry. Waxman was endorsing an appropriation bill rider that would prevent the Environmental Protection Agency (EPA) from imposing a construction ban on states failing to meet the Clean Air Act's 1982 deadline for attaining health-based air quality standards. He and his allies railed against former EPA Administrator Anne Gorsuch Burford's threat to impose such a ban in the 213 counties throughout the nation that exceeded those standards, calling her action "heavy-handed" and advising her successor to be more "flexible" in accommodating states that make "good faith" efforts to comply with the act. Dingell—who in 1982 led an effort to weaken the entire Clean Air Act—opposed Waxman's rider, warning, "If you vote for this amendment, you are voting for dirty air."[1] No wonder one House member announced that she was "astounded at this debate" of June 2, 1983, and another admitted to being "totally confused."[2]

The paradox of Clean Air Act opponents asking for rigorous enforcement, and supporters calling for administrative flexibility, becomes all the more striking when one considers the history of the Act. Ever since its passage in 1970, the Clean Air Act has been billed as an "action-forc-ing" statute. In place of vague commands to regulate in the "public interest" or to establish "reasonable" or "feasible" requirements, one finds in the act explicit, often numerical, standards coupled with strict time limits. The requirement that automakers reduce new car emissions by 90 percent within five years was the most visible element of this regulatory strategy. Such clear standards, environmental advocates have maintained, protect Congress's prerogative to set public policy, prevent agency "capture" or mismanagement, and allow citizens to seek relief in court whenever administrators fail to do their job. If ever an agency was in need of supervision it was the EPA under Administrator Gorsuch. Not only were the political executives appointed by President Ronald Reagan hostile to many of the statutes they were charged with carrying out; they were also frequently incompetent and, in at least one case, even dishonest. This hardly seemed to be the year for environmental advocates to put their trust in administrative discretion.

These unexpected positions, however, become understandable once one examines the immediate political context. The 97th Congress had witnessed a long and acrimonious battle over the revision of the Clean Air Act. Considering the Act far too restrictive, the Reagan administra-tion and many sectors of the business community sought to revise it as soon as possible. Environmental groups and congressional sponsors of the legislation of 1970 and 1977, in contrast, remained satisfied with the basic structure of the Act and opposed any set of amendments that failed to tackle such growing problems as acid rain and airborne carcinogens. By the end of 1982, weeks of committee hearings and markups had produced only stalemate. Administrator Gorsuch saw that an announce-ment of the construction ban was a convenient way of forcing Congress to open the Act to amendment. There can be little doubt but that her actions were, as environmentalists charged, politically motivated. At the same time, however, her opponents' efforts to delay the sanction were motivated by an equally political calculation of legislative strategy. They were determined to block any action until the political climate became more favorable to environmental protection. They were also willing to gamble that their cause would find more support after—or just before—the 1984 election. Meanwhile, they wanted no one to rock the boat.

Even before the appropriations rider became law, Gorsuch's replace-ment, William Ruckelshaus, announced that he opposed rapid, wholesale application of the construction ban. If this solved the immediate difficul-ties of the environmental advocates, it only highlighted their long-stand-ing problem. Congress and the EPA once again showed that they would not stand behind the standards and deadlines previously announced with great seriousness. Every major participant now knows that loopholes will always appear in the nick of time, thus obviating the need to impose sanctions in areas that fail to meet air quality standards. Yet the charade continues. Both bills considered by the House and Senate in 1982 extended rather than eliminated deadlines for meeting health-based standards. Put in this context, the debate of June 1983 carries lessons that are more important than the old saying that "politics makes strange bedfellows." An analysis of the dispute shows that "action-forcing" regulatory statutes seldom work as planned, and also shows why many Congressmen refuse to acknowledge this failure.

A DECADE OF DELAY

Section 109(b)(1) of the Clean Air Act requires the EPA to establish "primary" air quality standards that, "allowing an adequate margin of safety, are requisite to public health." The states are delegated the principal responsibility for writing and enforcing so-called implementation plans to achieve these air quality goals.

In 1970, agency officials advised Senator Edmund Muskie (D-Maine), the chief sponsor of the Act, that most areas of the country could probably meet health-based air quality standards by 1980. Muskie, trying to show that he cared more about the environment than did his chief political rival, Richard Nixon, cut in half the time allotted for reaching the goal. This political one-upmanship was later dubbed "technology forcing." But it did not "force" the development of pollution control technology nearly enough. By 1975, almost every metropolitan area in the country was still violating one or more standards. As this first deadline passed, Senator Muskie, who had previously berated the EPA for allowing polluters' compliance schedules to extend past the statutory deadline, suddenly urged administrators to find "flexibility" in the act. Just as Waxman did not want to open the Act to amendment in 1983, Muskie and his allies did not want to expose the Act to a full-scale congressional debate while the country was in the 1975 recession and while the "energy crisis" was the leading topic of political discussion. The EPA temporized until Congress passed the 1977 Amendments.

The 1977 Amendments extended the deadlines to 1982 for most areas and to 1987 for areas with especially serious "mobile source" pollution problems. The amendments also contained provisions to ensure that the deadlines would not slip a second time. The EPA received authority to impose large fines on recalcitrant polluters. At the same time, the amendments prohibited the EPA from using enforcement discretion to create de facto extensions. Only depriving administrators of such flexibility, the authors of this legislation indicated, would convince industry and the states that this time the federal government meant business. The most powerful expression of Congress's no-nonsense approach was the automatic ban on construction of new facilities in states failing to implement plans that would provide for attainment of national primary ambient air quality standards by the end of 1982.

Sponsors of the 1977 Amendments expected to make mid-course corrections as 1982 approached. However, as early as 1979, the EPA was already "conditionally" approving state plans that failed to meet all the requirements of the 1977 Amendments. These conditional approvals were designed both to lift the construction ban and to relieve the EPA of its responsibility to promulgate fully adequate plans. (The EPA's single prior attempt to write an implementation plan by itself had proven disastrous.) It was no secret that many of the plans approved by the EPA could not possibly produce attainment of the standards by 1982. Early in 1981, the National Commission on Air Quality (established by the amendments to examine progress under the statute) reported that the EPA had

approved virtually all states' projections that they would meet the air quality standards even though federal, state, and local officials privately acknowledged that such projections often were based on imprecise emission inventories and inadequate projection techniques, and that they were overly optimistic. . . . Where states obviously were unable to support a projection of meeting the standards, EPA conditionally approved plan revisions based on the states' commitment to study further measures for control.[3]

In other words, failure to meet the 1982 deadlines was not, as those environmentalists supporting the 1983 appropriation rider disingenuously implied, a last-minute surprise, but rather a long-awaited inevitability. The only surprise was that, since 1977, the EPA's strategy had garnered the support of environmentalists both inside the Carter administration and out. EPA Assistant Administrator David Hawkins, formerly an attorney for the Natural Resources Defense Council (NRDC) and subsequently chief lobbyist for the National Clean Air Coalition, had convinced the environmentalists that the massive imposition of sanctions would have "disastrous effects," and he hoped the sanctions would become a "historical footnote."[4] Thus, environmental groups played along with the game and agreed not to challenge the EPA's strategy in court—that is, until they decided that the Reagan administration was being *too* lenient. A chief characteristic of "action-forcing" statutes is that they allow private litigants and the courts to decide which actions to "force."

Nevertheless, the EPA did make significant progress in reducing air pollution under the 1977 Amendments, and the use of sanctions was a key element of this effort. By imposing civil penalties on some polluters, the federal government spurred many of the country's largest and most recalcitrant polluters to reduce their emissions. Moreover, the EPA announced that it would cut off certain federal funds and ban new construction in states that failed to adopt the automobile "inspection and maintenance" programs required by the 1977 Amendments. It showed it was serious about inspection and maintenance by applying these sanctions in two states (California and Kentucky) that failed to meet the EPA halfway.

It is quite clear that the EPA's threats do become credible and produce results when the agency demands that states and polluters take selective actions (installing scrubbers or instituting auto inspection and maintenance programs) that Congress has clearly endorsed and, thus, will most likely stand behind. Conversely, neither threats nor cajoling work when regulators make open-ended demands that states do absolutely everything and anything necessary to attain national standards or insist on the use of expensive or disruptive controls not clearly supported by Congress. The reality of pollution control is that regulators and polluters bargain over what controls are "reasonably available," with each side keeping in mind the extent of its political support. If application of these "reasonably available" controls fails to result in the attainment of national standards by statutory deadlines, then Congress either provides new deadlines (as it did for the steel industry in special legislation passed in 1982) or it lets the deadlines quietly slip by.

Recognizing that further deadline extensions would fool no one and would succeed only in diverting administrative resources to an elaborate shell game, the National Commission on Air Quality recommended that Congress eliminate statutory deadlines and instead require periodic updating of the "reasonably available control technology" requirement for polluters in nonattainment areas. Yet chances for congressional adoption of this sensible recommendation are remarkably slim. The recommendation drew a strong dissent from the most ardent environmentalists on the Commission, who claimed that "abolition of deadlines would legitimize the perpetual failure to provide healthful air quality for 50 to 100 million people" and would remove "the 'action-enforcing' quality needed to assure attainment."[5] Each of the bills considered by congressional committees dealt with the problem by extending the deadlines to 1985 and 1993. Evidently, the political appeal of deadlines has outlived its environmental usefulness.

SHIFTING JUSTIFICATIONS

If deadlines for "forcing" the attainment of air quality standards have had nine lives, it is largely because their advocates have been quicker than cats in jumping from one justification to another. As each rationale has collapsed under the weight of experience, another has risen to take its place. The deadline has become a hollow symbol in search of a tenable underpinning.

The sponsors of the 1970 Act originally claimed that deadlines were justified by the urgency of protecting public health. "The health of people," the 1970 Senate report declared, "is more important than the question of whether early achievement of ambient air quality standards protective of health is technically feasible."[6] The first blow to this argument was the recognition that primary standards do not constitute "thresholds," that is, points at which adverse health programs begin and end. The health effects of pollution generally increase in severity with dose, without sharp discontinuities. This means both that no standard other than zero will fully protect the health of the most sensitive individuals and that the health threat posed by pollution levels just above any given standard is only slightly more serious than the threat posed by pollution levels just below that standard. The second blow came when regulators, Congressmen, and polluters realized that the standards established in 1971 (all but one of which are still in force today) were based on amazingly tenuous evidence and relatively mild adverse effects. The third blow was the recognition that attaining these arbitrary and restrictive standards would cost billions of dollars and disrupt the lives of millions of citizens.

This does not mean, however, that the rapid attainment of primary standards is always unimportant or unreasonable. Despite the huge increase in the cost of low-sulfur fossil fuels during the 1970s, only a handful of areas failed to meet primary standards for sulfur dioxide. Additionally, there is substantial evidence that these standards do protect the public from the serious health risks created by sulfur dioxide derivatives or from the damage caused by acid rain. The difficulty is that the costs and benefits of meeting the deadlines vary tremendously, not just from pollutant to pollutant but also from area to area.

Consider the case of ozone, commonly known as smog. In revising its ozone standard in 1979, EPA relied predominantly on a study showing that when six healthy adults exercised heavily (the equivalent of running six miles in an hour) while exposed to ozone levels of 0.15 parts per million (ppm), several of them experienced such discomforts as headaches and chest tightness. Adding a 20 percent "margin of safety," EPA set the standard at 0.12 ppm. It is not unusual for Los Angeles to experience ozone concentrations of almost four times this level, and attaining the standard there would require massive industrial closures and restrictions on auto use. Few doubt that such controls would cause misery far exceeding that caused by air pollution. Clearly, urgency cannot be divorced from a consideration of the widely varying cost, feasibility, and benefit of attaining primary standards.

As the urgency argument lost force, deadline advocates switched their focus. In the words of Henry Waxman (who, representing Los Angeles, admits that shutting down the city is not an environmental necessity), "The purpose of deadline is simple: to force the development of better technologies to control air pollution."[7] By stimulating innovation, so the argument goes, deadlines make the previously infeasible become feasible, and thus reduce the cost of pollution control. One problem, of course, is that deadlines can stimulate technological innovation only if they are believable. Time after time, Congress has backed down, not just on deadlines for attaining air quality standards but on deadlines for meeting new car emission standards as well. Congress has cried wolf too often. The future of "technology forcing" lies not in further use of phony deadlines but rather in those pollution control strategies that make emission rights scarce and valuable.

CONGRESS AS POLICYMAKER

The final rationale for deadlines is more sophisticated and more overtly political, but ultimately unconvincing. This argument concedes that deadlines must be adjusted and that such adjustments undercut technology forcing, but it stresses that political choices about the pace of pollution control should be made by Congress rather than by faceless bureaucrats negotiating with polluters in back rooms. Today both liberals and conservatives proclaim that Congress should set policy directly rather than delegating such responsibility to agencies, and that it should write detailed legislation rather than trying to exert post hoc control through such means as the legislative veto. What these advocates of legislative specificity generally ignore is the institutional capacity of Congress.

To use air quality deadlines to exercise real control over the pace of pollution reduction, Congress must first set deadlines that are realistic, striking a rough balance between expected environmental benefits and the cost Congressmen are willing to impose on their constituents. Since the extent of pollution, and thus the cost of cleanup, varies from area to area, Congress must take the second step of setting different deadlines for different parts of the country. And since it is hard to know in advance the cost, or even the benefits, of control, it will always be necessary to take the third step of revising deadlines on a regular basis. The need for regional variation leads one to wonder why such important political choices should be made by Congress rather than by state and local elected officials. But leaving this highly charged issue to one side, one cannot but be impressed with the extent of responsibility this scheme places on Congress. The "action-forcing" deadline strategy sets deadlines not just for polluters and administrators, but for Congress as well.

It is hardly surprising that Congress has never—neither in 1975 nor in 1982—lived up to its responsibility to revise outmoded deadlines. Part of the problem has been that committee leaders want to have their cake and eat it too, to guide policy-making through statutory revision but to act only when the political time is right. There is, though, a more basic institutional cause of the congressional failure to act in a timely fashion. The many steps in the legislative process afford any of a number of actors an opportunity to block or delay action. While in 1975 it was Senator Muskie who dragged his feet, in 1976 his chief senatorial opponent, Jake Garn (R-Utah) was able to kill Muskie's bill with an end-of-the-session filibuster. In 1982, Representative Dingell suspended the House committee's work on his bill after losing several close votes; in 1983, Representative Waxman was the one advocating caution.

While it is always good fun to ridicule the glacial speed with which Congress proceeds, the legislative branch's proclivity for slow, painstaking deliberation is one of its chief virtues. Its many veto points allow large numbers of interests to be heard and, in some way, accommodated. Liberals who decried congressional "deadlock" in the 1960s could, by 1981, easily recognize the danger of Congress being "stampeded" by a huge, hastily prepared (even hand-written) budget reconciliation bill. "Action forcing" seldom works on Congress. And when it does, it threatens to rob that body of its most cherished institutional advantages.

The American constitution makes coalition building in Congress difficult in order to guard against the danger of faction, both minority and majority. It also places the "energy" necessary for "good administration," as the Federalist puts it, in the executive branch. The energetic branch can respond to new circumstances in ways that the deliberative branch cannot. The history of air pollution control shows that the real adjustment of deadlines comes in negotiation among state and federal administrators and polluters. While Congressmen regularly berate administrators for failing to meet statutory deadlines, Congress has always either changed the deadlines to reflect administrative policy or quietly indicated that administrators should ignore the law.

Setting unattainable deadlines has several advantages for Congressmen. They can take credit for establishing ambitious environmental goals, criticize administrators for failing to meet them (a move that is especially attractive when the president belongs to the other party), and even condemn the poor bureaucrats for threatening to impose "unreasonable" sanctions. These advantages for individual Congressmen, though, do not make the choice made by Congress as a whole any less illusory. In this case, institutional capacity is destiny.

THE SYMBOLS OF ENVIRONMENTALISM

The most curious aspect of the politics of deadlines is not that most Congressmen vote for them, or even that business and the states make little effort to eliminate them (having learned not to pay any attention), but that leading environmental advocates, both in public interest groups and in Congress, cling to them so tenaciously. It is possible that environmentalists still believe that deadlines will in some way help the EPA reduce the emissions of a few polluters. Perhaps federal regulators can convince some states and businesses that the deadlines have teeth: GM may have learned the game by now, but perhaps the local paper mill has not; if California cannot be pushed around, maybe New Hampshire can. Of course, the small—and decreasing—payoff from this game must be balanced not only against its unfairness but also against the required expenditure of administrative time and credibility. Not surprisingly, many air pollution control officials argue that retaining deadlines can actually impede environmental protection.

Not to be overlooked is the fact that litigation plays a major role in the strategy of environmental groups and that unmet deadlines make for easy courtroom victories. For example, when the NRDC decided that the Reagan administration's EPA had let Illinois get away with too much, it filed suit to compel the EPA to enforce on a selective basis provisions of the law that the NRDC itself conceded should not be applied across the board.[8] Such suits give private litigants, such as the NRDC, an enviable opportunity to amend policy set by public administrators. Environmental groups, though, are politically savvy and recognize that they must watch out for political backlash. This limits the potential of litigation for achieving real environmental benefits and helps explain why these groups have filed so few suits, either directly against polluters or against states for failing to meet the deadlines.

Speculation about the incremental advantages of deadlines for environmental groups should not distract us from the obvious: The value of deadlines is primarily symbolic. But what do they symbolize? Most immediately, environmentalists fear that dropping deadlines will indicate that their movement is in retreat. But they could easily employ the strategy George Aiken suggested for the United States in Vietnam—they could announce victory and get out. While the value of deadlines, they could argue, was great during the 1970s, the value has slowly been eroded. Let us now cash them in for a more effective strategy, such as regular upgrading of control-technology requirements.

The leaders of the environmental movement refuse to make this trade, because for them the symbolism of deadlines goes deeper than concern over their political reputation. Deadlines—or, perhaps more accurately, the ghost of deadlines passed—constitute a reminder of how much remains to be done. In a very real sense, deadlines are made to be broken. Each time we fail to meet a deadline, we are reminded that more effort is needed, that our environment is not yet clean. Deadlines are a time for soul searching and rededication. Although deadlines do not directly advance the process of cleaning up the environment, abolishing them, as the National Commission On Air Quality's dissenters said, "would legitimize the perpetual failure to provide healthful air quality." While we can tolerate this failure for years—perhaps forever—we should never deem it "legitimate."[9]

Thus, deadlines are, to put it bluntly, a symbol of government failure. Another deadline missed, another right violated, another promise unfulfilled. Perpetual failure to meet deadlines gives those who advocate more pollution control a key rhetorical advantage. Why is the government still refusing to do what is right? How can it condone this miserable situation? How long must we tolerate dirty air?

One can answer those questions with another (albeit less rhetorically powerful) question: Why is it illegitimate for Los Angeles to continue its present level of activity and to accept a peak ozone concentration of (to be optimistic) 0.20 ppm, not just for 10 years, but forever? The health risk associated with this level of pollution is quite small compared either with the other risks of urban life or with the benefits of prosperity. What many people like about that city—its climate, its size, its sprawling freeway system—is precisely what makes its smog so bad. Los Angeles is quite literally a sight fit for sore eyes, and is proud of it.

I suspect that most sophisticated environmentalists do not see anything "illegitimate" about government's failure to keep ozone levels below 0.12 ppm in Los Angeles. Many have listened to economists long enough to realize that a riskless society is either impossible or incredibly boring. But they are not willing to give up their rhetorical advantage on rights, health standards, and deadlines because they believe that the political deck is stacked against them. Without a noble lie (such as the commission dissenters' claim that "the Clean Air Act recognizes a basic right of the American people to air that is fit to breathe") industry would use its political clout in the legislative and administrative processes to allow more pollution than "the people" would "really" choose.[10] Conveniently, the fact that deadlines are always ignored or extended produces more evidence of the tremendous power of polluters. Belief in the dominance of industry becomes a self-fulfilling prophecy.

THE SUCCESS NO ONE ADMITS

What is often overlooked is that, by many standards, the federal government's effort to reduce air pollution has been a remarkable success. While gross national product (GNP) has grown and the price of clean fuels has skyrocketed, air quality has improved in almost all major cities. Between 1974 and 1978, the number of "unhealthy days" (as determined by the Council on Environmental Quality) dropped by 18 percent, "very unhealthy days" by 35 percent, and "hazardous days" by 55 percent. Think what would be said if similar gains were discovered in welfare or crime statistics. To be sure, serious problems such as acid rain remain. And regulation has produced serious inefficiencies and inequities, especially by protecting existing sources and discouraging the construction of new ones. Moreover, these gains have frequently come not because the Clean Air Act is "fundamentally sound" (as environmentalists claim) but despite the fact that it is fundamentally flawed (as most air pollution control professionals readily admit). But when one discards the arbitrary standards proclaimed in the act, it is hard to conclude that government has indeed failed again.

Capitalism has proved remarkably effective in making much of this country prosperous. Like all industrial systems it has produced externalities that harm the public health and threaten some of our most cherished wilderness areas. Government regulation has ameliorated some of these problems. But it, too, has produced an externality that has gone untreated because—like pollution before regulation—it is not considered anyone's business or anyone's problem. This externality is cynicism about government. Liberals and conservatives, environmentalists and polluters, all tell us that government has failed. Congressmen, as political scientist Richard Fenno tells us, run for Congress by running against Congress, and every president elected after 1964 has tried to show that he has less faith in the government he hopes to lead than does his opponent.[11]

Reading the debate of June 1983 over air quality deadlines may leave one with a cynical smile. Cynicism in private can be comic, but the spread of public cynicism can be tragic. Just as surely as pollution is harmful to public health, our Byzantine strategies for protecting the environment have become hazardous to the public spirit. In some policy areas, perhaps, our symbols are laudable but our practices are disappointing. In pollution control, however, our symbols are more in need of reform than our practices.

EPILOGUE, 1991

This article was written in 1983. Subsequent years have witnessed significant progress in reducing some forms of air pollution. The EPA reports that from 1979 to 1988, ambient levels of sulfur dioxide fell 30 percent, carbon monoxide levels fell 28 percent, and lead levels fell 89 percent.[12] For smog, though, little has changed. Ambient ozone levels increased by 2 percent, and 101 urban areas continue to violate the national air quality standard. This means that about half the nation's population lives in areas with air deemed "unsafe" by the federal government. For eight years, Congress and the Reagan administration remained at loggerheads over the revision of the Clean Air Act. During that period, the EPA did virtually nothing to punish states that continued to violate the ozone standard nearly a decade after the "technology-forcing" deadlines had passed.

In 1990, Congress and President George Bush finally agreed on a massive revision of the Clean Air Act. The acid rain title of the bill imposed extensive and specific controls on coal-fired power plants. Another section of the new law significantly tightened emission limits for new cars and trucks. A third made regulation of toxic pollutants much more stringent. With all this to fight and write about, legislators and the media paid little attention to the complex new rules for ozone nonattainment areas. *Congressional Quarterly* reported that "after weeks of dawdling progress on relatively minor differences between House and

Senate clean air bills," the conferees reached agreement on smog rules with "lightening speed."[13]

With little fanfare, Congress virtually abandoned nationally uniform deadlines. The new law created six categories of nonattainment areas. Table 5.1 provides an outline of the new regulatory regime.

Each category not only has its own compliance deadline, it has a separate set of control requirements as well. All but the "marginal" cities must reduce volatile organic compound (VOC) emissions by 15 percent within 6 years and 3 percent per year after that. The more severe the pollution problem, the smaller the sources that are subject to regulation. In "severe" and "extreme" areas, new regulations will fall on dry cleaners, auto paint shops, and even local bakeries. For "serious" problem areas, states must include plans for "enhanced inspection and maintenance" of auto emission equipment, a clean fuels vehicle program, and transportation controls. In "severe" areas the state must devise and enforce transportation control plans adequate to prevent any increase in "vehicle miles traveled"—no mean feat in light of past traffic growth. Complex additional requirements fall on Los Angeles, which has one section of the Act all to itself.

Table 5.1
1990 Clean Air Act Amendments: Air Quality Attainment Deadlines

Classification	Ozone "Design" Value (PPM)	New Deadline	Cities (Examples)
Marginal (41 areas)	.120 - .138	1993	Albany, NY Toledo, OH Paducah, KY
Moderate (32 areas)	.138 - .160	1996	St. Louis Phoenix Miami Greenville, SC
Serious (18 areas)	.160 - .180	1999	Atlanta Boston El Paso Portsmouth, NH
Severe I (5 areas)	.180 - .189	2005	Milwaulkee Philadelphia San Diego
Severe II (3 areas)	.190 - .280	2007	New York Chicago Houston
Extreme (1 area)	.280 - up	2010	Los Angeles

It takes 30 pages of the statute to spell out these rules—the same length as the entire Social Security Act of 1935. The law combines mind-numbing specificity (among the emission reductions "not creditable toward the 15 percent" VOC reduction are "regulations concerning Reid Vapor Pressure promulgated by the administrator by the date of enactment of the Clean Air Act Amendments of 1990 or required to be promulgated under section 211[h]") with a surreal detachment from political reality. The principal example of the latter is the requirement that states must compose and enforce transportation control plans and that EPA must establish its own federal implementation plans if the states balk. Large-scale transportation control plans proved such a disaster in the 1970s that they were abandoned by even the most ardent regulators in EPA. Now, like bad movie sequels, they're back. It is obviously hard for members of Congress and their staff to take seriously rules that will not go into effect for many years.

There was a time, not so very long ago, when only a national crisis could produce such extensive regulation of business and such intrusive control over state and local government. In 1990, though, these legislative changes simply rode the coattails of the more important and controversial sections of the bill. Most of these provisions met with little resistance since inside players figured they would never actually be enforced.

The political response to these new rules will depend on how visible they are to the average citizen. The only new regulations likely to be imposed are those on stationary sources. Dry cleaners, bakers, and owners of auto paint shops and gas stations will at first resist, and then comply, passing most of the costs along to consumers. This, however, will do precious little to make the air cleaner. State plans to make "inspection and maintenance" more rigorous, to impose a new round of transportation controls, to turn backyard barbecue equipment into illegal contraband, and to place other restrictions on the behavior of private citizens, in contrast, will be greeted with a barrage of criticism. Surely, before long Jay Leno will intervene, and criticism will become ridicule. Members of Congress will condemn EPA, EPA will search for loopholes, and many years later Congress will rewrite the Act—once again.

NOTES

This article originally appeared in substantially identical form—but without the epilogue—under the same title in *The Public Interest*, no. 75 (Spring 1984): 123–34. It is reprinted here by permission.

1. *Congressional Record*, June 2, 1983 (daily ed.), H3507.

2. Congressional Record, June 2, 1983 (daily ed.), H3504 (Congresswoman Martin), H3514 (Congressman Molinari).

3. National Commission on Air Quality, *To Breathe Clean Air* (Washington, D.C.: GPO, 1981), 2.1–21.

4. *Environment Reporter (BNA)—Current Developments* 9 (1979), 1351.

5. Ibid., 5–36, 5–38.

6. U.S. Congress, Senate Report No. 91–1196, 1970, 2.

7. *CQ Almanac* (1981), 514.

8. Testimony of Robert Yuhnke (Environmental Defense Fund), Hearings before the Subcommittee on Health and the Environment of the House Committee on Energy and Commerce, 97th Congress, 1st Session (Washington, D.C.: GPO, 1981), 92–125.

9. *To Breathe Clean Air*, 5–36.

10. *To Breathe Clean Air*, 5–35.

11. Richard Fenno, "If, As Ralph Nader Says, Congress is 'The Broken Ranch,' How Come We Love Our Congressmen So Much?" in Norman J. Ornstein, ed., *Congress in Change: Evolution and Reform* (New York: Praeger, 1975), 280.

12. 1988 EPA Trends Report, cited in U.S. Congress, House Report No. 101–490, 1990, Part I, 196.

13. Alyson Putte, "Conferees Reach Agreement on Urban Smog Provision," *Congressional Quarterly Weekly Report*, 15 September 1990, 2903.

6 PRIVATE ENFORCEMENT, PRIVATE REWARDS: HOW ENVIRONMENTAL CITIZEN SUITS BECAME AN ENTITLEMENT PROGRAM

Michael S. Greve

One of the most distinctive features of environmental law is the broad role it affords to private law enforcers. With only one exception, every federal environmental statute contains a so-called "citizen suit" provision allowing "any citizen" or "any person" to sue private parties for noncompliance with the statute.[1] Plaintiffs suing under these provisions need not have suffered, and usually have not suffered, a specific harm or injury as a result of the conduct they seek to redress. Rather, citizen suit provisions allow private citizens to step into the government's shoes and to act as "private attorneys general," without the consent and even over the objections, of the actual attorney general.

Congress has consistently endorsed citizen suit provisions as an efficient and participatory mechanism that allows concerned citizens to redress environmental problems. Since the first such provision was written into the 1970 Clean Air Act, Congress has repeatedly broadened the scope of citizen suit provisions and expanded the remedies that are available to environmental citizen-plaintiffs. Nonetheless, the legislative histories of environmental statutes "indicate some congressional caution about giving private parties the power to enforce regulatory statutes."[2] This caution is appropriate, for it is exceptionally difficult to put citizens to work for public goals and values. Private individuals are ordinarily good judges of their own rights and interests, and can therefore be relied on to right the civil wrongs that are done to them, such as trespasses or breaches of contract. But they are terrible at judging the interests of others, including, and especially, public interests. Private enforcers are driven by a desire to collect whatever rewards are offered, irrespective of the social consequences of their actions.

This would not matter if all enforcement actions under a given statute were socially beneficial. However, laws are usually overinclusive; they tend to prohibit at least some desirable or innocent activities, along with those that they rightly prohibit. For example, the full enforcement of meat inspection laws would shut down every meat processor in the country, and the full enforcement of speed limits would slow highway traffic to a much greater extent than the limits are intended to attain. Since private enforcers are indifferent to this consideration, they tend to overenforce the law.[3]

The danger of excessive enforcement explains why law enforcement has traditionally been left to the discretion of public officers. Of course, public officials are not always and automatically better judges of the public interest than a conscientious and resourceful private enforcer; like every political agency, the executive suffers from institutional and political biases. Nonetheless, in contrast to private enforcers, public officials are subject to political pressures and sanctions, including removal, which permit the public and its elected representatives to express their preferences for more or less stringent enforcement. Moreover, and more important, public officials face budgetary constraints that prevent overenforcement.[4] Private parties, in contrast, do not depend on appropriations and are, therefore, much harder to direct and, if need be, to discipline.

The congressional authors of environmental citizen suit provisions were not indifferent to the threat of excessive enforcement. Congress did want private environmental law enforcement mechanisms to be readily available and widely used. For these reasons, environmental statutes typically instruct courts to award attorneys' fees to plaintiffs "when appropriate." At the same time, however, citizen suit provisions contain several mechanisms designed to guard against excessive enforcement. Foremost among these is a prohibition on *profitable* enforcement: Citizen-plaintiffs are not permitted to collect rewards or bounties. Statutory fines obtained in a citizen suit are payable not to the plaintiff but to the U.S. Treasury. And attorneys' fees provisions allow plaintiffs to recover their expenses, but they are not intended to let enforcers profit from their activities.

The premise behind this altruistic structure of citizen suits seems straightforward and compelling: Where no rewards are to be had, excessive enforcement is not a threat; enforcers will be guided solely by the prospective environmental benefits of their actions. In practice, however, considerations of private economic reward have come to play a prominent role in determining how and by whom environmental laws will be enforced. Altruism—the prohibition on profitable enforcement— has failed to serve as an adequate proxy for efficient enforcement and as an effective safeguard against erratic and excessive enforcement. Citizen suit provisions essentially became an off-budget entitlement program for the environmental movement when inventive environmental lawyers discovered a way of utilizing the citizen suit provision of one environmental statute, the Clean Water Act, as a vehicle to secure funding for environmental causes. This practice is arguably at odds with the statutory purpose and intent of citizen suit provisions, and its environmental merits are questionable at best. However, Congress has failed to contemplate more efficient enforcement mechanisms because no other system would lend itself equally well to the purpose of subsidizing the environmental movement.

THE CASE OF THE CLEAN WATER ACT

The term *citizen suit* evokes the image of a more or less spontaneous action by "concerned citizens" who seek to remedy some environmental problem in their neighborhood. However, this picture is very misleading: Citizen suits are almost always brought by nationally organized, professional advocacy groups such as the Sierra Club Legal Defense Fund or the Natural Resources Defense Council (NRDC). Proving ongoing, site-specific violations of environmental standards is costly and difficult; often it cannot be done at all without the alleged violator's cooperation, which is rarely forthcoming. Few individuals have sufficient time, money, or incentives to overcome these obstacles. Environmental groups, in contrast, do possess sufficient expertise and resources to monitor how the Environmental Protection Agency (EPA) administers environmental statutes and to take legal action when they consider it necessary.

In the early 1980s, a handful of environmental groups organized a campaign to enforce one environmental statute, the Clean Water Act, against private industry.[5] With the help of a seed grant, the NRDC established a self-sustaining enforcement program by recovering attorneys' fees and using them to fund future cases. Five advocacy organizations, including the Sierra Club Legal Defense Fund and Friends of the Earth, joined the NRDC's campaign.

As a result, the number of citizen suits increased dramatically, as did the number of notices of intent to sue. (These notices, which must be sent to the alleged violator, the EPA, and state environmental agencies 60 days before a suit is filed, are better indicators of enforcement activity than actual suits because they include the large number of claims that are settled before trial.) A 1984 study of citizen actions conducted by the

Environmental Law Institute (ELI) showed that of a total of 349 notices of intent to sue filed under all federal environmental statutes between January 1978 and April 1984, fully 214 were issued under the Clean Water Act after the beginning of 1982.[6] Claims filed by six environmental groups accounted for 162 of these notices. Table 6.1 shows that between April 1984 (the end of the ELI study) and September 1988 (when the EPA ceased collecting data on citizen suits), the EPA received more than 800 notices of intent to sue under the Clean Water Act. Environmental organizations account for two-thirds of these actions. More than half of all notices were filed by only five environmental groups.

The surge in private enforcement after 1982 did not result from the accidental preferences of environmental groups, a sudden deterioration of water quality, or a slackening of governmental enforcement. (While

Table 6.1
Private Enforcement of the Clean Water Act: Notices of Intent to Sue Filed with the EPA (May 1984–September 1988)

Plaintiff	Defendant				
	Private Industry	Gov't.	Other	N.A.	TOTAL
National/Regional Environmental Group					
SC/SCLDF	90	12	61	0	163
ASLF	135	9	2	3	149
NRDC	59	7	0	0	66
PIRG	12	4	0	0	16
FoE	2	4	0	0	6
Other	27	23	3	1	54
Coalition	76	2	0	0	78
Total	401	61	66	4	532
Local Group/ Individual	119	76	6	8	209
Other (including Govt't., Industry)	17	24	2	3	46
N.A.	13	4	0	2	19
TOTAL	550	165	74	17	806

Source: Environmental Protection Agency, Consolidated Docket Enforcement System (all regions); Clean Water Act citizen suits. See appendix for an explanation of the data.

environmentalists' concerns over a drop in EPA enforcement under the Reagan administration may have played a role, EPA enforcement of other environmental statutes also declined, yet without triggering a rush of private enforcement.) The explanation is more prosaic: Environmental groups had come to realize that enforcement actions under the Clean Water Act are cheap to bring, easy to win, and financially rewarding. This is due to statutory and regulatory features that distinguish the Act from other environmental statutes.[7]

Foremost among these features is an elaborate permit and record-keeping system. The Clean Water Act prohibits all waterborne discharges not made in compliance with a permit. By the early 1980s, the EPA had issued thousands of permits. At the same time, regulations issued under the statute had created a record-keeping system that reveals each permit holder's specific violations of regulatory standards and permit conditions. It takes less than one day for environmental organizations to train student volunteers to scan these records and identify infractions. Record-keeping requirements, in other words, drastically reduced the search and detection costs potential enforcers would incur. They also created economies of scale: Large numbers of companies can be served with identical, form-letter notices of intent, on which only the dates, names, and a few specifics have to be changed.

A second peculiarity of the Clean Water Act is that its citizen suit provision—in contrast to analogous provisions in other environmental statutes—allows private citizens to sue not only for injunctive relief but also to enforce the civil fines provision of the Act. These fines are substantial: District courts are authorized to impose civil penalties of up to $25,000 per day per violation. Violators are thus confronted with potentially ruinous liability. Private enforcers, on the other hand, possess enormous leverage, both because of the sheer magnitude of the fines that may be assessed and because the courts have disallowed virtually all defenses against alleged liability.[8]

This explains why citizen suits under the Clean Water Act are usually settled prior to litigation. Settlements typically contain four elements: a fine payable to the Treasury; provisions for achieving compliance with permit conditions (for example, an agreement to install additional pollution control equipment); payment of attorney's fees and costs to the plaintiff-group; and, finally, so-called "mitigation" or "credit" programs, to be paid for by the defendant in lieu of or in addition to civil fines. Such payments may finance research projects on the effects of water pollution, grants to local or regional environmental organizations for educational or outreach purposes, grants for land acquisition, and the like.

Substantial portions of such settlements constitute direct transfer payments to environmental groups. First, environmental groups can, and often do, insist on obtaining attorneys' fees and litigation reimbursements in excess of their actual costs. (Attorney's fees are commonly calculated on the basis of the going rates of for-profit attorneys and are, therefore, well above the costs incurred by nonprofit groups.) Second, and more important, payments for "mitigation" or "credit" programs almost always involve payments to environmental groups, ranging from a few thousands to millions of dollars in a single case.[9]

It is obvious why environmental groups can exact such payments: They threaten targets with an expensive trial and offer to settle the matter for a smaller sum—so long as the defendant agrees to make the payment not to the U.S. Treasury but to an environmental group or cause. For the defendants, such bargains are much cheaper than either going to trial or dealing with EPA enforcement.

The result is that credit projects are much more common and account for a far larger share of the total settlement value in settlements obtained by private enforcers than in those obtained by the government. The EPA's enforcement guidelines permit credit projects only under exceptional circumstances and on certain conditions; for example, credit projects are acceptable in addition to but not as a substitute for fines, and they must remedy the environmental damage done by the violator. Environmental groups, on the other hand, virtually always demand and obtain credit projects—many of them without a remedial nexus to the underlying violation—well in excess of the fines assessed. An analysis of 29 cases between 1983 and 1985 showed that more than 65 percent of the settlements, totaling slightly under $1,000,000, went to environmental groups.[10] Another analysis of 30 Clean Water Act citizen suits against alleged polluters in Connecticut between 1983 and 1986 showed that the total settlement of more than $1.5 million included $492,036 in attorney's fees to the NRDC and the Connecticut Fund for the Environment (who had brought the vast majority of these cases) and $869,500 to the Open Space Institute, an organization established by and affiliated with the NRDC. No fines were paid to the Treasury in these cases.[11]

PUBLIC BENEFITS, PRIVATE REWARDS

The fact that transfer payments to environmental organizations constitute the overwhelming portion of settlements of Clean Water Act citizen suits might lead one to suspect that the pattern and scope of private enforcement are determined *not*, as intended, by its expected public benefits, but rather by the enforcers' expected rewards or, more precisely, the "spread" between the costs and the benefits of enforcement *to the enforcer*. A closer examination of the Clean Water Act enforcement campaign shows this suspicion to be correct.

We have already seen that the heavy concentration of enforcement activity under the Clean Water Act is attributable to the Act's unique combination of low search and enforcement costs and high potential rewards. The Clean Water Act enforcement campaign began when environmentalists discovered that this combination made a self-sustaining, remunerative enforcement project a viable option. Similarly, of the 162 recorded enforcement actions brought by environmental groups between 1978 and 1984, not one was brought against a municipal entity.[12] As is shown in Table 6.1, between 1984 and 1988, organized enforcers filed more than six times as many notices against private industry as they did against governmental entities. (Local groups and individuals, in contrast, proceed almost as frequently against municipal or other governmental parties as they do against private industry.) There are no *environmental* reasons why environmental groups would display such a pronounced preference for proceeding against corporate polluters: Governmental facilities cause far more water pollution than private industry and violate their permits far more frequently.[13] Rather, environmental groups prefer suing private corporations because their capacity for fast, authoritative decision making makes settlement negotiations less complicated and expensive, and potentially more rewarding, than negotiations with government officials who worry about the legality of settlements and their own accountability to the electorate. Actions against industry also have more public relations value than actions against local governments; proceedings against government seem less of a "free lunch" to the public than actions against corporations, especially if taxes go up as a result of enforcement.

The list of private enforcers' successful efforts to minimize enforcement costs and maximize private rewards could easily be extended. A group called the Atlantic States Legal Foundation, for example, has brought scores of actions, not over substantive environmental violations but over violations of the voluminous paperwork requirements of the Clean Water Act. While these actions generate tens of thousands of dollars in attorneys' fees and credit projects, they produce no discernible environmental benefits. In short, the targets of private enforcement are not necessarily the parties who did the most damage but those who are likely to accede to substantial settlement demands.

One may be tempted to ascribe this phenomenon to less-than-altruistic motives, and, in fact, the environmental movement's practice of demanding payments for credit projects has sparked an acrimonious debate about the true intentions of citizen-enforcers. Industry representatives have denounced private enforcement actions as "hold-up operations" and "extortion"; environmental organizations have responded that they are genuinely concerned about the environment and that citizen suits do not make them rich.[14] In order to avoid the appearance of self-dealing, environmental groups have even created shells—such as the Open Space Institute, mentioned earlier—"as a repository for cash settlements in Clean Water Act permit violation suits."[15]

However, the universal preoccupation with motives obscures a more fundamental problem: Even the best-intentioned private enforcers will invariably be guided by the costs and benefits of litigation to themselves, not to society. Private attorneys general must choose among enforcement targets, and they should worry about an optimal level of enforcement. Since social costs and benefits are highly uncertain, even the most altruistic enforcers can calculate them only impressionistically. The only factors enforcers *can* assess with certainty and, thus, use as a reference point for selecting cases and enforcement priorities are their own costs and benefits. And since enforcers—altruistic or not—act under budgetary constraints, they will seek to minimize their costs and maximize their rewards.

On occasion, this calculus may lead to enforcement choices that would appear to be rational from the perspective of public benefits. For, example, environmental groups tend to target firms whose discharge records show multiple and recent violations. This strategy makes sense, inasmuch as frequent violations are grounds for suspecting that the damage is substantial and that violations occurred through ill will or negligence rather than through accidental circumstances. However, such suspicions are not based on elaborate cost-benefit analyses; indeed, environmental groups rely on student volunteers—instead of expensive economists and scientists—to select enforcement targets. Environmentalists focus on repeat offenders and recent violations because this, too, permits them to minimize costs and maximize rewards. Under the Clean Water Act and its regulatory progeny, accidental permit violations may be discounted as nonpunishable "upsets." Moreover, judicial interpretations of the Act require citizen-plaintiffs to make a good-faith allegation of an ongoing violation.[16] Private enforcers can keep enforcement costs low by avoiding complicated disputes over isolated violations and the times of their occurrence.

Unfortunately, though, this congruity of economic incentives and public benefits is the exception, not the rule. An enforcer who considered nothing but environmental benefits of alternative enforcement strategies would scarcely focus virtually his entire energy and resources on proceedings against industrial facilities (which, as noted, do less environmental damage and have a far better compliance record than government entities). For that matter, a perfectly altruistic enforcer would scarcely focus his energies on the enforcement of the Clean Water Act. There is no evidence whatsoever to suggest that the Clean Water Act is a particularly "underenforced" environmental statute—quite the contrary: For reasons described below, the result of the aggressive enforcement of the Act against industrial facilities is likely a lot of expensive treatment for treatment's sake that produces few, if any, environmental benefits.

CITIZEN SUITS: RATIONALES AND IRRATIONALITIES

The availability of private rewards does more than distort enforcement priorities; it also undermines the rationales on which the present citizen suit regime is ostensibly based. The most common argument for environmental citizen suits is that private citizens may be better situated than the EPA to detect and apprehend environmental polluters in their neighborhood. By addressing types of violations that tend to escape the EPA's attention, private enforcement could thus fill "gaps" in the government's enforcement program, while leaving public officials in charge of designing and implementing that program. Accordingly, provisions in several environmental statutes—including the Clean Water Act—direct private enforcement toward ongoing, localized pollution and away from past pollution.

However, due to the availability of rewards, the citizen suit provision of the Clean Water Act has produced an enforcement pattern wholly unlike the one purportedly envisioned by Congress. Private enforcement has *not* been directed, as ostensibly intended, against local violations that tend to escape the EPA. If citizen suits served this purpose, they would typically be brought by individual citizens or ad hoc neighborhood associations. Instead, private environmental law enforcement is the domain of national advocacy groups, which are no more attuned to local conditions than the EPA. Since these organizations try to minimize their costs, moreover, they act only when the government and private industry have already paid a substantial portion of the detection costs (such as data collection). They direct their energies away from discovering the violations that tend to escape the EPA because such investigative efforts are expensive. Instead, they focus on the retroactive punishment of known violations (primarily under the Clean Water Act), which requires only record scanning.

Congress is well aware that private enforcers do not bring the types of cases they were ostensibly supposed to bring and that private suits are normally brought, not by concerned citizens, but by professional lobbying and litigation groups. The Clean Water Act enforcement campaign has been examined by the EPA and in a widely used, government-funded study.[17] It was also the subject of extensive congressional testimony during the 1987 revision of the Act. If Congress wanted to correct the reward-induced distortions of private environmental law enforcement—in other words, if Congress seriously intended altruism to serve as a proxy for efficient enforcement choices—it could prohibit the private enforcement of civil fines or legislate a prohibition on mitigation projects and above-cost attorneys' fees. Yet Congress has consistently refused to take such measures.

Charitably interpreted, the reluctance to abolish credit projects and excessive reimbursements for attorneys' fees reflects a genuine dilemma: While Congress wants the scope and direction of enforcement to be determined entirely by the potential public benefits, it *also* wants private enforcement to be extensive. The problem is that one cannot preclude remunerative private enforcement without running a serious risk of eliminating virtually all private enforcement. When payoffs are unavailable, environmental organizations stay out of the market, and private enforcement adds little or nothing to governmental enforcement; this has been the pattern under every environmental statute except the Clean Water Act. When payoffs *are* readily available, on the other hand, private enforcement will no longer be merely supplementary and "gap-filling." In fact, the flood of complaints under the Clean Water Act has eclipsed governmental enforcement and produced a shift in control over enforcement priorities from public to private hands—a result the congressional authors of environmental legislation ostensibly sought to prevent. Congress, though, has come to tolerate attorneys' fees and credit projects because it prefers extensive—though not strictly altruistic—private enforcement to less enforcement.

Congress has justified this preference on grounds that are quite different and, in fact, at odds with the limited, gap-filling conception of citizen suits. Private enforcement, the argument goes, provides much-needed compensation for the EPA's allegedly lax and wholly insufficient enforcement efforts. The perceived lack of stringent law enforcement by public authorities is ascribed to a lack of resources or to the EPA's supposed recalcitrance, foot dragging, and solicitude toward corporate interests.

The claim that environmental laws are systematically underenforced presupposes some independent measure of what would constitute an appropriate level of enforcement. Advocates of citizen suits commonly base the claim of inadequate enforcement on the uncompromising language of environmental statutes, many of which require the attainment of exceedingly ambitious environmental goals without regard to cost.[18] The Clean Water Act, for example, establishes a legal standard of zero discharge; its official goal is not to eliminate harmful pollution but all pollution, however harmless and insignificant it may be and however expensive its prevention. When measured by the yardstick of such absolutist goals, underenforcement is indeed rampant, and private enforcement would make some sense even in its current form and with all its distortions: More enforcement would automatically be better enforcement, and it would no longer matter how many private enforcers enter the market and what choices they make. However, such an attempt to determine the appropriate level of enforcement without reference to anything in the real world is highly problematic. The Clean Water Act illustrates the point.

In mandating the total elimination of discharges, Congress sidestepped what one would believe to be the central question of water pollution—namely, the link between discharges and water quality. From the assumption that *any* discharge is too much, regardless of its effects, flowed a system of technology-based regulatory standards that makes no systematic reference to water quality. On the one hand, the standards are too lax to ensure the integrity of relatively pure streams; on the other, they impose extravagantly strict and expensive requirements to prevent discharges that have no discernible impact on water quality. At the same time, the regulatory system has a strong bias toward regulation of and enforcement against so-called point sources, such as sewerage plants and, especially, private industrial facilities. These are easy to regulate, but they account for a far smaller part of water pollution than nonpoint sources (such as runoff from agricultural fields, construction sites, and roads). As of 1986, industrial point sources accounted for a mere 9 percent of stream pollution, and municipal sources for another 17 percent.[19] The economic and environmental results of this regulatory scheme are sobering. According to the EPA, the country spent about $200 billion on water pollution control between 1970 and 1984.[20] Yet, "the best of admittedly poor statistics show essentially no change in water quality" since 1972.[21]

These considerations cast considerable doubt on the utility of the private enforcement campaign and, more generally, on the assumption that private enforcement is a remedy for an alleged governmental enforcement deficit. As noted, the industrial point sources against which environmental organizations have directed their enforcement efforts account for less than 10 percent of all water pollution. In light of the unimpressive cost-benefit ratio of water pollution controls, one must assume that the marginal environmental gains from enforcement in this area are exceedingly small, and that they are bought at enormous cost. "Underenforcement" would thus be a rational way of preventing a lot of treatment for treatment's sake.

The absolutist language of environmental statutes, then, does not obviate the need to make difficult judgments about the optimal level of enforcement; since absolutist statutory requirements generate overbroad regulatory schemes, they *increase* that need. Since the requisite trade-offs have not been made at the legislative stage, they must be made in the enforcement process, and the most basic and effective way of achieving this is through budgetary constraints. The "lack of resources" which advocates of citizen suits persistently cite as evidence of governmental underenforcement is not really a lack but rather Congress' way of guarding against the potentially destructive application of absolutist statutes. A "lack of resources" means that we prefer to spend existing revenues on something else and that we are unwilling to impose a tax to finance additional enforcement. In other words, the existing level of governmental enforcement reflects the costs that we are willing to pay to improve the environment.

If Congress believed that more enforcement would be unambiguously beneficial, it could remedy a lack of resources by raising the fines under environmental statutes—thus increasing their deterrent effect—or by increasing the EPA's enforcement budget. This would be easier and more effective than the use of private attorneys general, whose decisions are hard to predict and even harder to control and correct. Moreover, if we knew environmental statutes to be underenforced, it would no longer make sense to prohibit *profitable* enforcement. Why should the enforcers' motives matter, if we know that every additional enforcement proceeding generates environmental benefits?[22] The fact that Congress has never even contemplated the option of permitting environmental bounty hunting shows that Congress does *not* believe that more enforcement is automatically better enforcement. Hence, that argument cannot serve as a rationale for the existing enforcement scheme.

A final justification and, historically, perhaps the most important rationale for citizen suit provisions is a general presumption of recalcitrance and sheer ill will on the part of the executive branch. Prompted by a reflexive distrust of executive power, Congress structured citizen suit provisions so as to allow private enforcers not only to fill gaps in the government enforcement scheme but also to prod the government into tougher, more aggressive enforcement. Private enforcers are not quite on a par with the government; they must give notice to the government of their intent to sue, and citizen suits are automatically preempted by governmental enforcement measures. However, *only* by starting its own "diligent enforcement" action can the government stop private enforcers.

This scheme of coordinating private and public enforcement has been recognized as problematic even by staunch supporters of environmental citizen suits.[23] Since the government cannot stop citizen suits by any means short of instituting its own proceedings, private parties can force the government into enforcement actions, including pointless and counterproductive ones. At the same time, the Justice Department insists that citizen suits and private settlements do not bar the government from bringing its own suits over the same violations. It *must* so insist; otherwise, it could not remedy inadequate private settlements or effectively ensure that at least a portion of the assessed penalties goes to the U.S. Treasury instead of being diverted into credit projects. Given the department's position, however, violators are confronted with the possibility of what amounts to the civil equivalent of double jeopardy. Moreover, the government's position weakens the bargaining leverage of the citizen-plaintiffs who act on its behalf: A private settlement that may subsequently be upset by the government is worth less to an alleged polluter than a final disposition of the charges. Consequently, settlements are reduced, and the law is selectively *underenforced*. It would be pure coincidence if the net result were an optimal level of enforcement; erratic enforcement is much more likely.

One might argue that these problems would not arise if the executive, being inherently untrustworthy, were relieved of its responsibility to oversee private enforcers, who are much better judges of the public good. This argument is quite extraordinary in its own right, for the alternative to the selection of enforcement priorities by public officials—who may be biased but are, after all, accountable—is not impartial and efficient law enforcement but rather the selection of enforcement priorities by individuals such as the NRDC's staff attorneys, who are also biased but are unaccountable. Moreover, the argument for relinquishing private enforcers entirely from government oversight—much like the argument that we need not worry about reward-induced distortions of enforcement priorities because more enforcement is always better enforcement—rests on premises Congress itself has explicitly disavowed: Congress has steadfastedly maintained that the executive must retain control over the scope and direction of environmental law enforcement. As is briefly described below, Congress has, on several occasions, even legislated modest expansions of government oversight of citizen plaintiffs.

THE ENVIRONMENTAL ENFORCEMENT CARTEL

In their present form, then, environmental citizen suit provisions rest on premises that are confused at best and mutually exclusive at worst. Private enforcement is supposed to be altruistic; yet, in the interest of encouraging extensive enforcement, Congress and the courts have come to tolerate transfer payments that undercut the proffered rationales for altruism. The flood of private enforcement actions triggered by the available rewards is said to be desirable because it compensates for a lack of government enforcement; but, on that basis, one can no longer explain why environmental law should not be enforced by bounty hunters—an idea that Congress and the courts (and, for that matter, environmental advocates) have never seriously contemplated. Finally, Congress insists that the government is supposed to set enforcement priorities; yet at the same time, private enforcers are supposed to prod the government—an exercise that would be pointless if it were *not* intended to change the government's enforcement priorities.

Periodic congressional debates over citizen suit provisions still call forth a great deal of rousing rhetoric about citizen participation and efficient law enforcement. In truth, however, citizen suits have little to do with either democratic participation or efficiency. Since the provisions are utilized overwhelmingly by organized interest groups and their attorneys, they increase citizen participation only in the most attenuated sense of the term. As to efficiency, citizen suit enforcement has been overwhelmingly concentrated in a single area—industrial water pollution—where the marginal environmental gains from added enforcement are likely to be very small and the costs very large. Contrary to the contention that citizen suits should fill the gaps in the EPA's enforcement scheme, private enforcement has *not* increased the likelihood of detection and apprehension of environmental violators. Some observers have speculated that private enforcement may have ratcheted up the penalties for violators.[24] But even if so, it is far from clear that this has produced any environmental benefits. More likely than not, private enforcement of the Clean Water Act has reduced industry's incentives for voluntary compliance with the law, thus necessitating additional private and governmental investment in enforcement. It may have impeded technological innovation by making permit holders prefer fail-safe equipment to more advanced gadgetry that, although more effective, is untested and may lead to technical violations. And it may have given potential enforcement targets incentives to pollute the air and the land rather than the water or to channel discharges into already overloaded municipal wastewater treatment facilities. Depending on the extent to which these effects have occurred—and they have indeed occurred, at least to some extent—private enforcement may have done more environmental harm than good.[25]

More efficient private enforcement schemes can easily be imagined; in fact, they could be implemented with comparatively minor changes of the statutory language. If Congress truly believed in altruistic enforcement, it could prohibit credit projects and attorneys' fees in excess of actual costs and, at the same time, reduce private enforcers' search and enforcement costs to the extent possible and under all environmental statutes. If, on the other hand, it is judged more important that private enforcement be extensive than that it be altruistic, environmental bounty hunting under stricter governmental oversight would be far more efficient than the current system. Private attorneys general would act as the government's deputies. Although they would possess full governmental powers, the Department of Justice would have the authority to preempt ill-advised citizen suits by issuing a simple notice to the parties and to the court that enforcement is undesirable. Fee recovery and credit projects would be abolished; in order to entice private enforcers, the government would make grants for enforcement actions to environmental groups or, for that matter, to bounty hunters. (The grants would be discretionary; the government would be entitled to refuse payment of rewards for useless or counterproductive cases.)[26] Such a simple system would end coerced wealth transfers and greatly reduce the threat of excessive and erratic enforcement, while allowing private enforcers to collect adequate rewards and securing the environmental benefits that allegedly result from extensive private enforcement.

Congress has not contemplated—never mind adopted—either of these models. The reason for this failure is not confusion or a lack of attention but a conscious effort to preserve the character of citizen suit provisions as an off-budget entitlement program for the environmental movement.

Above-cost attorneys' fees and credit projects—a currency valued exclusively by the environmental movement—makes private enforcement attractive to environmental interest groups. At the same time, the prohibition of other profits limits the pool of enforcers—not the number but the *type* of enforcers. Simply put, congressional policy is to lure environmental organizations into the enforcement market while keeping everyone else out of it. The practical result is an enforcement cartel consisting principally of the environmental movement.

No other system of private enforcement would sustain such a cartel. A strictly altruistic system of private enforcement would fail to generate rewards. A bounty hunter system, on the other hand, would be open to all comers, not just environmental groups. Moreover, rewards would be discretionary and subject to political controls in the form of executive oversight and legislative appropriations. Obviously, this would be less advantageous to the intended beneficiaries than the current system, under which transfer payments are off-budget and sanctioned by the courts.

Congress is well aware of the conditions that sustain the environmental enforcement cartel. Reauthorizations of major environmental statutes routinely give rise to squabbles over the extent to which these provisions may serve as a funding vehicle for advocacy organizations; and, by and large, Congress has sustained and even expanded this use of citizen suits. During the 1987 reauthorization of the Clean Water Act, for example, the Department of Justice (DOJ) argued that the flood of enforcement actions under the Act was coming dangerously close to producing the result Congress had ostensibly meant to prevent—namely, a shift of control over enforcement from the government to private parties. DOJ officials further argued that the unsupervised substitution of credit projects for fines might create a potential for abuse and constitute a diversion of public funds, on the theory that payments for credit projects are made in lieu of penalties. Environmental groups, predictably, opposed the Department of Justice's requests for greater oversight authority over private settlements of citizen suits.[27] Responding to the government's concerns, Congress expanded government oversight over the settlement process; proposed private settlements must now be submitted to the Department of Justice, which may submit its comments to the court within 45 days. However, Congress took great care to avoid any action that might endanger the environmental enforcement cartel. Obviously, the government's authority to comment on proposed consent decrees stops far short of an authorization to *veto* the entry of inappropriate consent decrees. Citizen enforcers were, thus, left free to exact transfer payments more or less regardless of the government's objections.

Indeed, Congress may have endorsed the solicitation of credit projects, albeit in a very underhanded way. The sole reference to the practice appears in the conference report on the Amendments:

In certain instances settlements of fines and penalties levied due to . . . permit and other violations have been used to fund research, development and other related projects which further the goals of the Act. In these cases, the funds collected in connection with these violations were used to investigate pollution problems other than those leading to the violation. Settlements of this type preserve the punitive nature of enforcement actions while putting the funds collected to use on behalf of environmental protection. Although this practice has been used on a selective basis, the conferees encourage this procedure where appropriate.[28]

Since this passage appears at the end of a lengthy discussion of *government* enforcement policy, its qualified endorsement of fines for projects may not apply to private enforcers. On the other hand, the twisted, passive construction also allows the opposite interpretation.[29]

Congress has not only been very deliberate in maintaining the statutory mechanisms of the Clean Water Act that permit environmental groups to collect rewards, it has also attempted to create similar mechanisms under other environmental statutes. Seemingly technical provisions that reduce search and enforcement costs—such as requirements for record keeping, data collection, and public access to information—have proliferated in environmental law. The biggest single accomplishment in this respect is Title III of the 1986 Superfund Amendments, which may eventually allow private enforcers to discern any violation of any environmental statute with the same ease with which violations of the Clean Water Act can now be detected and prosecuted.

Perhaps most tellingly, the 1990 Amendments to the Clean Air Act assimilated the enforcement provisions of the statute to the Clean Water Act. The Amendments contain an elaborate permit system explicitly modeled on the Clean Water Act, and private parties were authorized to enforce the civil fines provision of the Act, much as they are under the Clean Water Act. For the first time, Congress provided statutory authority for the substitution of civil penalties with payments for "beneficial mitigation projects which are consistent with [the Act] and enhance the public health or the environment." However, evidently in recognition of the problematic nature of this policy, Congress limited such payments to $100,000 per case and provided the government with authority to intervene in private enforcement proceedings. (In previous Clean Water

Act cases, environmental plaintiffs had disputed, with mixed success, that the government possessed such authority.)

The reauthorization of the Clean Water Act, due in 1992, will see renewed efforts by environmental groups to expand opportunities for citizen enforcement and the solicitation of transfer payments. For example, the groups will renew their efforts to obtain an explicit congressional declaration to the effect that credit projects need not be related to the violation that is being remedied, which would greatly facilitate the use of citizen suits for general environmentalist purposes. Environmentalists will also continue to press their erroneous and, ultimately, destructive notion that increasing the compliance of industrial sources with permit requirements is *the* key to improved water quality. Already, some of the environmental groups that have been most active in the enforcement of the Clean Water Act are desperately trying to keep Congress focused on the noncompliance of point sources rather than endorsing tentative moves toward examining nonpoint source pollution—a vastly more important problem from an environmental perspective, yet one for which private enforcement provides no remedy.[30]

CONCLUSION

The creation of an environmental enforcement cartel may not have been the original purpose of citizen suit provisions. In 1970, when the first such provision was written into the Clean Air Act, Congress may have believed that enforcement proceedings would ordinarily be brought by individual citizens or neighborhood associations and not by environmental-advocacy groups (most of which were young and small then, as well as less numerous than they are today). On the other hand, environmental lawyers with close ties to the existing groups played a significant role in designing the Clean Air Act and its citizen suit provision, and they did want environmental organizations to have a hand in law enforcement.

In any case, environmental groups, Congress, and the EPA now know, and have known for some time, that citizen suit provisions do more to secure funding for environmental causes than they do to reduce pollution. Yet Congress has done nothing to bring private environmental enforcement more closely in line with the enforcement pattern it purportedly sought to achieve. In fact, Congress has repeatedly endorsed the solicitation of credit projects and expanded the opportunities to solicit such payments. Considerations of public participation and efficiency have long ago given way to interest group transfers.

Of course, it is hardly unusual for Congress to create entitlement programs for favored constituencies and to proffer somewhat specious public rationale for such programs. From this perspective, the use of citizen suit provisions as a funding device for environmental causes seems unexceptional. However, citizen suits differ from more ordinary special interest programs in crucial respects. In contrast to, say, agricultural marketing orders and similar policies that cartelize a private market, citizen suit provisions authorize private parties to step directly into the government's shoes and to exercise its inherent authority—a concept traditionally considered troublesome and odious. Moreover, environmental programs are not normally viewed as entitlement programs; in contrast to farm subsidies, environmental protection is widely believed to be a genuinely public purpose. The fact that Congress permits and, indeed, encourages the direct exercise of public authority for private reward shows that Congress is unwilling to distinguish the exercise of public authority from special interest programs and, perhaps, is no longer capable of doing so.

APPENDIX

Table 6.1 is based on the EPA's Consolidated Docket of private enforcement actions filed under the Clean Water Act. The docket—which was discontinued in 1988—permits the identification of most defendants; unidentified defendants were classified as "N.A." Of the defendants in the 74 cases categorized as "Other," 61 are Alaskan gold miners who were served with complaints by the Sierra Club as part of an effort to end placer mining in Alaskan streams.

The five national or regional groups that filed the largest number of notices are identified as follows:

SC/SCLDF: Sierra Club/Sierra Club Legal Defense Fund
ASLF: Atlantic States Legal Foundation
NRDC: Natural Resources Defense Council
PIRG: Public Interest Research Group
FoE: Friends of the Earth

The many cases in which the EPA's docket lists multiple plaintiffs were "assigned" to one plaintiff. Coalitions among local and national groups were assigned to the "national" category because these groups tend to be the dominant force in enforcement proceedings. Coalitions among

Table 6.2

Private Enforcement of the Clean Water Act: Participation by Major Environmental Organizations (May 1984–September 1988)

	Sole Plaintiff/ Coalition With Local Group	Coalition With Other Nat'l/Regional Group	TOTAL
SC/SCLDF	163	57	220
ASLF	149	0	149
NRDC	66	63	129
PIRG	16	12	28
FoE	6	13	19

Sources: Environmental Protection Agency, Consolidated Docket Enforcement System (all regions); Clean Water Act citizen suits

national groups were listed as a separate category and *not* simultaneously under the name of the groups involved. Hence, Table 6.1 gives only a partial account of the enforcement activity of major environmental groups. Table 6.2 gives a better impression.

NOTES

Portions of this essay have previously appeared in the following articles: "Environmentalism and Bounty Hunting," *The Public Interest* no. 97 (Fall 1989): 15; and "The Private Enforcement of Environmental Law," *Tulane Law Review* 65, no. 2 (1990): 339. Permission to reprint these passages is gratefully acknowledged.

1. Citizen suit provisions typically also allow "any citizen" to sue the EPA administrator for a failure to perform a nondiscretionary duty under the respective statute. However, this article deals only with citizen suits against *private* parties. Citizen suit provisions are contained in environmental statutes such as the Clean Air Act, the Clean Water Act, the Resource Conservation and Recovery Act, and the Superfund Amendments and Reauthorization Act. The only major environmental statute lacking a citizen suit provision is the Federal Insecticide, Fungicide, and Rodenticide Act (FIFRA).

2. Barry Boyer and Errol Meidinger, "Privatizing Regulatory Enforcement," *Buffalo Law Review* 34 (1985): 846.

3. A sophisticated demonstration of private overenforcement is William M. Landes and Richard A. Posner, "The Private Enforcement of Law," *Journal of Legal Studies* 4 (1975): 1. For a somewhat different perspective, see Mitchell N. Polinsky, "Private versus Public Enforcement of Fines," *Journal of Legal Studies* 9 (1980): 105.

4. Landes and Posner, "Private Enforcement," 36–37.

5. The origin of the citizen suit campaign is described by Adeeb Fadil, "Citizen Suits against Polluters: Picking Up the Pace," *Harvard Environmental Law Review* 9 (1985): 36; and Jeffrey G. Miller, "Private Enforcement of Federal Pollution Control Laws Part III," *Environmental Law Reporter* 14 (1984): 10, 424.

6. Environmental Law Institute (ELI), "Citizen Suits: An Analysis of Citizen Enforcement Actions under EPA-Administered Statutes," 1984, III-10.

7. The following discussion, which ascribes the surge of private enforcement actions under the Clean Water Act to the ease of proving violations and the availability of civil fines, is based on the following sources: Fadil, "Citizen Suits," 73–75; Boyer and Meidinger, "Privatizing Regulatory Enforcement," 917–920; and Note, "Citizen Suits under the Clean Water Act," *Rutgers Law Review* 38 (1986): 820–21.

8. For example, the courts held that records compiled and submitted pursuant to regulatory requirements constitute admissions of punishable violations. For example, see *Sierra Club v. Simkins Indus.*, 617 F.Supp. 1120, 1130 (D. Md. 1985), aff'd, 874 F. 2d 1109 (4th Cir. 1988), cert. denied, 109 S.Ct. 3185 (1989). The courts also rejected constitutional challenges to citizen suit provisions: for example, *Chesapeake Bay Foundation v. Bethlehem Steel Corp.*, 652 F.Supp. 620, 622–26 (1987); and *Student Public Interest Research Group, Inc. v. Monsanto Co.*, 600 F.Supp. 1474, 1478–79 (1985).

9. See, for example, *Wall Street Journal*, 23 February 1990, p. B2; "Bethlehem Steel Settles Bay Suit: $1.5 Million Pact Said Largest of Kind," *Washington Post*, 17 February 1987, p. B1; and *Hui Malama Aina O Laie v. Brigham Young University*, D. Hawaii, Civil No. 90-00638, 7 December 1990 (consent decree providing, inter alia, for payment of $2,250,000 "to a Hawaii non-profit corporation yet to be formed").

10. The remainder was split in roughly equal amounts between the U.S. Treasury and state and local agencies. Boyer and Meidinger, "Privatizing Regulatory Enforcement," 933 n. 237.

11. Brief of *Amicus Curiae, Connecticut Business and Industry Association, Gwaltney of Smithfield v. Chesapeake Bay Foundation*, 484 U.S. 49 (1987), Appendix D. Thirty-one cases outside Connecticut during the same time span settled for a total of $5,136,438, consisting of $720,488 in attorneys' fees; $723,900 in treasury fines; and $3,692,050 to others (usually, environmental groups). Yet another study showed that more than 90 percent of the penalties paid by industry in response to citizen suits in 1983 went to environmental organizations, not to the U.S. Treasury. William H. Lewis, Jr., "Environmentalists' Authority to Sue Industry for Civil Penalties Is Unconstitutional under Separation of Powers Doctrine," *Environmental Law Reporter* 16 (1986): 10, 101–2.

12. ELI, "Citizen Suits," III-16.

13. As of July 1977, only 40 percent of municipal sources had attained water pollution requirements, compared to 80 percent of industrial sources. Council on Environmental Quality, *Tenth Annual Report* (Washington, D.C.: CEQ, 1979), 113–114, 137–139. In 1986, the EPA estimated that 37 percent of municipal facilities were still not in compliance. Management Advisory Group to the U.S. EPA Construction Grants Program, *Municipal Compliance with the National Pollutant Elimination Discharge Elimination System* (1986), 11–12.

14. "Citizen Suits Become a Popular Weapon in the Fight against Industrial Polluters," *Wall Street Journal*, 17 April 1987, p. 17.

15. Donald W. Stever, "Environmental Penalties and Environmental Trusts—Constraints on New Sources of Funding for Environmental Preservation," *Environmental Law Reporter* 17 (1987): 10361.

16. *Gwaltney of Smithfield v. Chesapeake Bay Foundation*, 484 U.S. 49 (1987).

17. ELI, "Citizen Suits."

18. See, for example, Mark C. van Putten and Bradley D. Jackson, "Dilution of the Clean Water Act," *University of Michigan Journal of Law Reform* 19 (1986): 863. Boyer and Meidinger, "Privatizing Regulatory Enforcement," 885–959, discuss this view in a sympathetic way.

19. EPA, *Environmental Progress and Challenges: EPA's Update* (Washington, D.C.: EPA, 1988), 46.

20. The projection for the period from 1981 to 1990 is $250 billion. EPA, Office of Policy Analysis, *The Cost of Clean Air and Water Report to Congress 1984: Executive Summary* (Washington, D.C.: EPA, 1984), Table 3.

21. William F. Pedersen, "Turning the Tide on Water Quality," *Ecology Law Quarterly* 15 (1988): 69. The paragraph in the text is based on Pedersen's article.

22. It will not do to argue that "credit projects"—but not profits in a strict sense—promote environmental values. Congress never intended or expected private enforcement environmental benefits other than those accrued to enforcement itself. Moreover, in this crucial respect, it makes no difference that credit projects are not profits. As we have seen, the fact that rewards take the form of credit projects does nothing to ensure that private plaintiffs select the right targets and the right level of enforcement.

23. Miller, "Private Enforcement, Part III," 10, 424–28, argues that the existing scheme of coordinating private and public enforcement poses awkward (though manageable) problems. Boyer and Meidinger, "Privatizing Regulatory Enforcement," p. 839 passim, consider the coordination of private and public enforcers—one of the key problems of private enforcement.

24. Ibid., 931.

25. See, for example, Note, "Citizen Suits," 840–41.

26. Otherwise, the government could not prevent excessive or erratic enforcement. Precisely for this reason, the bounty hunter statutes of the

nineteenth century gave the government the authority to determine the size of awards and even to deny the payment of any awards to private enforcers. See *The Confiscation Cases*, 74 U.S. (7 Wall) 454 (1868).

27. In litigation, environmental plaintiffs have argued that the parties to a citizen suit may settle it on almost any terms they see fit and even over the government's objections. See, for example, *Sierra Club v. Electronic Controls Design*, 703 F.Supp. 875, 878 (D. Ore. 1989).

28. H.R. Conf. Rep. No. 1004, 99th Cong., 2nd Sess. 139 (1986); reprinted in, 132 *Congressional Record*, 132 (daily ed.), 15 October 1986, H10, 571.

29. The Ninth Circuit Court of Appeals read it that way. *Sierra Club v. Electronic Controls Design*, 909 F. 2d 1350, 1355 (9th Cir. 1990).

30. Jeannie Jenkins, Zoe Schneider, and Rob Stewart, *Permit to Pollute: Violations of the Clean Water Act by the Nation's Largest Facilities* (New Brunswick, N.J. and Washington, D.C.: New Jersey Public Interest Research Group and U.S. Public Interest Research Group, June 1991).

7 OZONE LAYERS AND OLIGOPOLY PROFITS

Daniel F. McInnis

On September 16, 1987, 24 countries and the European Economic Community (EEC) signed the Montreal Protocol on Substances that Deplete the Ozone Layer. The Preamble of the Protocol states the parties' bold commitment

to protect the ozone layer by taking precautionary measures to control equitably total global emissions of substances that deplete it, with the ultimate objective of their elimination on the basis of developments in scientific knowledge, taking into account technical and economic considerations.

Signatories of the Protocol committed themselves to a 50 percent reduction of chlorofluorocarbons (CFCs) over 1986 levels by 1999, with the ultimate goal of a total CFC phaseout.

CFCs are a component of dozens of familiar consumer products. They are used as aerosol propellants, refrigeration coolants, foam-blowing agents, and cleaning solvents, among other applications. Many CFC products contribute to our convenience and high standard of living; some are almost necessities. For example, CFCs are one of the most efficient coolants, and some 70 percent of the nation's food supply depends on chilling at some point of the processing and distribution chain. Blood supplies and many medicines also require refrigeration.[1]

The Montreal Protocol "sounded the death knell for an important part of the international chemical industry, with implications for billions of dollars in investment and hundreds of thousands of jobs in related sectors."[2] CFCs are still a big business for the chemical industry; the 1990 global market for CFCs totaled approximately $1.8 billion dollars.

But, as the Montreal Protocol and the 1990 London Agreement—which accelerated the phaseout schedule agreed on in the Protocol—are implemented, this lucrative market will gradually disappear.

The Montral Protocol has been widely heralded as a victory of international cooperation and good sense over powerful corporate interests that sought to block regulation. However, the perception that producer interests obstructed an international agreement—and that they had to be subdued to secure whatever environmental benefits the Protocol may generate—is seriously misleading. The role of business, and of American business in particular, was considerably more complicated.

In fact, at critical junctures, American CFC producers *supported* the Montreal Protocol. In 1985, for example, negotiations on the Vienna Convention—the forerunner agreement to the Montreal Protocol—ran into political resistance on the part of the Reagan administration, which harbored objections to the transfer of multilateral powers to the United Nations and had become increasingly skeptical about the wisdom of a CFC phaseout based on limited scientific knowledge. Then-secretary of state for economic affairs Allen Wallis recommended that Secretary of State George Schultz withhold authority for the U.S. delegation to sign the Vienna Convention. When the U.S. representatives in Vienna received word of this recommendation, they lobbied industrialists and scientists in the United States through a series of frantic late-night phone calls. These parties, in turn, pleaded with the administration to support the Vienna Convention. According to Richard Benedick, the State Department's lead negotiator of the Montreal Protocol, "Eleventh-hour private-sector interventions with the Administration . . . enabled the United States to join in signing the Vienna Convention."[3]

It is probably too much to say that the Montreal Protocol came about *because* of industry demand. Public and political pressure did much to shape the Protocol, and scientific discoveries about CFCs, atmospheric chemistry, and skin cancer—whether correct or not—informed much of the debate. Still, business, and American CFC producers in particular, provided crucial support for the Montreal Protocol—all the while publicly insisting that a CFC ban would entail near-catastrophic disruptions.[4] This essay describes the reasons that account for the CFC industry's seemingly perplexing role in bringing about an agreement widely hailed as a model of international environmental cooperation.

FROM MIRACLE SUBSTANCE TO ENVIRONMENTAL MENACE

Among the ironies of the current concern over CFCs is that these chemicals had long been thought of as "miracle" substances. Before their invention in the early 1930s by Thomas Midgley of General Motors, standard refrigeration fluids were ammonia, sulphur dioxide, and even ether vapor. These substances posed substantial safety hazards. Ammonia, for example, is flammable and toxic; ether can be used as an anesthetic. CFCs, in contrast, are nonflammable, noncorrosive, very low in toxicity, and extremely stable. Moreover, CFCs can be easily liquified under pressure, an important energy-saving consideration in refrigeration. CFC production is also simple and generally economical.

The combination of increased safety, effectiveness, and economic efficiency made CFCs a chemical of choice for many applications. Initially, CFCs were used almost exclusively as a refrigerant. By the 1960s, though, entrepreneurs had successfully developed CFCs and chemically similar substances as foam-blowing agents, solvents, fire suppressants, and propellants. As a result, demand for the most common types of chlorofluorocarbons skyrocketed. Worldwide production of CFC-11 (a common type of CFC used mostly as a foam-blowing agent) increased almost fivefold, from 49,715 metric tons in 1960 to 238,136 metric tons in 1974; production of CFC-12 (an aerosol propellant) more than tripled during the same period, from 99,428 to 321,099 metric tons.[5] As Figure 7.1 indicates, 1974 was a peak year for CFC production; due in large part to the government interventions discussed below, CFC production fell for the remainder of the 1970s. Production recovered in the 1980s but topped the 1974 peaks only in 1987, the year of the signing of the Montreal Protocol.

Concerns over the global environmental effects of CFCs began to surface around 1970. Scientists began to suspect that CFCs might be dangerously increasing the rate of the natural breakdown of ozone formed in the stratosphere. Ozone, a molecule combining three oxygen atoms, is formed naturally in the upper atmosphere in a band between 15 and 35 kilometers from the earth's surface. In this sphere, normal ozone background levels (around 2 parts per million) are increased fivefold. This "layer" of ozone results from high levels of ultraviolet radiation (UV), which breaks apart oxygen molecules. The "free" oxygen combines with normal oxygen to produce a layer of ozone, which shields the earth's surface against excessive ultraviolet radiation: Ozone molecules absorb ultraviolet radiation and break apart. CFCs are suspected of

Figure 7.1
World Production of CFC-11 and CFC-12, 1960–1987

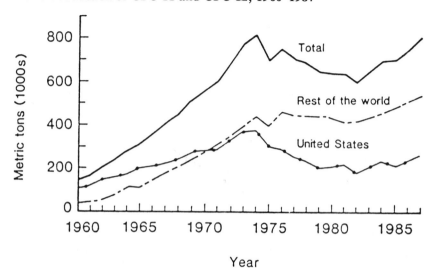

Source: Reprinted by permission of the publishers from *Ozone Diplomacy: New Directions in Safeguarding the Planet* by Richard Elliot Benedick, Cambridge, Mass.: Harvard University Press, copyright © 1991 by the World Wildlife Fund & The Conservation Foundation and the Institute for the Study of Diplomacy, Georgetown University.

accelerating this naturally occurring breakdown of ozone, thus depleting the ozone layer.

The process of stratospheric ozone formation has been relatively well understood since it was first explained in the 1930s. There is also agreement among scientists about some of the consequences that would be entailed by a serious depletion of the ozone layer. For example, almost all scientists believe that increased UV-B radiation (that is, biologically active UV radiation) would have adverse effects on many plants and plankton. UV-B radiation is also thought to be an important factor in both malignant and nonmalignant skin cancers.

What we know about the ozone layer pales in comparison to what we do *not* know. Even after two decades of extensive research efforts (which are briefly described below), the relative contribution of CFCs and other manufactured substances to the rate of stratospheric ozone depletion, the scale of the effects of such depletion on ground-level UV-B radiation, and other crucial questions remain surrounded by uncertainty. They were a complete mystery when the ozone layer first came to public attention.

The concern over the potential impact of human activity on the ozone layer first played a political role in the early 1970s in a controversy over proposed government subsidies to build two prototype Super Sonic Transports (SSTs), high-flying jet airplanes. Scientists argued that the exhaust from a fleet of 800 SSTs might have a catastrophic impact on the atmosphere by depleting 70 percent of the ozone layer, and they claimed that a thinning of the ozone layer would lead to greater incidence of skin cancer.[6]

Although SST proponents defended the project as a critical step toward ensuring the continued U.S. dominance of the aerospace industry, the U.S. Senate eventually voted, in March 1971, against funding an American prototype. (Britain and France followed through with their program, but the Concorde has never been the economic success envisioned by SST advocates.) The concerns over the SST's environmental impact on the atmosphere played a relatively minor part in defeating the SST project; economic considerations—the enormous subsidies to private industry that would have been required for SST development—and concerns over local air pollution and the sonic boom were more prominent. However, the global atmosphere and the ozone layer had appeared on the environmental agenda, never to disappear again.

The SST debate triggered large-scale atmospheric research projects such as the Climate Impact and Assessment Project (CIAP), a three-year research effort involving over 500 scientists and costing over $20 million. CIAP's output included a report of findings, six monographs, and the proceedings from four international conferences totaling over 9,000 pages. The project was followed by large-scale scientific inquiries by the United Nations Environmental Programme (UNEP) and the World Meteorological Organization (WMO). Business became a major funder of many CFC research programs. After questions began to be raised about CFCs in the early 1970s, E. I. Du Pont de Nemours and Company—the world's largest producer of CFCs—sponsored a seminar on the ecology of fluorocarbons. (Later, Du Pont would claim to be among the first to recognize the health risks posed by ozone-depleting chemicals.[7]) Many companies shared Du Pont's concern, and the conference directly led to the 1973 formation of the Fluorocarbon Technical Panel (FTP), composed of the representatives of 20 international CFC producers and administered by the Chemical Manufacturers Association. Over its 18 years of existence, FTP spent more than $25 million on direct funding of independent studies. An equivalent amount was spent by company scientists who worked with the FTP and conducted their own research projects.

The information produced by these research efforts gave scientists a somewhat better understanding of the frustratingly complicated interactions of the atmosphere and forced many of them to revise or discard their previous assumptions and hypotheses. Certainly, the weight of scientific evidence disproved the fears of SST opponents. Summarizing the research trends for a lay audience and in a popular journal, S. Fred Singer, an expert on environmental sciences and former chief scientist for the Department of Transportation, commented that it was

discovered that there were also natural sources of stratospheric NOx [the element of jet exhaust thought to deplete ozone], and the SST effect soon fell to 10 per cent [depletion]. But then laboratory measurements yielded better data, and by 1978 the effect had actually turned positive: SSTs would add to the ozone![8]

On the other hand, the voluminous research failed to produce certainty about the actual amount of ozone depletion caused by CFCs. Changes in the ozone level may be accounted for by natural mechanisms such as sea spray or volcanoes. The 1982 eruption of El Chichon in Mexico, for example, spewed huge amounts of sulphur aerosols into the upper atmosphere, causing easily measurable changes in the local ozone level. Large amounts of sea spray may be carried into the atmosphere by hurricanes and other natural mechanisms, adding substantial amounts of ozone-depleting chlorine atoms to the ozone layer. Solar cycles—the cyclical increase or decrease of sunspots and, thus, solar radiation—may also be a significant variable in explaining variations in ozone levels.[9] Moreover, the ozone layer constantly adjusts to natural factors; most likely, it will adjust to manufactured factors. For example, Petr Beckman, a professor emeritus at the University of Colorado, has argued, "Like all layers in the atmosphere, the ozone layer is stable: if the ozone concentration changes, due to whatever cause, [the natural formation of ozone] will simply form the layer at a different altitude: lower if the concentration decreases."[10]

Similar uncertainty continues to surround the health risks—specifically, the danger of increased skin cancer—of stratospheric ozone depletion. While skin cancer rates have been increasing since the 1930s, ground-based measurements show that UV-B levels have remained constant or even, perhaps, may have decreased. The observed increase in skin cancer rates may be a result of life-style changes, such as the (until very recently) increased popularity of sunbathing. Some individuals go so far as to argue that small decreases in the ozone layer are not particularly dangerous. For example, Singer has argued that "the increase of UV-B radiation that is feared to result from the thinning of ozone does occur simply as a result of moving closer to the equator. Thus ozone decreases of five percent would correspond to a move of less than 100 miles" toward the equator.[11] Similarly, skeptics have pointed out that long-term percentage changes in ozone levels are dwarfed by natural seasonal variations, which may reach 50 percent. One climatologist has likened attempts to measure long-term changes in such a volatile environment to "measuring the level of the sea during a typhoon" and has claimed that, occasionally, "seasonal declines themselves have been used as 'proofs' of depletion."[12]

For all the research, the dynamics of the atmosphere remained mostly a mystery, as did the potential health effects of whatever atmospheric changes may be occurring and whatever may be causing them. However, scientific uncertainty did little or nothing to silence vociferous demands to regulate or ban man-made substances that might affect the ozone layer. For instance, nuclear weapons testing, already a highly charged political topic, came to be criticized on the basis of its ozone-depleting potential; the use of nitrogen-based fertilizers was questioned on the same grounds. Environmental groups and the public increasingly demanded a role in political decisions concerning global environmental risks.[13] The enormous scientific uncertainty surrounding CFCs and their effects did little to curb demands for government action; in fact, science itself threatened to become a lever of interest groups. Singer observed that in the ozone debate, "scientists, by and large, behaved honorably, although egos and ambitions sometimes collided with facts, leading to a temptation to ignore the facts."[14] Doubts and uncertainties, even when clearly stated in scientific studies, often got lost in the translation of those studies into media reports: Announcements from the scientific community detailing new findings about the ozone layer produced lurid headlines and fairly outrageous claims and counterclaims.[15]

THE AEROSOL WARS

In 1974, two California scientists demonstrated the possibility that normally inactive CFCs would gradually percolate into the upper atmosphere, decompose, and release chlorine atoms, which would attack ozone.[16] In the wake of these findings, the ozone debate shifted toward a ubiquitous household product: aerosol spray cans.

At the time, CFCs were used extensively as propellants in aerosols. They were nontoxic, nonflammable, and easy to produce. For consumers, they were easy to use and delivered a high-quality spray. Environmental activists targeted aerosols in large part because they personalized the issue of ozone depletion: Just about every consumer used spray cans of some sort. CFCs were only as far away as the local supermarket.

The antiaerosol campaign was soon joined by business interests whose products had the potential to replace CFCs as aerosol agents. "Get off the Spray, Get on the Stick" was one prominent ad campaign for a solid deodorant product. Improved pumps also began to be developed, and they promised substantial savings for consumers: An antiperspirant could be delivered in a mechanical pump bottle for 46 cents, while an equivalent aerosol package cost 71 cents.[17] Most important, other types of propellants—hydrocarbons such as butanes and penthane—became available.

The reasons why pumps and non-CFC propellants had not already replaced CFCs were, respectively, convenience and safety. Consumers were willing to pay more for aerosols than for pumps. Aerosol hydrocarbons, on the other hand, are extremely flammable, which made the filling of cans in the production process extremely difficult. Whereas CFCs can be cooled, literally poured into cans, and sealed, hydrocarbons are too volatile for this simple process. However, by the mid-1970s, an improved insertion technology (specifically spray nozzles through which gases can be injected) allowed industry to switch.[18]

The CFC industry, then, found itself fighting a war on two fronts. While scientists and environmental activists attacked CFC use in aerosols as a dangerous addiction to a trivial use, competing industries advertised environmentally "safer" and often cheaper products—and consumers listened:

Many in the aerosol industry attributed the failing fortunes of the aerosol industry primarily to the aggressive advertising of nonaerosols by marketers who had jumped ship. [A] rebounding economy notwithstanding, the aerosol industry continued to fret over the continuing encroachment of the nonaerosol. In early 1976, nonaerosol deodorants had jumped 800 per cent over the previous year, and nonaerosol hair sprays had taken over nearly a quarter of the market, compared with 4 per cent in 1973.[19]

Once the CFC industry's competitors had developed viable, economical alternatives to CFC aerosols, CFC producers found it impossible to defend so-called trivial uses of their product against aggressive demands for regulation. Competing industries such as the manufacturers of deodorant roll-ons or sticks actively supported proposed CFC aerosol bans, and the existence of convenient alternative products allowed legislators to treat CFC aerosols as dispensable. As one state legislator put it: "If we err on one side, we'll lose some spray cans. If we err on the other side, there's the possibility we'll doom mankind."[20]

Government intervention began at the state level. By 1976, two dozen states had considered and two states had passed antiaerosol legislation: New York required warning labels on CFC aerosol cans, and Oregon legislated an outright ban on the sale of such products. State regulation slowed as federal legislation became a certainty. In 1976, Congress passed the Toxic Substance Control Act (TSCA), which gave the administrator of the EPA broad power to regulate all nondrug and pesticide chemicals, including CFCs. The enactment of TSCA led to the eventual ban of CFCs as aerosol agents. In March 1978, the EPA and FDA issued final regulations under TSCA and the Federal Food, Drug, and Cosmetic Act, which prohibited the use of CFCs as propellants in pressurized containers for virtually any purpose, unless the FDA Commissions deemed a particular use "essential." The ban was implemented in December 1978.

In 1977, Congress passed Amendments to the Clean Air Act that gave the EPA administrator power to regulate "any substance . . . which in his judgment may be reasonably anticipated to affect the stratosphere, especially ozone in the stratosphere, if such effect may reasonably be anticipated to endanger public health or welfare." No definitive action was taken under this provision. Although, in 1980, the EPA issued an Advance Notice of Proposed Rulemaking for the purpose of determining whether regulatory action was warranted, President Ronald Reagan's appointees to the EPA squelched any further action in this proceeding. Still, the broad mandate of the Clean Air Act exposed CFCs to a continous threat of regulatory action.

The various anti-CFC aerosol regulations and, in particular, the December 1978 ban, affected nearly $3 billion worth of sales in a wide range of household and cosmetic products, from hair spray to furniture polish. As noted, American consumers had already been shying away from CFC aerosol products for both environmental and economic reasons, but the 1978 ban destroyed what had, until then, been the largest segment of the domestic CFC market: U.S. production of CFCs for aerosols fell by 95 percent.[21] The more extensive use of CFCs for refrigeration and other purposes was insufficient to compensate for the virtual elimination of CFC aerosols.

Figure 7.2
FC-11/12/113/114/115 Volume by Industry: United States, 1976 and 1985

1976 U.S. 750 mm lbs

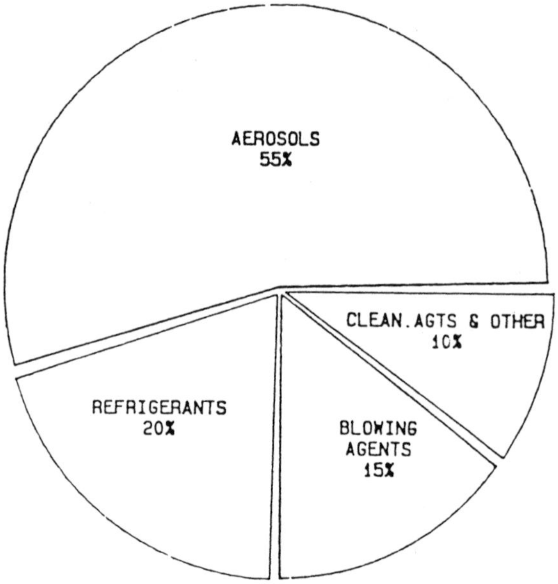

AEROSOLS
55%

CLEAN.AGTS & OTHER
10%

REFRIGERANTS
20%

BLOWING
AGENTS
15%

1985 U.S. 650 mm lbs

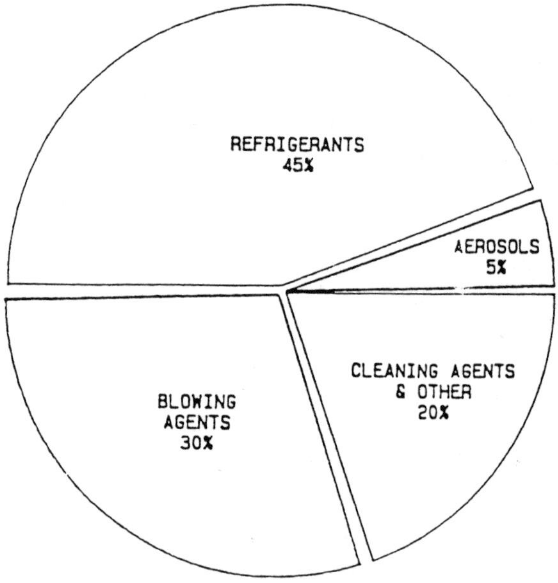

REFRIGERANTS
45%

AEROSOLS
5%

BLOWING
AGENTS
30%

CLEANING AGENTS
& OTHER
20%

Source: Alliance for Responsible CFC Policy.

Figure 7.3
FC-11/12/113/114/115 Volume by Industry: Worldwide, 1976 and 1985
(excluding the USSR, Peoples Republic of China, and Eastern Europe)

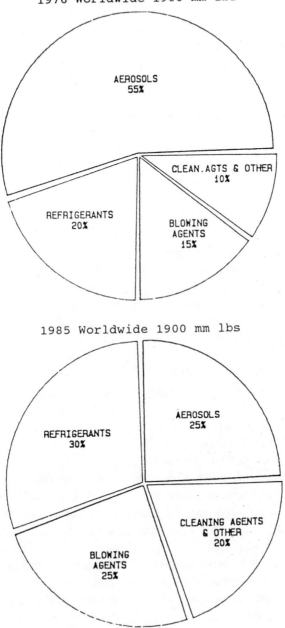

1976 Worldwide 1900 mm lbs

AEROSOLS
55%

CLEAN.AGTS & OTHER
10%

REFRIGERANTS
20%

BLOWING
AGENTS
15%

1985 Worldwide 1900 mm lbs

REFRIGERANTS
30%

AEROSOLS
25%

CLEANING AGENTS
& OTHER
20%

BLOWING
AGENTS
25%

Source: Alliance for Responsible CFC Policy.

The aerosol ban was not fatal to the American CFC industry. At no point did U.S. production fall below 180,000 metric tons, the approximate mid-1960s level. However, the aerosol ban did doom the U.S. manufacturers to high production capacity within a smaller market. It led to a sudden and sharp price drop and exacerbated a tough situation in an increasingly tight market. To many industry analysts, CFCs had become a "mature" product in the developed world. CFCs now held no promise of great growth, and they were less profitable than they had been in the past. (Du Pont products usually have a 6 percent profit margin; CFCs were running at about 4 percent in the early 1980s.)

Moreover, the unilateral U.S. ban on aerosols put American producers at a substantial disadvantage in global competition. Worldwide production of CFC-11 and CFC-12 reached its peak in 1974 at nearly 374,000 metric tons. At that time, U.S. production was 46 percent of the world total; the 12 EEC countries accounted for another 38 percent.[22] In later years, and to this day, the United States has remained the largest producer and consumer of CFCs. The largest CFC-producing company, Du Pont—which accounts for about a quarter of world production—has factories in the United States, Canada, the Netherlands, Japan, and Latin America, but it is headquartered in the United States.

Partly as a result of changing consumer preferences, but primarily as a result of government regulation and the continuing threat of additional regulation in the United States, the world market share of American producers nosedived to 40 percent in 1976, whereas the market share of European producers expanded to 43 percent. By 1985, the European CFC market share was 45 percent; the U.S. share, due largely to unilateral government action, had dropped to 28 percent.[23]

Throughout the latter half of the 1970s, the U.S. government, responding to the demands of domestic CFC producers, attempted to pressure European governments to follow the American example of banning CFC aerosols. However, these efforts met with little success. Britain and France were still smarting over the wounds they had suffered as a result of the American resistance to transatlantic flights, which had led to endless delays and, eventually, only a grudging and limited grant of landing rights. In Europe, U.S. lobbying for CFC bans was often characterized as "environmental neocolonialism" that was based on economic interest rather than environmental concern.[24] In any event, European governments were under less pressure to "do something" about CFCs than the American government. Many European countries lacked an environmental movement as powerful as the American movement. European CFC manufacturers, on the other hand, firmly resisted restrictions on CFC use, and, throughout the 1970s, they prevailed in their countries' legislatures.

Canada, Norway, and Sweden joined the United States in banning CFCs for aerosol use, but none of them were major producers or users. In the early 1980s, West Germany agreed to cut CFC aerosol use by 30 percent over 1976 levels, but this was largely a symbolic step since aerosol use had dropped by almost that amount already. In short, while the unilateral ban on the aerosol business had shrunk the American CFC market, European manufacturers had gained a relative advantage.

THE CFC INDUSTRY CHANGES ITS STRATEGY

The results of the aerosol wars were painful for American CFC producers. The industry had put up a long, hard fight—and lost. Environmental activists and advocate scientists had swayed public opinion; the CFC industry's competitors had seized on environmental concern to promote their own, alternative products; and CFC producers were pushed out of a large and lucrative market. The industry's response to this experience proved to have a profound influence on future CFC regulation.

In the wake of the aerosol ban, the CFC industry stepped up its funding of research. Industry backing went into computer modeling, ozone trend measurements by satellites, studies of CFC lifetimes, and even a 1986 expedition to examine an atmospheric phenomenon that came to be known as the Antarctic "ozone hole." Of course, the industry funded these efforts in large part to obtain evidence with which to counter future scare campaigns and exaggerated accounts of the environmental impact of CFCs, but there were also broader reasons. In order to make long-term investment decisions involving millions or even billions of dollars, business needed sound information. If CFCs were depleting the ozone layer, the industry needed to know. In fact, industry funded a large number of *independent* research projects, some of which suggested that CFCs were dangerous to the ozone layer. For example, an industry-sponsored project conducted at the National Oceanic and Atmospheric Administration laboratory in Boulder, Colorado, led to a doubling of the estimate of CFC-induced ozone depletion.[25]

At the same time, the CFC industry initiated efforts to create a united front. In 1980, a coalition of industrial producers and users of CFCs and similar products such as hydrochlorofluorocarbons (HCFCs) and hydrofluorocarbons (HFCs) formed the Alliance for Responsible CFC Policy. The formation of the Alliance was a direct result of the lessons that the CFC industry had learned in the "aerosol wars." First, CFC producers became convinced that they had lost the aerosol wars in large part because their opponents, by attacking a particular—and seemingly nonessential—*use* of CFCs, rather than the product itself, had managed to divide the industry. The Alliance, then, sought to provide a response to the dangers of a divided industry front. By banding together, all segments of the CFC industry would be able to marshal their combined forces.[26] This task was of considerable urgency in the early 1980s. Kevin Fay, the executive director of the Alliance, explained that "the environmental community was once again going to push a regulatory initiative on CFCs. We didn't want them to just start picking off industries one by one because that meant that everyone was going to be eventually dead."[27]

The second concern that prompted the formation of the Alliance was the fear of unilateral U.S. regulation. The CFC aerosol ban had shown that the American government was quite willing to regulate producers, regardless of the effects on their international competitiveness. It had further shown that unilateral actions failed to prompt other producer countries to take similar actions. Quite the contrary: As an Alliance official observed, "If the United States takes unilateral action, it takes the pressure off the rest of the world to act."[28] At all costs, then, unilateral regulation had to be avoided—even at the price of making *international* regulation a more likely prospect. Accordingly, an Alliance brochure states that the organization's goal was "to ensure that the establishment of reasonable government policies regarding further regulation of CFCs and protection of stratospheric ozone layer be pursued on an *international basis* and be based on sound scientific facts" (emphasis added). After the 1978 CFC aerosol ban, U.S. producers consistently emphasized the essential importance of international cooperation to allow American industry to remain competitive in world markets.

The industry's consolidated strategy produced measurable results. In 1980, the Alliance called for at least five years of additional study—and got it. Federal regulators backed off from further controls; for example, the rule-making proceeding under the Clean Air Act was stalled. This cease-fire at the regulatory front meant, of course, that existing CFC uses were allowed to continue.[29]

However, by 1985 (the year when negotiations on the Montreal Protocol began), American CFC producers faced a deteriorating picture. Regulatory pressures were building, largely in response to new scientific evidence on ozone depletion. Worldwide, CFCs were being increasingly used in car air conditioners, fire protection equipment, and electronics and computer production (mostly as a cleaner). By 1983, worldwide CFC demand took off and output soared at a rate of 5 percent per year; in 1986, production had reached the level of the mid-1970s.[30] Scientists warned that these trends would accelerate the rate of CFC-induced ozone depletion, and several studies seemed to confirm this assessment. Two studies released in 1985 warned that CFC production at present rates would have drastic consequences in the future. The first, a World Meteorological Organization (WMO) report, stated that significant ozone depletion could occur in 70 years if CFC emissions increased at an annual rate of 3 percent.[31] The second report, released by EPA/UNEP after a June 1986 conference, estimated that there could be over 150 million new cases of skin cancer in the United States alone by 2075. Three million of these people would die. Eighteen million additional people would develop eye cataracts, many leading to blindness.[32] Moreover, in the Antarctic spring (roughly late August to November) of 1985, a British group operating an ozone observation station at Halley Bay in Antarctica documented a dramatic fall in ozone levels at the South Pole. A review of the group's past measurements indicated that the decrease had been occurring since 1975. Its amplitude had grown steadily, eventually reaching nearly 50 percent of the total ozone.

The Antarctic "ozone hole" again brought ozone depletion to the forefront of public perception. An industry trade journal editorialized in 1986 that

a few members of Congress, spurred on by tantalizing new scientific data including the still-unexplained Antarctic ozone hole and by environmental activism, are gearing up to take action, perhaps even legislate control. Legislation is probably premature—and likely to be costly.[33]

While in the early 1980s, the Reagan administration's antiregulatory attitude had stalled EPA action on CFCs, the 1983 ouster of the politically embattled EPA administrator Anne Gorsuch reinvigorated the agency. The stratospheric ozone program, in particular, received a substantial boost in terms of resources and agency commitment.[34] For the industry, the buildup of public concern and regulatory resolve looked like an ominous repeat of the events leading up to the aerosol ban.

In September 1986, the Alliance announced a startling change in policy: It declared that it would support "a reasonable global limit on the future rate of growth of fully halogenated CFC production capacity." The same month, Du Pont also called for a limit of worldwide emissions of CFCs.[35] (Two years later, the company called for a complete phaseout of CFCs.) This change in position was widely portrayed as an overdue adjustment to new scientific evidence. The editors of *Atmosphere*, a quarterly publication of Friends of the Earth, a leading anti-CFC environmental group, commented on Du Pont's 1988 call for a CFC phaseout, "Cold hard facts converted du Pont [*sic*]. Now no one dares dismiss scientists as doom and gloom painters of worst case scenarios or environmentalists as dreamers of a CFC-free utopia."[36]

However, this explanation is unsatisfactory. For one thing, an enormous amount of money was at stake. For the industry, CFCs were a billion-dollar business, and over $135 billion dollars of equipment is dependent on CFCs in the United States alone. Moreover, the CFC industry continued to insist—and insists to this day—that current scientific knowledge is insufficient to condemn CFCs. For example, the final report of the Chemical Manufacturers Association's Fluorocarbon Technical Panel declares that "By the mid-1980s, the preponderance of research results . . . showed that there had been no detectable depletion of the ozone layer and [that] little would be expected if the CFC emission level remained stable."[37] Similarly, the industry continued—and continues—to dispute dire assessments of the public health effects of ozone loss. Kevin Fay of the Alliance has observed, "Every study we've seen—despite the data that we're getting large ozone losses in the stratosphere—[shows that] you're not getting the resulting increases in the ground level UVB radiation . . . even today."[38] It is unlikely that industry was persuaded by what it viewed, with some justification, as highly circumstantial scientific evidence.

Rather, the U.S. CFC industry's switch was the result of a rising tide of bad public relations, hostile legislation, and continued uncertainty. The industry saw the handwriting on the wall—another round of unilateral regulation and a replay of the disastrous aerosol ban. At the same time, the international position of the U.S. CFC industry had deteriorated badly, despite the surge in worldwide CFC demand. As previously noted, the world market share of U.S. producers had dropped to 28 percent in 1985, compared to 45 percent for European producers. The EEC was the almost unchallenged supplier of CFCs to the rest of the world, particularly developing countries; nearly one-third of European production was exported. In contrast, the United States consumed just about all the CFCs it produced.[39]

If these trends continued, U.S. manufacturers would steadily lose market share to the rest of the world, especially as other countries like India, China, and the Soviet Union began to develop their own CFC industries. Further U.S. regulation could make matters worse. In light of these circumstances, the American CFC industry began to push for an international agreement that would hopefully forestall unilateral regulation and protect the position of American manufacturers in global markets.

THE MONTREAL PROTOCOL AND ITS EFFECTS

The Montreal Protocol was the result of two years of contentious negotiations. Disputes arose not only over the levels to which global CFC output should be reduced and the time frames within which the reductions were to be achieved, but also, and prominently, over the appropriate regulatory *means* for CFC control. With regard to this issue, the principal split—which U.S. negotiator Richard Benedick has termed the "great divide"—was between the Toronto group (which included the Americans), on the one hand, and the Europeans on the other. Predictably, "each side was backing a protocol that would require no new controls for itself, but considerable adjustment for the other."[40] The central question was whether to limit the supply and production of CFCs or to ban particular *uses* of CFCs. The Toronto group and the United States, having already banned the use of CFCs in spray cans, advocated a worldwide ban of "nonessential" CFC uses. European countries took the opposite position: They adamantly opposed restrictions on CFC consumption or specific uses and, instead, advocated a cap on CFC *production*.

The compromise eventually agreed on was a cap on production *and* consumption. Each country committed itself to reduce production and consumption of CFCs and halons (a substance used mostly in fire extinguishers and, like CFC, suspected of inducing ozone depletion) to 1986 levels by 1989, by an additional 20 percent by 1993, and by yet another 30 percent by 1998. "Consumption" was defined in the protocol as production, plus imports, minus exports. Under this somewhat unorthodox definition, producer-countries, and especially the Europeans, can comply with the consumption mandates by shipping excess production to Third World countries.

To ensure ratification of the Montreal Protocol by Third World countries, who will have a harder time to adjust to higher CFC prices and to a CFC-free world than will richer, developed nations, the agreement provided a carrot and a big stick. While less-developed countries were given much more liberal time frames by which to attain the mandated reductions, the parties to the protocol agreed to apply very severe trade sanctions against nonsignatories. Signatories agreed to outlaw exports to nonsignatories not only of CFCs and products containing CFCs, but also of products that depend on CFCs at some point in the production process, such as computer circuit boards.

The regulatory framework of the Montreal Protocol, then, was closer to the European than to the American position, in that it provided for an—albeit modified—production cap. With respect to its economic implications, such a limit on *supply* differs profoundly from a regulation that limits *demand* by banning particular applications of CFCs: Instead of depressing the price of CFCs, a production cap raises prices and profit margins.

From an economic standpoint, these limits on production [agreed upon in the Montreal Protocol] are no different from the production targets set by OPEC in trying to enforce its cartel. Just as limits on oil production raise prices, so do limits on CFC and halon production.[41]

For the American industrial *users* of CFCs, such as the producers of cars, air conditioning and refrigeration equipment, and insulation materials, this result was highly disadvantageous: They would now have to pay higher prices for CFCs, and they would have to pay a very major portion of the costs accrued to converting products and processes to CFC substitutes—without having any firm assurance of being able to pass the costs on to consumers. In fact, it appears that the rapid movement toward, and the eventual agreement on, a production cap came as something of a shock to American industrial CFC users. Not without reason, these industries believed that the vital importance of their products to consumers and, indeed, to the functioning of the economy made them the least plausible target for regulation. It appeared that any international agreement would first and foremost ban, on a worldwide basis, the "nonessential uses" that had already been discontinued in the United States.

Moreover, industrial CFC users relied on CFC *producers* for protection. These CFC users did participate energetically in the Alliance for Responsible CFC Policy for a brief period in the early 1980s, largely for the purpose of stopping the EPA's anti-CFC rule-making proceedings which had been initiated by the Carter administration. However, as noted, the Reagan administration had discontinued these proceedings, and from then on, CFC users were, by and large, satisfied to have the case for continued CFC use made by their producers—who, after all, had done so for more than a decade. The producers', and, in particular, Du Pont's, sudden change of position in fall 1986 caught American CFC users by surprise.

For American CFC *producers*, on the other hand, the protocol was quite favorable. For one thing, it was surely much preferable to the dreaded—and very real—prospect of further unilateral regulation. Moreover, the production cap agreed on in the protocol and the attendant price increase promised to generate substantial profits: According to a 1988 analysis by the EPA, the phaseout mandated by the Montreal Protocol and the implementing U.S. regulations would create a $1.8 to $7.2 billion "windfall profit" for U.S. producers by the end of the century.[42]

Finally, the production cap gave CFC producers—including American producers—a very substantial advantage in developing substitutes. Producers had long realized that, if CFCs were going to be regulated out of existence, the best alternative was to capture the market with a substitute product—especially since substitutes promised subtantially better profits than CFCs. "If successful," noted the *Wall Street Journal*, "the substitutes business stands to bring much higher profits. Du Pont has referred to the current business as a 'cash trap,' the result of excess production and low prices."[43] However, previous efforts to find suitable substitutes had failed, largely (though not exclusively) for economic reasons. In the mid-1970s, when American CFC producers were confronted with an increasing threat of regulation, several companies studied the viability of developing and marketing alternative substances, only to discard the idea. CFCs worked so well and were so economical that chemical makers were unable to find viable alternatives.

Du Pont [terminated] a five-year, $15 million dollar research program in 1980, largely because preliminary results indicated that substitutes would be uneconomical to make, require difficult changes in manufacturing plants, take a minimum of ten years to develop and market, and involve controversial toxicity testing for adverse health effects.[44]

Explaining the difficulties involved in developing CFC substitutes, a Du Pont spokesman stated that "If we were able to produce [CFC substitutes], we know that they would be several times as expensive to produce as current products, and that's assuming we can overcome the remaining problems."[45]

Around the mid-1980s, however, when a new wave of public concern increased the likelihood of regulation, CFC makers again geared up their research departments to look for substitutes. The producers' support for the Montreal Protocol is, at least in part, explained as an effort to protect their investment in this research. Indeed, many industry representatives had long viewed an international agreement as a vital step toward creating incentives for the development of CFC substitutes, and the Montreal Protocol had precisely this effect.[46] In contrast to the replacement gases for CFC aerosols, new substitutes will be more expensive for consumers—up to five times more expensive, by some estimates.[47] In an open market, no substitute could possibly compete with CFCs. However, the CFC phaseout required by the Montreal Protocol will drive up the price of CFCs to the point at which substitutes will be economically viable.

CFC producers were well positioned to take advantage of the enhanced economic viability of CFC substitutes. A 1988 EPA review of patents on potential CFC substitutes indicated that the existing CFC producers in the United States were also the most likely producers of alternatives.[48] Du Pont, for instance, announced as early as 1988 that it planned to start producing an HFC variant, HFC-134a, to replace the refrigerant CFC-12 at its Corpus Christi, Texas, production facility. Allied-Signal announced the discovery of a new lubricating system that will permit the use of HFC-134a in automobile air conditioning and refrigeration applications.[49] By June 1989, Du Pont had begun building its first large-scale production plant for an HCFC variant, HCFC-123, in Canada. This HCFC would be used to replace CFC-11, the foam-blowing agent, and CFC-113, an industrial solvent.

Moreover, the Montreal Protocol and the implemeting EPA regulations effectively created barriers to entry for smaller, nonproducing firms. The development of CFC substitutes will be costly and time-consuming. Enormous resources are required to obtain regulatory approval for the new products. Du Pont, for example, expects to spend $1 billion in the next 10 years developing substitutes, but even such research represents a minor part of the conversion costs. "Du Pont estimates that retrofitting and shifting all the world's processes to alternative compounds will cost the world between $50 and $100 billion by the year 2000.[50] Throughout the promulgation of the CFC regulations, industry lobbyists defended the potential windfall profits caused by the phaseout as necessary to fund the development of substitute products. Of course, firms not presently producing CFCs would not benefit from those profits.

The CFC industry has even formalized its advantage in producing substitutes on a global scale. Thirteen major producers of CFCs from the United States, Japan, and Europe have formed the Program for Alternative Fluorocarbon Toxicity Testing, a cooperative effort for the toxicity testing of CFC alternatives. Although the Montreal Protocol was merely intended to give the industry some "breathing room" to phase out CFCs and to develop substitutes, joint testing may give member firms greater control on the rate at which CFC substitutes reach the market-place. This could further increase oligopoly profits.[51]

The Montreal Protocol solved the CFC industry's short-term profitability problems. CFC prices began to rise even before capacity cuts had to be made. In 1989, a major trade journal noted that "Montreal Protocol provisions for CFCs have wrought a turnaround in the market. . . . CFC-11 and CFC-12 are in tight supply worldwide and prices are rising, up 30%–60% over the past year in the U.S. and around 15% in Europe."[52]

Similarly, the implementation of the agreement by the EPA was, by and large, favorable to American producers. The EPA began formulating U.S. policy to conform with the agreement. A rule proposed in December 1987 and issued as final in August 1988 set up a quota system to allocate production "rights" based on 1986 levels, thus effectively precluding any company that was not a producer at that time from getting into the CFC-producing business.[53]

Whether the CFC industry was well advised to support an international agreement in the long term is far less certain. One of the industry's central objectives was to produce sufficient certainty at the regulatory front to permit rational long-term investment decisions; an orderly phaseout that would provide some breathing room was considered far preferable to an atmosphere of utter uncertainty. On this score, the protocol has been a disappointment for the industry. Once in place, the agreement created regulatory leverage for interest groups, bureaucrats, and environmental advocates. Consequently, far from settling the questions of how and on what schedule CFCs should be phased out, the protocol opened a virtual Pandora's box of proposed regulation. The already stringent regulatory mandates of the protocol created a precedent for setting yet more stringent mandates and applying them to substances other than CFCs. In Helsinki, Finland in May 1989, and again in London in June 1990, the signatories agreed to accelerate the schedule of the Montreal Protocol, leading to a complete CFC phaseout by January 1, 2000. Carbon tetrachloride (an industrial solvent used by dry cleaners as a spotting agent) and methyl chloroform (a solvent for degreasing and cleaning computer chips) were added to the list of substances to be phased out. More critically for the industry, the London Accord included a resolution to phase out HCFCs, a probable CFC replacement, by the year 2030. Although this resolution was nonbinding, the 1990 Clean Air Act Amendments committed the United States to an HCFC phaseout in accordance with the terms of the resolution.

The failure of the Montreal Protocol to provide a stable regulatory environment may well doom the CFC industry's hope to be compensated for the CFC phaseout through the development and marketing of successor products. A Du Pont spokesman explained: "We need a twenty year life cycle to pay for these investments. So if you say 'Phase out by 2010' that means do not build after 1990." (Du Pont favors using the materials until some time between 2030 and 2050.[54]) A phaseout of HCFCs by the year 2030 would still permit producers to amortize the capital investments that would be required for the large-scale production of these substances. However, experience has taught the industry that such schedules and deadlines are not cast in stone; they may be accelerated at the next international environmental conference. Thus, it comes as no surprise that some companies, including Du Pont, are already balking at building plants to produce HCFCs.

Other benefits conferred on U.S. CFC producers as part of the Montreal Protocol and its regulatory progeny may prove equally transient. As part of the fiscal year 1990 budget reconciliation, the Senate Environment and Public Works Committee proposed a tax on CFCs. Under the thin pretense of seeking to encourage the development of CFC substitutes—a purpose already accomplished by the Montreal Protocol and the EPA's implementing regulations—Congress easily persuaded itself to tax "windfall profits." The tax started in 1990 at a rate of $1.37 per pound of CFC production; it is scheduled to rise to $2.65 in 1993 and 1994, and by 45 cents per pound each successive year. (The tax will raise an estimated $450 million the first year alone.[55]) CFC producers have learned the hard way that government can not only create oligopoly profits, it can also confiscate them.

CONCLUSION

CFCs are not irreplaceable. Refrigerators, computers, fire extinguishers, and even ordinary foam rubber cushions are crucial products. The benefits that CFCs provide will continue to be provided, albeit less efficiently and at much higher prices. The Third World will pay dearly for these added costs.

Whether these costs are worth the environmental benefits cannot be determined. Stratospheric ozone depletion has been called an impending global apocalypse and, at the same time, a poor retelling of the story of Chicken Little; the simple truth is that there is enormous uncertainty over the scale of ozone depletion, its likely consequences, and the relative contribution of CFCs to atmospheric problems.[56, 57] It may be that 50 or 100 years from now, the Montreal Protocol will have proven an example of remarkable foresight. It is equally possible that, in hindsight, it will appear that the CFC phaseout was a correct decision for reasons not contemplated by the signatories: CFCs are increasingly suspected of being greenhouse gases, and their phaseout is being praised as an important step toward controlling the global climate. However, it is also quite possible that the phaseout will prove to be an overreaction to concerns that, however urgent they appeared at the time, are unwarranted.

In the end, the political lessons of the Montreal Protocol may be of greater consequence. The fact that an international environmental agreement was signed to prevent a distant and, as yet, hypothetical threat—as opposed to averting an impending catastrophe—has been celebrated as a victory of reason and public concern over narrow self-interest. Environmentalists and a burgeoning international bureaucracy clearly view the protocol as a prelude to even more comprehensive agreements. For example, UNEP President Mostafa Tolba has declared that "the mechanisms we designed for the Protocol will—very likely—become the blueprint for the institutional apparatus designed to control greenhouse gases and adaption to climate change."[58]

Especially in light of this enthusiasm for increased international environmental regulation, it must be stressed that the Montreal Protocol is, in many respects, an old-fashioned cartel arrangement. To be sure, the industry was highly concentrated even prior to the agreement, a circumstance that made it vulnerable to regulation in the first place.[59] However, it was only *after*, and by virtue of, the agreement that producers were able to secure above-market rate returns and oligopoly profits.

The prospect of such profits, of course, accounts for the CFC producers' support for the Montreal Protocol. It appears at this stage, though, that the industry miscalculated. Soon after putting the CFC cartel in place, international and U.S. regulators began to confiscate the proceeds; in this crucial respect, the protocol differs from the local taxi commission or the Department of Agriculture. Moreover, by cooperating with the regulators despite its continued insistence that the evidence on the environmental and public health effects of CFCs was insufficient to warrant drastic regulation, the CFC industry may have set a dangerous precedent for the proposition that international environmental regulation should proceed even if the threats are distant and as yet unproven, and even at the cost of enormous economic dislocations.

NOTES

1. John Holusha, "Ozone Issue: Economics of a Ban," *New York Times*, 11 January 1990.

2. Richard E. Benedick, *Ozone Diplomacy: New Directions in Safeguarding the Planet* (Cambridge, Mass.: Harvard University Press, 1991), 1.

3. Benedick, *Ozone Diplomacy*, 46. The entire paragraph in the text is based on Benedick's account.

4. Our high standard of living is in part provided by the benefits of CFCs. "Society can't simply junk all this [CFC] equipment overnight, not without disruption," says former Du Pont chairman, R. E. Hackert. Ronald Bailey, "The Ozone Hole That Didn't Eat the World," *Forbes*, 30 October 1989, 225.

5. Chemical Manufacturers Association, *Production, Sales, and Calculated Release of CFC-11 and CFC-12 through 1988* (Washington, D.C.: CMA, 1988), 7–8.

6. See H. Johnston, "Reduction of Stratospheric Ozone by Nitrogen Oxide Catalysts from Supersonic Transport Exhaust," *Science* 173 (6 August 1971): 517–22.

7. "Grappling with the Cost of Saving the Earth's Ozone," *New York Times*, 17 July 1990.

8. S. Fred Singer, "My Adventures in the Ozone Layer," *National Review*, 30 June 1989, 35.

9. See Hugh W. Elsaesser, "A Reassessment of Stratospheric Ozone: Credibility of the Threat," *The Journal of Climate Change* 1 (1978): 257–66; and Elsaesser, "The Holes in the Ozone Hole II," paper presented at the Cato Institute Conference, "Global Environmental Crisis," May 1991 (Washington, D.C.: Cato Institute, 1991).

10. Petr Beckmann, *Access to Energy* 18 (Boulder, Colo.: Access to Energy, May 1991): 9.

11. S. Fred Singer, *Global Climate Change: Human and Natural Influences* (New York: Paragon House, 1989), 161.

12. "Holes in the Ozone Theory," *Orange County Register*, 25 June 1989, p. K2.

13. Peter M. Morrisette, "The Evolution of Policy Responses to Stratospheric Ozone Depletion," *The University of New Mexico Natural Resources Journal* 29 (Summer 1989): 803.

14. Singer, "My Adventures," 34.

15. Lydia Dotto and Harold Schiff, *The Ozone War* (Garden City, N.Y.: Doubleday, 1978), 5.

16. Mario J. Molina and F. Sherwood Rowland, "Stratospheric Sink for Chlorofluoromethanes: Chlorine Atomic Catalyzed Destruction of Ozone," *Nature* 249 (1974): 810–12.

17. Robert A. Leone, *Who Profits: Winners, Losers and Government Regulation* (New York: Basic Books, 1986), 33.

18. Still, even today, "every six months or so you get a new story of some filling plant blowing up." Author's interview with Kevin Fay, director for the Alliance for Responsible CFC Policy, the major industry lobbying group, 2 May 1991.

19. Dotto and Schiff, *Ozone War*, 254.

20. Ibid., 196.

21. Benedick, *Ozone Diplomacy*, 24.

22. Ibid., 26.

23. Ibid.

24. Morrisette, "Evolution of Policy Responses," 801.

25. Chemical Manufacturers Association, *Searching the Stratosphere: Industry's Contribution to Scientific Understanding of the Ozone Depletion Issue* (Washington, D.C.: CMA, 1991), 8. Commenting on an industry-funded search for CFC "sinks"—natural storage places of CFCs which would remove CFCs from the atmosphere before they reached the ozone layer—Pauline Midgley of the FTP dryly noted, "From our point of view, we did not find what we hoped." Cited in Lois R. Ember, Patricia Layman, Wil Lepkowski, and Pamela S. Zurer, "Tending the Global Commons," *Chemical and Engineering News*, 24 November 1986, 22.

26. Whether the Alliance represents the interests of the entire industry, however, is an open question. It is widely believed that Du Pont, the world's largest producer, had a great deal of control over the positions taken by the Alliance. CFC users do not seem to have played a great role in CFC policy. Economists Robert Hahn and Albert McGartland argue that "The small users may have made an early decision that teaming up with producers would minimize their lobbying and research expenses yet still promote what, from their perspective, would be a reasonable outcome." See Hahn and McGartland, "The Political Economy of Instrument Choice: An Examination of the U.S. Role in Implementing the Montreal Protocol," *Northwestern University Law Review* 83 (1989): 607 and the brief discussion on page 146 of this chapter.

27. Fay interview.

28. Ember et al., "Tending the Global Commons," 49.

29. Richard Hoppe, "Ozone: Industry Is Getting Its Head Out of the Clouds?" *Business Week*, 13 October 1986, 110–11.

30. Morrisette, "Evolution of Policy Responses," 809.

31. Chemical Manufacturers Association, *Searching the Stratosphere*, 10.

32. Benedick, *Ozone Diplomacy*, 21.

33. Ember et al., "Tending the Global Commons," 15.

34. Morrisette, "Evolution of Policy Responses," 809.

35. Ember et al., "Tending the Global Commons," 48.

36. Liz Cook, "Barometer," *Atmosphere* [published by Friends of the Earth International] 1 (Spring 1988): 2.

37. Chemical Manufacturers Association, *Searching the Stratosphere*, 10.

38. Fay interview.

39. Benedick, *Ozone Diplomacy*, 27.

40. Richard E. Benedick, "Ozone Diplomacy," *Issues in Science and Technology*, Fall 1989, 48.

41. Hahn and McGartland, "Political Economy of Instrument Choice," 594.

42. "Protection of Stratospheric Atmosphere," *Federal Register* 53 (12 August 1988): 30604.

43. "Du Pont Plans to Produce Refrigerant Harmless to Ozone," *Wall Street Journal*, 30 September 1988, Sec. 2, p. 32.

44. Hoppe, "Ozone," 111.

45. Ember et al., "Tending the Global Commons," 52.

46. Ember et al., "Tending the Global Commons," 47–56.

47. Bailey, "Ozone Hole," 225.

48. *Federal Register* 53 (12 August 1988): 30606.

49. Liz Cook, "Du Pont Sets Up 134a Plant," *Atmosphere* 1 (Fall 1988): 10.

50. Bailey, "Ozone Hole," 225.

51. Hahn and McGartland, "Political Economy of Instrument Choice," 603.

52. David Hunter, "CFC Prices Soar as Capacity Is Cut," *Chemical Week*, 26 April 1989, 14.

53. Hahn and McGartland, "Political Economy of Instrument Choice," 601 passim.

54. "Ozone Issue," *New York Times*, 11 January 1990, p. D6.

55. David E. Gushee, "Stratospheric Ozone Depletion: Regulatory Issues," *Congressional Research Service Issue Brief* No. IB89021, updated 17 December 1990, 7–8.

56. "It's terrifying," one overwrought government scientist told the *New York Times*. "If these ozone holes keep growing like this, they'll eventually eat the world." Bailey, "Ozone Hole," 224.

57. See Dotto and Schiff, *Ozone War*, 145. "We beg to differ with Chicken Little," reads one aerosol industry press release.

58. Benedick, *Ozone Diplomacy*, 7.

59. Production was concentrated in the United States, Europe, and Japan, with only 16 worldwide producers of CFC-11 and C-12. In the United States, CFCs are produced by only 4 companies (5 at the time of the signing of the protocol); Du Pont and Allied Signal account for approximately 49 and 25 percent, respectively, of total U.S. production. Furthermore, CFCs are only one of the many chemicals these large companies produce; for example, CFCs account for only 2 percent of Du Pont's sales. Peter M. Morrisette, "Lessons from Other International Agreements for a Global CO2 Accord," Discussion Paper ENR91-02, Resources for the Future, October 1990, 15.

8 THE PUBLIC INTEREST MOVEMENT AND AMERICAN TRADE POLICY

David Vogel

In recent years, environmental and consumer organizations have become active participants in the making of American trade policy. They have played an important role in placing on the political agenda the impact of American trade policies on consumer and environmental protection in the United States, as well as on the citizens of other countries. They have accomplished this in part by entering into alliances with constituencies both in the United States and overseas whose economic interests lie in restricting international trade.

The public interest movement's aggressive involvement in international trade issues marks a significant shift in its historical political agenda. Beginning in the latter half of the 1960s, consumer and environmental organizations emerged as a major force in American politics, gradually replacing trade unions as the central locus of political opposition to business. However, for the first decade of their political existence, consumer and environmental groups paid little attention to the international dimensions of health, safety, and environmental regulation; their political energies were focused almost exclusively on American domestic policies. A book of essays on consumerism published in 1972 made no references to the safety, price, or quality of imported or exported goods.[1] The first edition of *The Politics of Environmental Concern*, an influential treatise on environmental politics published in 1973, did not discuss the relationship between environmental protection and international trade.[2] Of the more than a score of books criticizing virtually every aspect of American health, safety, and environmental regulations published by Ralph Nader and his associates during the late 1960s and early 1970s, not one examined either the impact of American trade and regulatory policies on the citizens of other countries or the impact of foreign policies or practices on American consumers.

It was only during the late 1970s that American environmental and consumer organizations started to pay attention to the relationship between American health, safety, and environmental regulations and the international economy. One of the public interest movement's initial concerns in this area was the health hazards posed by imports to American consumers. For example, the November 1979 issue of the muckraking magazine *Mother Jones* featured an article entitled, "The Boomerang Crime," which contended that American consumers were still being exposed to many of the pesticides that had been recently banned in the United States.[3] Many of these chemicals, including DDT, were produced in the United States for export. Farmers in other countries sprayed the chemicals on fruits and vegetables, which were, in turn, exported to the United States—thus completing what became widely referred to as a "circle of poison."

American consumer advocates were also troubled by the impact of American exports on the health of foreign consumers and workers, particularly in less developed nations. "The Corporate Crime of the Century," by Mark Dowie (also published in the November 1979 issue of *Mother Jones*), described numerous products that, having been banned in the United States, were subsequently "dumped" on unsuspecting Third World consumers.[4] The most widely publicized example of such a product was children's pajamas that had been treated with the flame retardant Tris. After the Consumer Product Safety Commission (CPSC) had prohibited sales in the United States on the grounds that Tris was a potential carcinogen, 2.4 million garments containing the chemical were exported, primarily to developing countries.

Public criticisms of American "double standards" prompted Congress to amend several statues that regulated hazardous products in the United States to encompass exported goods. A 1978 amendment to the Flammable Fabrics Act, the Federal Hazardous Substances Act, and the Consumer Product Safety Act required foreign governments to be notified before consumer goods banned in the United States were exported. A similar amendment to the Federal Insecticide, Fungicide, and Rodenticide Act (FIFRA) required exporters, before shipping a domestically banned pesticide overseas, to obtain a statement from the foreign purchaser acknowledging that the pesticides could not be used in the United States. EPA was then required to notify the appropriate foreign official of the transaction.

In 1980, shortly before leaving office, President Jimmy Carter accepted the recommendations of an interagency working group that had been established to formulate a comprehensive hazardous export policy for the United States. Executive Order 12,264 strengthened formal export notice requirements already required by various statutes and established formal exporting licensing controls for "extremely hazardous substances." One month later, on February 17, 1981, President Ronald Reagan revoked Carter's executive order and substituted his own. Entitled "Federal Exports and Excessive Regulation," it directed the Departments of State and Commerce to review American policy on hazardous exports in order to find ways to accomplish the goals of the existing policies at a lower cost. Environmental and consumer advocates sharply criticized this decision; one critic accused the Reagan administration of having "wiped out two-and-one-half years of study and hard bargaining among more than twenty federal agencies, two sets of Congressional hearings, and the participation of over 100 business, labor, environmental and consumer organizations here and abroad."[5] During the 1980s, consumer and environmental groups pressed for legislation to restore the thrust of the Carter executive order or even go beyond it. One such proposal would have amended FIFRA to require exporters to provide more detailed information to importers and to write labels in the language of the country to whom the pesticides were exported. This proposal was supported by a broad and unusual coalition of environmental and industry groups as part of an elaborate compromise designed to strengthen and streamline the federal government's regulation of pesticides. Although the legislation came within a hair's breadth of passage in 1986, the coalition eventually split apart over unrelated issues and the legislation remained stillborn. Other legislative initiatives to expand government oversight of exports on health and safety grounds fared no better.

While these skirmishes illustrate the public interest movement's gradual discovery of international trade issues, they were hardly central to American trade policy. Neither the 1978 and 1985 statutes nor the Carter and Reagan executive orders were especially controversial outside a narrow circle of advocates and lobbyists, and their impact on American exports was negligible. Consumer and environmental organizations played virtually no role in the fierce debates over American trade policy during the 1970s and 1980s; they showed no interest in the various rounds of the General Agreement on Tariffs and Trade (GATT) negotiations or the numerous trade disputes between the United States and its major trading partners that periodically surfaced during these years.

Only during the late 1980s did the public interest movement become actively involved in a wide range of issues that directly affected America's economic relations with other countries and the competitiveness of a number of important American industries. Consumer groups, including Ralph Nader's Public Citizen, began to lobby Congress on trade issues. For the environmental movement, trade policy has become an integral part of its political agenda. Less than five years ago, few public interest activists had even heard of GATT; now, no gathering of environmentalists is complete without a panel or workshop devoted to the implications of international trade for the environment.

The public interest movement's political initiatives on American trade policy fall into two broad categories. One set of policy goals aims at restricting the export of various domestic products, such as cigarettes, pesticides, and timber, on the grounds that these products either are harmful to foreign consumers or threaten consumer safety or environmental quality in the United States. A second priority is broader in scope: Environmental and consumer groups have opposed American efforts to liberalize world trade—multilateral as well as bilateral—on the grounds that the expansion of world trade threatens to undermine American health, safety, and environmental standards and to impair environmental quality in other countries. Both sets of policy goals are essentially protectionist; both provide anticipated or unanticipated benefits to various businesses and other economic interests.

EXPORT RESTRICTIONS

Cigarettes

During the 1980s, the United States ran substantial trade deficits, especially with Japan and the rapidly growing economies of East Asia. In order to increase American exports, the Office of the United States Trade Representative (USTR) began to scrutinize the policies of America's trading partners that restricted their purchases of American-made goods. At the request of the United States Cigarette Export Association, the USTR began to investigate the allegedly unfair tobacco trading practices of Japan, Taiwan, and South Korea. All three countries had large number of cigarette smokers. Yet their governments had enacted quotas and protective tariffs that almost tripled the price of American cigarettes, and they restricted the advertising of foreign brands—thus managing to preserve almost their entire domestic markets for cigarettes produced and marketed by state-controlled monopolies.

Indeed, in South Korea, the mere possession of a pack of imported cigarettes was illegal.

Between 1986 and 1988, the Reagan administration twice threatened to invoke trade sanctions against Taiwan, South Korea, and Japan in order to pressure them to eliminate their import restrictions on cigarettes. As one official put it, "All we wanted was a fair crack at their markets. Just the chance to compete on equal footing with their domestic brands; nothing more, nothing less."[6] These pressures proved effective. Japan liberalized its laws in 1986, South Korea in 1987, and Taiwan in 1988. All three governments either reduced or eliminated their tariffs and quotas on imported cigarettes and agreed to permit American and British cigarette companies to advertise their products more widely.

In 1989, an international trade panel was convened under the GATT in response to a complaint from the United States about similar restrictions on American cigarettes imposed by Thailand. A spokesman for the American trade office stated that since "tobacco products are harmful, countries have a sovereign right to protect the health of their citizens. . . . But what . . . Thailand has done is create a monopoly under which they alone sell cigarettes. It is simply discriminatory."[7] In fall 1990, the GATT panel ruled that Thailand's ban on the import, sale, and distribution of imported cigarettes was illegal.[8]

The result of these concessions by foreign governments was a dramatic increase in American exports to the developed economies of Asia. American exports of cigarettes to East Asia nearly tripled in 1987 and went up an additional 40 percent between 1987 and 1989. Prior to 1986, foreign cigarettes accounted for only 2 percent of Japanese domestic sales. Their market share tripled in 1987, approached 10 percent the following year, and in 1990 reached 15 percent. In all, U.S. tobacco exports totaled $5 billion in 1989. They expanded another 25 percent during the first nine months of 1990—making cigarettes one of America's most successful and rapidly growing exports.[9]

The American government's pressures on foreign governments to open their markets to American cigarettes have come under sharp criticism. U.S. Surgeon General C. Everett Koop characterized the position of the American government as, "unconscionable[,] . . . deplorable[, and] . . . the height of hypocrisy," and described the export of tobacco products as a "moral outrage."[10] The American Heart Association proclaimed that "the U.S. government should not be in the business of encouraging exportation of cigarettes. . . . Every country including the United States, should be doing everything possible to discourage [tobacco] use worldwide."[11] Representative Chet Atkins (D-Massachusetts) complained that by allowing the export of cigarettes without the health warnings required under American law, "Washington is sending Asians a message that their lungs are somehow more expendable than American lungs."[12] Atkins submitted legislation to subject exported cigarettes to the same health warnings and advertising restrictions that apply in the United States. This legislation was endorsed by the American Medical Association, whose Council on Scientific Affairs noted that tobacco use was increasing on a global basis and was responsible for 5 percent of all deaths worldwide. Another bill submitted by Atkins sought to prevent the president from seeking the "removal or reduction by any foreign country of any restrictions" on the advertising, manufacture, packaging, importation, sale, or distribution of cigarettes.[13]

American cigarette exports were also opposed by the Advocacy Institute, a public interest lobbying group headed by former Federal Trade Commission (FTC) chairman Michael Pertschuk and David Cohen, who previously headed Common Cause; and by the Coalition on Smoking OR Health, which was established by the American Heart Association, the American Lung Association, and the American Cancer Society. These groups claim that the relaxation of import restrictions has led to a dramatic increase in cigarette advertising, much of it by foreign manufactures, and that the aggressive, "Madison Avenue-style" marketing efforts by American firms have contributed to an increase in overall cigarette consumption, especially among teenagers and women in Asia.

The impact of American cigarette imports, in general, and American marketing practices, in particular, on cigarette consumption in the developed nations of Asia remains a matter of dispute. Adult male smoking rates in Japan, South Korea, Taiwan, and Thailand averaged between 60 and 70 percent before imported cigarettes became widely available. While total cigarette sales did increase in all four countries during the second half of the 1980s, smoking rates do not show the same trend; for example, in 1989, the percentage of smokers in Japan hit an all-time low. At the same time, smoking rates remain extremely high in China, where no foreign cigarettes are marketed. According to an industry official, there is no evidence that cigarette consumption trends overseas "are affected by whether or not the U.S. product is there."[14] Moreover, while it is true that American trade negotiators did press for a relaxation of advertising restrictions as part of their market-opening demands, most Asian countries have made little effort to discourage cigarette smoking—which, outside Hong Kong, remains dominated by domestic brands. For example, the label required on cigarette packages sold in Japan reads, "Please Do Not Smoke Too Much For Your Health," while in Taiwan, the best-selling government-issued brand is called "Long Life."

Still, antismoking activists in both Japan and Taiwan have joined American advocacy groups in opposing the liberalization of restrictions on cigarette imports. David Yen, the chairman of a Taipei-based public health lobby, and Bungaku Watanabe, who heads the 60,000 member Japan Antismoking Liaison Council, urged President Reagan not to "push American cigarettes on us."[15] Both individuals have close ties with American antismoking groups. Watanabe has held a number of press conferences in Washington, D.C.; at one such media event, he accused American firms of particularly targeting women and youth.[16]

However, American antismoking activists have also received support from a less likely source—namely, East Asian governments. To the extent that American cigarette exports reduce the market share of domestic cigarette companies in Asia, import restrictions benefit not only non-American tobacco companies, but, equally important, the governments who are their primary stockholders. For precisely this reason, the Thai government approached American antismoking activists for help in resisting American pressure to open up the Thailand market. According to Alan Davis of the American Cancer Society, "The Thais came to us and said: 'Your government is trying to force U.S. cigarettes down our throats.' "[17] The result was a "strange de facto alliance . . . between the local tobacco monopoly . . . and anti-smoking forces."[18]

The Thai government justified the retention of its ban on imported cigarettes on the grounds that it served to control a social ill. However, the government's case was weakened by the fact that it banned cigarette advertising only after American firms began to increase their marketing efforts in Asia. At the same time, the government monopoly's harsh blend is both more unpleasant and more harmful than are American brands. More generally, American firms have charged that at least some part of the recent increase in antismoking activism in much of Asia really represents an attempt to discourage foreigners from competing with state-run monopolies. According to Richard Synder, executive vice-president of Philip Morris, "It's just covert protectionism."[19]

Pesticides

American pesticides, like American cigarettes, are highly competitive in global markets: American exports account for one-quarter of the $17 billion world pesticide market. U.S. companies annually export between

400 and 600 million tons of pesticides, or approximately one-third of their domestic production. Of these pesticides, approximately one-quarter (by weight and volume) have not been approved for use in the United States. While the 1978 FIFRA Amendments did impose some controls on pesticide exports, its provisions were not strictly enforced. According to Michael Synar (D-Oklahoma), chairman of the House Subcommittee on Environment, Energy and Natural Resources,

when it comes to the export of unregistered pesticides, foreign governments have been kept in the dark, the public has been kept in the dark and the agencies responsible for inspection of U.S. food imports have been kept in the dark.[20]

Environmentalists have been criticizing American pesticide export policies for more than a decade. Greenpeace has declared it "outlandish that current pesticide law permits the uncontrolled export of these dangerous products," and the National Coalition Against the Misuse of Pesticides—a coalition of more than 300 organizations—has demanded that "U.S. corporations must be held accountable for standards of health and safety in this country and must uphold those same standards around the world."[21]

The case against the export of unregistered pesticides rests on their alleged harm to the health and safety of both Third World workers and American consumers. The World Health Organization contends that nearly 1 million farmers in the Third World suffer acute poisoning from pesticides each year and approximately 20,000 are killed. The regulations established by most Third World governments are poorly enforced and farmers in these countries, many of whom are illiterate, are not able to understand instructions for proper pesticide use. Compounding this problem has been a substantial increase in pesticide use in a number of developing countries; this is, in part, a result of efforts to increase agricultural exports to the developed nations.

American environmental groups also claim that many unregistered pesticides wind up being consumed by Americans. As exports of pesticides from the United States have increased in recent years, so have American imports of fruits and vegetables, many of which are grown or processed with chemicals that have not been approved for use in the United States. Fresh fruit imports more than doubled between 1979 and 1986; currently, one-quarter of all the fruits and vegetables consumed by Americans are imported. While the FDA is responsible for monitoring the safety of imported as well as domestic foods, import controls are highly uneven: according to a 1986 General Accounting Office (GAO) study, less than 1 percent of the estimated 1 million food shipments that enter the United States each year are checked for pesticide residues.[22]

In 1990, Senator Patrick Leahy (D-Vermont) and Representative Synar introduced the Pesticide Export Reform Act. The bill required that imported foods be accompanied by documentation describing the pesticides used on them in order to facilitate American border inspections. (Leahy argued that "Because FDA waves through virtually all imported foods without inspection, these chemicals often end up on America's dinner tables."[23]) The most important provision of the bill was a total ban on the exports of pesticides not approved for use in the United States—thus, presumably, putting an end to the "circle of poison." Leahy subsequently modified his proposal to allow for the export of some unregistered pesticides, provided that the FDA had established "tolerance levels" for them. In this form, and largely at Leahy's initiative as the chairman of the Senate Agriculture Committee, the amendment was included in the farm bill reported out by the Senate Agriculture Committee and passed by the Senate in the fall of 1990. A somewhat weaker version—which permitted the export of unregistered pesticides as long as they had been registered for use in at least 1 of the 24 member-states of the Organization for Economic Cooperation and Development (OECD)—was adopted as part of the House farm bill.

The Leahy-Synar Amendments were strongly opposed by the American chemical industry. The National Agricultural Chemicals Association described the Amendments as a form of "environmental imperialism" and predicted that their passage would provoke a trade war that would undermine the American chemical industry.[24] The group also argued that restricting American exports would increase sales of locally produced pesticides, many of which are more dangerous than those manufactured in the United States. Further, the chemical industry pointed out that many pesticides were unregistered for use in the United States not because they could not meet American regulatory standards but because there was simply no domestic demand for them. Now, in order to continue to export these products, American manufacturers would have to go through the trouble and expense of obtaining American regulatory approval. Finally, critics of the bill argued that the issue was American jobs, not the safety of the food supply, since the passage of the Leahy Amendment would either force American chemical firms to shift production to other countries or encourage foreign farmers to purchase from chemical firms in their own country.

Although the pesticide export provisions in both the House and Senate versions of the farm bill were all but eliminated in conference committee, it is striking how close they came to being enacted. (Indeed, they have already been reintroduced.) How was this possible? In particular, how did Leahy's Amendment pass the Senate Agricultural Committee, which is traditionally dominated by the interests of large agricultural producers?

The key was a convergence of interests between American environmental and consumer groups and American farmers. The former supported the legislation for obvious reasons; the latter, because restrictions on the use of pesticides by foreign farmers, or improved border controls, are a form of agricultural protectionism. The most important economic beneficiaries of restricting the access of foreign farmers to U.S.-made pesticides are American farmers: If foreign farmers can no longer use pesticides that do not meet strict American health and safety standards, they will be deprived of an important competitive advantage. This, in turn, is likely to make it more difficult for them to produce fruits and vegetables for export to the United States. Thus, the playing field between them and their American competitors would become more level once both must use similar pesticides.

Congressional supporters of the Leahy bill often stressed this economic aspect. According to then-Senator Pete Wilson (R-California), the "export of dangerous pesticides creates a competitive inequality between foreign and American farmers and growers."[25] Congressman Leon Panetta (D-California), a member of the House Agricultural Committee, also made explicit the protectionist implications of restricting pesticide exports:

California fruit and vegetable producers have met the toughest food safety standards in the country. However, foreign produce has not had to meet these same strict standards. I believe that this double standard is not fair to American consumers or domestic producers who are competing with foreign producers for a share of the market.[26]

In light of the laxity of American border inspections, the adoption of the Leahy Amendment might well have had little or no impact on the quantity of food imported into the United States. Nonetheless, the coalition between public interest lobbies and American farmers is a phenomenon of political significance and a harbinger of the future nature of the political alliances that are likely to constitute the protectionist coalition.

Timber

On June 22, 1990, the Bush administration decided to list the Northern Spotted Owl as an endangered species. This decision threatened to impose severe restrictions on logging in the Pacific Northwest and Rocky Mountain states. The U.S. Forest Service estimated that the log-cutting restrictions necessary to protect the habitat of the endangered birds would cost 20,000 jobs in the timber and logging industries.[27]

American sawmills in the Northwest have suffered economically as a steadily growing share of the logs harvested in the Northwest have been shipped directly to Japan. The Japanese prefer to import the raw logs and then cut them in their own mills; this both supports their domestic mill industry and enables the logs to be cut according to their country's unique specifications. In order to preserve employment in the dying sawmills of their region, Senator Robert Packwood (R-Oregon) and other legislators from the Pacific Northwest have long urged a ban on log exports from state lands. (Exporting logs from federal lands is already prohibited.)

This proposed export restriction had been strongly opposed by the Bush administration on the grounds that it was protectionist. However, following the spotted owl decision, the sawmill operators gained a significant political ally—the American environmental movement. Environmentalists argued that the shortage of logs available for processing in domestic lumber mills was due, not to the restrictions on logging needed to protect the owls, but rather, to uncontrolled log exports. They supported an export ban on unprocessed timber for two reasons. First, it would help reduce foreign demand for American timber, thus helping to preserve the owl's habitat. Second, by promising to create upwards of 6,000 or 7,000 additional jobs in sawmills, it would soften the economic impact of the spotted owl decision, thus counteracting the growing perception that the environmental movement was indifferent to the loggers' jobs.

The Bush administration, now caught between pressures from the environmentalists and the logging industry, saw the export ban as a way of pleasing both constituencies. In August 1990, President Bush signed into law the Customs and Trade Act of 1990 which, among its other provisions, imposed a permanent ban on the export of unprocessed timber from public lands. In signing the bill, the president stressed its environmental significance: "There can be no doubt that high levels of export of unprocessed timber have contributed to the decline in habitat that caused this species to be listed as endangered."[28]

The president's decision to support the ban angered the Japanese, who regarded it essentially as a protectionist measure designed to save American jobs at the expense of Japanese employment. The legislation also created considerable concern at Weyerhaeuser, the largest private timber owner in the West: Following the passage of the ban on the export of timber from public lands, environmentalists indicated that their ultimate goal was an export ban on all timber, including logs harvested from private lands.

TRADE LIBERALIZATION

Public interest organizations have also become deeply involved in the domestic politics surrounding the "Uruguay" round of trade negotiations that was convened to renegotiate the General Agreement on Tariffs and Trade. Whereas previous GATT agreements only covered trade in manufactured goods, the Bush administration has proposed to expand the GATT's scope to include trade in agricultural products. This so-called "double zero plan" seeks to liberalize world agricultural trade by prohibiting GATT nations from imposing restrictions on the production, consumption, and prices of agricultural products; by forbidding the use of import or export controls on food and other natural resources; and by requiring nations to justify their environmental health standards for agricultural products on scientific grounds.

The purpose of the administration's proposals was to expand the market for American agricultural exports by reducing the agricultural subsidies and import restrictions of the European Community and Japan. In particular, the effort to "harmonize" world health and safety standards was in large measure prompted by the 1989 decision of the European Community to ban imports of U.S. beef treated with growth hormones. The United States had argued that the real purpose of this ban was not to protect European consumers (there was no evidence that the beef posed a public health threat) but rather to protect the European beef industry. By requiring nations to justify their health and safety regulations according to internationally recognized scientific criteria, the United States hoped to reduce the use of health and safety regulations as nontariff barriers by its trading partners.

The American position divided the American farm community. It tended to be supported by those export-oriented sectors that believed they stood to benefit from multilateral reduction in subsidies and trade restrictions. It was strongly opposed by farmers whose products were not competitive on international markets and who, therefore, favored continued government intervention in agricultural markets, including import restrictions. Organizations representing the latter approach viewed "the Bush administration as a tool of the multinational food processors, which profit from low grain prices and push the use of chemicals to maintain productivity."[29]

Opponents of the Bush administration's efforts to include agricultural trade in GATT stressed the linkage between the health and safety of the American public and the economic interests of American farmers. For example, the Farmers Union Milk Marketing Cooperative, which represents 9,800 dairy farmers in seven Midwest states who stood to suffer serious financial losses if barriers to milk imports were lifted or dairy subsidies reduced, urged Congress to "reject any new international trade agreement which puts American consumers and farmers at increased risk from unsafe food imports."[30] Opposition to the administration's GATT proposals was spearheaded by a coalition called the Fair Trade Campaign. It consisted of a number of local and national organizations representing the interests of family farmers, including the National Save the Family Farm Coalition—which represents 42 grass-roots farm and rural advocacy organizations in more than 30 states—as well as the National Toxics Campaign, itself a coalition of local and national environmental and consumer groups. The campaign particularly objected to the provisions of the GATT treaty requiring the international harmonization of national sanitary standards.

In order to prevent these standards from being used as nontariff barriers, the Bush administration had proposed to limit the right of federal and state governments to impose health and safety regulations on imported foods in excess of those established by the Codex Alimentarius, an international scientific body affiliated with the United Nations. The coalition argued that the Codex was dominated by executives from food and chemical companies and that, in many cases, its standards were less strict that those adopted by the American federal government or by certain state governments, most notably California. (In point of fact, while some Codex standards are laxer than American standards, some are stricter.) Members of the campaign further claimed that the administration's proposal threatened to undermine the ability of American governmental officials—and, by extension, American public interest groups—to determine safety standards for the food consumed by Americans, since their ability to apply these standards to imported foodstuffs would now be subject to review by an international body. The coalition's supporters feared that the ultimate result would be a lowering of state and federal standards, lest domestic farmers find themselves at a competitive disadvantage. According to the Natural Resources Defense Council:

The pesticide industry has lost the battle in Congress, in the courts, at the state level and in the court of public opinion. Now industry, with the administration's help, seeks to undermine state and federal pesticide regulations through the back door of international trade.[31]

Ralph Nader added, "More than one giant multinational corporation is watering at the mouth over the opportunities presented by the forthcoming GATT Treaty."[32]

In May 1990, Congressman James Scheuer (D-New York) introduced a resolution intended, according to a press release, to "prevent an international veto of U.S. environmental, consumer and trade laws." The resolution threatened congressional disapproval of the renegotiated GATT treaty unless the administration dropped its support for its "controversial" proposal to "diminish congressional control over domestic regulations." Scheuer observed that the United States "has the highest safety and consumer protection standards in the entire world" and warned that the "proposed GATT agreement could reduce our health regulations to those of the third world."

The Scheuer resolution rapidly became a focal point for opposition to the administration's proposed harmonization of health and safety regulations and to the GATT treaty itself. Scheuer's press conference announcing his proposal was attended by Ralph Nader and by representatives from major environmental groups. An Ad-Hoc Working Group on Trade and Environmentally Sustainable Development, consisting of six major national environmental organizations and a number of individual groups and coalitions representing family farmers, was formed to lobby for the Scheuer resolution. The ad hoc group focused on the environmental implications of the GATT treaty: It argued that the liberalization of trade in agricultural products would preclude "environmentally sustainable development" among Third World nations that wanted to gain access to the American and European markets and urged the convening of a special session of the GATT to focus on the environmental dimensions of liberalizing international trade.

The Scheuer resolution was never voted on, and by the time Congress was ready to vote on the extension of fast-track authorization for the GATT in May 1991, the Uruguay Round itself had become overshadowed by controversy over a proposed free-trade agreement between the United States and Mexico. (Congress voted on the extension of fast-track approval for both GATT and the U.S.-Mexico free-trade agreement at the same time.) In many respects, the former battle represented a kind of political dress rehearsal for the latter: The same environmental and consumer groups that supported the Scheuer proposal also campaigned vigorously against the free-trade agreement with Mexico. In both cases, political opposition to trade liberalization was based on an alliance between producers who feared the economic consequences of allowing foreign producers increased access to the American market and public interest organizations that regarded trade liberalization as a threat to consumer protection and environmental quality. However, the coalition of economic interests that stood in opposition to the free-trade agreement with Mexico was broader in scope than the one that supported the Scheuer Amendment. In addition to family and dairy farmers, it included citrus and vegetable growers, the American textile industry and, most important, the AFL-CIO. Winter citrus and vegetable growers feared competition from Mexican farmers; textile producers, from Mexican manufacturers. For its part, organized labor was worried that American firms would relocate to Mexico in order to take advantage of that nation's much lower wages.

Public interest groups argued, as they had in the controversy over the Scheuer resolution, that the free-trade agreement would compromise American health and safety standards. In her testimony before the International Trade Commission, Lori Wallach, a staff attorney with Public Citizen's Congress Watch, cited the American experience with the Canadian free-trade agreement that Congress had approved under fast-track procedures in 1988. She noted that American health and safety regulations were now subject to legal challenge from Canada on the grounds that they constituted nontariff barriers. For example, in May 1990, Canadian asbestos producers had filed a suit claiming that EPA asbestos regulations constituted an "unnecessary" barrier to trade. In addition, Wallach claimed that "one of the little-noticed results of the Canada FTA . . . was the dismantling of meat inspection along the U.S.-Canadian border." Under the new system, only 1 truck in 15 is inspected and the result, she contended, has been a "terrifying increase in meat imports contaminated with feces, pus-filled abscesses and foreign objects such as metal and glass." Wallach concluded:

If meat from Canada has proven a serious concern to American consumers, the danger of not reinspecting meat from Mexico, not to mention Mexican fruit and vegetables, is many times greater. . . . If the Mexico agreement follows the pattern of the U.S.-Canada agreement, effective border inspection would be all but stopped.[33]

The consumer and environmental coalition also contended that trade liberalization between the United States and Mexico would lead to a deterioration in the quality of Mexico's environment. Environmental organizations claimed that the quality of the Mexican environment had significantly declined in recent years, and they attributed this trend to increased foreign investment as well as the unwillingness or inability of the Mexican government to enforce adequate environmental standards. They predicted that if large numbers of American firms decided to take advantage of Mexico's low wages and permissive regulatory laws to shift production there, the result would be not only increased unemployment in the United States but also a substantial increase in air and water pollution in Mexico—some of which would then affect the American Southwest as well. The president of the National Toxics Campaign remarked, "We're fearful that the U.S.-Mexican border is already a 2,000 mile Love Canal."[34]

Ironically, while spokesmen for American public interest advocates repeatedly drew parallels between the health, safety, and environmental implications of the Canadian and Mexico free-trade agreements, the former treaty was approved without any opposition from American environmental groups. It was the *Canadian* environmental movement that opposed the treaty, fearing that it would result in a lowering of Canadian regulatory standards and in the accelerated exploitation of Canada's natural resources. For their part, most Mexican environmentalists supported the elimination of trade barriers between the United States and Mexico on the grounds that American pressure—along with American resources—would both encourage and permit Mexican authorities to tighten regulatory enforcement.

In order to help diffuse environmental opposition to the Mexican trade agreement, the Bush administration promised to include a set of environmental clauses in the final version of the treaty. In May 1991, Congress approved the Bush administration's request for an extension of fast-track negotiating authority for both GATT and the U.S.-Mexico free-trade treaty. However, although the environmentalists lost, they were able to extract some significant concessions. In August 1991, the United States and Mexico announced a draft plan to improve the quality of the environment along the border.[35] In addition, it has been speculated that Mexican president Carlos Salinas will negotiate the adoption of American EPA standards for Mexican plants located within 100 miles of the American border—a significant portion of which are American-owned.[36]

Equally important, the debate over the Mexico trade agreement was a historic one in that, for the first time in the long and bitter history of American trade policy, the health, safety, and environmental dimensions of international trade had become a focus of public debate. Previous disputes over American trade policy had primarily revolved around economic issues: They pitted coalitions of producers—and their employees—against one another. Now, a new set of interest groups had begun to participate in the shaping of American trade policy in Congress. Protectionist forces had acquired an important new political ally.

CONCLUSION

American consumer and environmental organizations have become active participants in the shaping of American trade policy. Consistently, their objective has been to prevent trade liberalization and to promote various forms of protectionism. The reasons for this orientation are not altogether self-evident; for example, inasmuch as trade barriers and subsidies increase the price of food and other consumer goods, one would ordinarily expect consumer groups to *favor* free trade and to *support*, rather than oppose, a reduction in agricultural subsidies.

One reason for the public interest movement's staunch protectionism is that expanded world trade reduces the ability of the American government to shape domestic regulatory policies. Fewer trade restrictions mean that a larger proportion of the goods and commodities that Americans consume will be produced outside the United States and thus, to some extent, will be beyond the control of American regulatory authorities. Similarly, a commitment to free trade places American regulatory officials under pressure to take the concerns of foreign producers and government officials into account in making American regulatory policies—lest such policies be challenged as nontariff barriers. Consequently, more liberalized trade policies threaten to undermine the power and influence of American regulatory agencies and their supporters in Congress. This, in turn, reduces the political influence of American public interest groups over American regulatory policies.

Moreover, the public interest movement's protectionist orientation reflects its broader political priorities and perspectives. The American consumer movement has, during the last two decades, become progressively less interested in protecting the pocketbook of consumers and more concerned about safeguarding their health. Indeed, on balance, the political triumphs of consumerism have made products *more*, rather than less, expensive. The consumer movement's current focus on the quality, as opposed to the price, of imported food is thus consistent with its domestic political agenda. For its part, the opposition of much of the American environmental movement to trade liberalization is as much philosophical as pragmatic. A significant strain within the American environmental movement distrusts economic development and international trade and favors self-sufficiency.[37] Environmental advocacy groups dislike development and trade because they view the two as causes of environmental degradation; the notion of economic self-sufficiency more closely approaches their vision of a sustainable society. The environmental movement's opposition to trade liberalization is of a piece with its general hostility to market forces.

Neither the increased interest in trade policy nor the support for protectionism on the part of consumer and environmental organizations are confined to the United States. In Germany and Japan, for example, environmental groups and their supporters have been strong supporters of agricultural protectionism. The *Economist* has commented that Germany's "environment-conscious voters see it as normal to rig the farm market so that their landscape is beautified by leather-trousered smallholders. The costs are ignored."[38] Japanese environmental organizations have entered into a de facto alliance with Japanese rice farmers, with the former contending that rice farming is needed to prevent the flooding of the Japanese countryside and protect the habitat of various waterfowl.[39] And, much in the way that American environmentalists oppose the destruction of America's old-growth forests, Japanese environmentalists have criticized their country's importation of hardwoods from Indonesia and other Asian nations on the grounds that it is destroying the jungles of these countries. Nor is the belief that there is an inherent tension between free trade and consumer health and safety confined to the American consumer movement. Japanese consumer organizations are among the strongest domestic supporters of retaining Japan's restrictions on agricultural imports from the United States; they justify their stance on the grounds that many imported agricultural products contain dangerous chemicals that are banned in Japan. Within the European Community (EC), many national consumer groups oppose the creation of a single European market in foodstuffs because they consider the food safety and inspection laws of other member states of the EC inferior to their own.

So far, consumer and environmental organizations have not played a decisive role in shaping American trade policies. Among the five cases examined in this article, only in one—log exports—were public interest organizations effective in achieving their policy goals. The same holds true for other industrialized democracies: Farmers, not consumer or environmental groups, are responsible for keeping American rice out of Japan and for preserving the EC's Common Agricultural Program.

Still, it would be wrong to dismiss the political and economic significance of "green" or "eco-protectionism."[40] The formerly distinctive policy arenas of protective regulation and trade policy have begun to converge. Policymakers and the public have become aware of the extent to which international economic activity, no less than domestic economic activity, affects health, safety, and the quality of the environment. To the extent that producers and employees who stand to suffer financially from liberalized trade find themselves on the defensive, they are apt to make greater use of health, safety, and environmental arguments to justify their case for trade restrictions. These arguments resonate with significant segments of the electorate in a way that economic defenses of protectionism no longer do. Indeed, the public interest movement appears to have replaced the trade union movement as the most "legitimate" liberal source of nonproducer opposition to trade liberalization. Producers are likely to find the political appeal of their position substantially enhanced to the extent that they can claim the support of public interest organizations. These groups, in turn, have learned that economic interests represent an important source of political support for their efforts to preserve national controls over social regulation and slow the movement toward more liberalized world markets.

NOTES

1. Ralph Gaedeke and Warren Etcheson, *Consumerism: Viewpoints from Business, Government and the Public* (San Francisco: Canfield Press, 1972).

2. Walter Rosenbaum, *The Politics of Environmental Concern* (New York: Praeger, 1973).

3. David Weir, "The Boomerang Crime," *Mother Jones*, November 1979, 40–48.

4. Mark Dowie, "The Corporate Crime of the Century," *Mother Jones*, November 1979, 23–39.

5. Ruth Norris, A. Karim Ahmed, S. Jacob Scherr, and Robert Richter, *Pills, Pesticides and Profits* (Croton-on-Hudson, N.Y.: North River Press, 1982), 97.

6. Peter Schmeisser, "Pushing Cigarettes Overseas," *New York Times Magazine*, 10 July 1988, p. 20.

7. "Thailand's Cigarette Ban Upset," *New York Times*, 4 October 1990, p. D19.

8. However, the panel also held that since cigarettes were hazardous, Thailand was within its rights to ban cigarette advertising, provided that the same restrictions applied to both national and foreign products. This ruling constituted something of a setback to the United States, which had argued that Thailand's advertising ban constituted a de facto trade barrier, since it made it more difficult for newly introduced—that is, foreign—brands to gain market share.

9. Schmeisser, "Pushing Cigarettes Overseas," 22.

10. Paul Magnusson, "Uncle Sam Shouldn't Be a Travelling Salesman for Tobacco," *Business Week*, 9 October 1989, 61. See also "Medical Association Assails U.S. Policy on Tobacco Exports," *New York Times*, 21 June 1990.

11. John Burgess, "Cigarette Sales Overseas Light a Fire under U.S. Tobacco's Tail," *Washington Post National Weekly Edition*, 24–30 December 1990, p. 21.

12. Schmeisser, "Pushing Cigarettes Overseas," 22.

13. "Tobacco Exports Rile American Lawmakers," *Journal of Commerce*, 2 March 1989, 5A.

14. "Medical Association Assails U.S. Policy on Tobacco Exports," A5.

15. Schmeisser, "Pushing Cigarettes Overseas," 22.

16. "Non-smokers to Urge Stop of US Tobacco Exports," *Mainichi Daily News* (Japan), 14 February 1988. In fairness, Japanese antismoking activists have also criticized Japan Tobacco, 100 percent of whose shares are owned by the Ministry of Finance, for its 1984 decision to begin exporting Japanese cigarettes. Japanese cigarette exports have since grown substantially; in 1989, Japan Tobacco began marketing its own brand, Mild Seven, in the United States.

17. Pete Engardio, "Asia: A New Front in the War on Smoking," *Business Week*, 25 February 1991, 66.

18. Burgess, "Cigarette Sales Overseas," 21.

19. Engardio, "Asia: A New Front," 66.

20. "Concern Rising over Harm from Pesticides in Third World," *New York Times*, 30 May 1989, sec. 3, p. 4.

21. Chris Bright, "Pesticide Export Reform Act Tries to Break the Circle of Poison," *In These Times*, 9–15 May 1990, 3.

22. "As Food Imports Rise, Consumers Face Peril from Use of Pesticides," *Wall Street Journal*, 26 March 1987, p. 1.

23. David Cloud, "Attacking the 'Circle of Poison,' " *Congressional Quarterly*, 9 June 1990, 1783.

24. Bright, "Pesticide Export Reform Act," 3.

25. Quoted in C. Ford Runge, "Trade Protectionism and Environmental Regulations: The New Non-Tariff Barriers," *Northwestern Journal of International Law and Business* (Spring 1990): 48.

26. Correspondence with author, 24 August 1990.

27. Ronald Elving, "Congress Ships Trade Bill to Bush for Signature," *Congressional Quarterly*, 4 August 1990, 2490.

28. "Logging on Protectionism," *Wall Street Journal*, 6 September 1990, p. A14.

29. Nancy Dunne, "U.S. Sees a Health Hazard in GATT," *Financial Times*, 1 August 1990, p. 3.

30. Press Release, 15 May 1990. On file with the author.

31. Brian Ahlberg, "Administration Trade Proposal Endangers US Health, Food-Safety Standards," National Family Farm Coalition, May 1990.

32. Ralph Nader, "GATT Could Get Us," *National Forum*, 16–22 July 1990, 1.

33. Lori Wallach, "The Consumer and Environmental Case against Fast Track" (Testimony before the International Trade Commission, Washington, D.C., 12 April 1991): 11.33.

34. William Burke, "The Toxic Price of Free Trade in Mexico," *In These Times*, 22–28 May 1991, 2.

35. "U.S. and Mexico Draft Plan to Fight Border Pollution," *New York Times*, 4 August 1991.

36. John Ross, "The Annexation of Mexico," Z, July/August 1991, 143.

37. See, for example, Diana Johnstone, "GATTastrophe; Free Trade Ideology Versus Planetary Survival," *In These Times*, 19–25 December 1990, 12–13.

38. "Trade Betrayed," *Economist*, 27 October 1990, 16.

39. Michio Matsuda, "Will Wildlife Be Harmed by Importation of Rice?" *Japan Times Weekly International Edition*, 3–10 December 1990, 10.

40. See C. Ford Runge and Richard Nolan, "Trade in Disservices: Environmental Regulation and Agricultural Trade," *Food Policy* 15 (February 1990): 3–7, and Runge, "Trade Protectionism."

9   CONCLUSION: ENVIRONMENTAL POLICY AT THE CROSSROADS

Fred L. Smith, Jr.

> The cynics are probably the least frustrated, for they never expected
> public problems to be solved in ways that satisfy the common good.
> Those who have other expectations expose themselves to greater
> hazards than that threatened by even the most hazardous product.[1]

It has always been with us, and it always will be. Dealing with it requires
good judgment and a sense of balance; it involves degrees of uncertainty
and, invariably, an element of danger. Dealing with it politically is quite
another matter.

It is risk. This collection of essays has illustrated the ways in which,
and the extent to which, the Environmental Protection Agency's risk
management policies have gone astray. Some of EPA's failures—clean
fuels regulations that benefit ethanol producers; a Superfund program
that has created a vast pork barrel—conform to the traditional political
pattern of favoring special interests under the guise of serving the public
interest. Other failures fall in the category of misguided risk selection:
The Clean Water Act requires enormous investments to abate so-called
pollution that has no discernible effect on water quality, while Superfund
mandates extravagantly expensive "permanent" treatment options, with
the result that hundreds of sites remain entirely untreated.

The challenge to improve on this performance is evident and urgent.
According to the EPA, America now invests well in excess of $100 billion
per year in environmental protection. We should seek to ensure that these
vast resources are directed to abate genuine risks and that they are used
as efficiently as possible.

However, inefficiency and misguided risk selection may not be the EPA's most serious failures. As disappointing as these outcomes are, they are not altogether surprising in light of our experience with grand social schemes in general. When it comes to inefficiency and misdirection of resources, there is no great difference in principle between the war on poverty and the war on environmental risk. Rather, the distinctive, and most fateful, consequence of environmental regulation has been a complete transformation of public expectations regarding risk. We expect insurers to mitigate the effects of unfortunate events, not to prevent their occurrence, and we expect doctors to cure diseases (most of them, anyway), not to make us immortal. Not so with governmental risk managers: We have come to expect that the EPA—and, for that matter, the Food and Drug Administration (FDA) and other "social" regulatory agencies—will *eliminate* risk. This expectation is as much the *result* of modern environmental risk management as it is its source: As described by several contributors to this volume, statutes such as Superfund, the Clean Air Act, and the Clean Water Act incorporate binding commitments to zero risk and an absolutely clean environment.

By promising the impossible, though, government sets itself up for failure. The result is an environmental version of Gresham's law: Utopian but horribly flawed regulatory schemes drive out more realistic, imperfect, but acceptable, policies. Having been promised, and having come to expect, a totally clean environment, the public is not readily persuaded that it must make do with less. The utopian pretensions of environmental programs, and the public misperceptions induced by those pretensions, pose a most serious obstacle to environmental policy reform.

One may be tempted to conclude that the combination of government-sponsored ignorance and entrenched interests may doom any prospect for more sober, realistic, and effective environmental risk management. However, growing disenchantment with current "command and control" policies may create a basis for reform. Moreover, one can at least hope that the dynamics of inflated public expectations will, in the long run, do more to undermine than to sustain the demand for comprehensive regulatory schemes. Government cannot possibly succeed in attaining the unattainable, and as the real and perceived failures multiply, we may eventually begin to address the question of what has gone wrong with the seriousness it deserves.

Broadly speaking, the reforms now under discussion fall into two categories. One of these comprises managerial reforms such as an emphasis on sound science, improved risk assessment procedures, and better interagency cooperation. As I will argue below, such reforms can remedy the more fundamental flaws of environmental regulation only to a limited extent and only if they change or at least counteract the political and institutional incentives that currently produce inefficient regulation and biased risk selection. The second category of reforms contains "incentive-based" or "market-based" regulatory tools, such as emission fees and tradable emission permits. Such devices represent a welcome departure from the exclusive reliance on command and control regulation, and some of them might result in more efficient, less wasteful environmental regulation, which is a worthy goal. However, as I shall argue, incentive-based environmental regulation is no panacea and may even exacerbate some of the defects of command and control regulation. The fundamental problem of market-based regulation is that risks would continue to be selected and regulated on political grounds, with all the attendant opportunities for special interest mischief, political abuse, and false promises.

For this reason, the case for *private* environmental risk management deserves consideration. Reconsideration would be the more accurate term: Until not so very long ago, risk management was considered predominantly a private responsibility. Most significant resources at risk were privately owned, and their owners protected them—in the extreme case, through use of the courts—against trespass, theft, and other risks. Individuals negotiated on risk matters, typically through contractual agreements. Private parties paid to shift risks to private insurance firms; private rating services provided information about the nature and level of risk in countless fields.

Today, however, private risk management devices are frequently dismissed as impractical or as objectionable for other reasons, at least in the environmental context, and such dismissals are usually accepted as soon as they are voiced. America seems to have fallen in love with political risk management. How did this romance start?

SOURCES OF POLITICAL RISK MANAGEMENT

The beliefs that government must manage and even eliminate environmental risk, and that only government can do so, can be traced to two sources. First, and most obviously, America has become obsessed with risk. Americans are among the healthiest, wealthiest people in history. And yet, we worry.

This is not a paradox: The taste for zero risk is one in which only the richest and most advanced societies can indulge. Indeed, our growing wealth and health are partially responsible for the growing discontent over the remaining residual risks we face: Having attained much, we want it all. We want no changes that entail risks. We are no longer content to take the bitter of uncertainty with the sweet of progress; instead, we insist on having the sweet only and rely on government to protect us in advance from the bitter.

However, as Aaron Wildavsky has shown, the effort to "have it all" is both paradoxical and futile.[2] It is paradoxical because societies become safer only by replacing the old with the new. Familiar products give way to newer ones that turn out to be safer (commercially canned foods instead of home canning) and less polluting (electric heating instead of wood stoves). This is itself a risky course; it involves reliance on such engines of change as science and technology, and it requires us to overcome our fears of the unknown. At the same time, we underestimate the extent to which scientific progress and increased economic wealth have made us safer and healthier; nostalgia has a way of concealing the unpleasant aspects of the past. When we think of travel by horse in the preautomotive era, we tend to forget the huge disposal problems created by horse wastes and carcasses. When we think of man's effect on nature, we forget nature's often cataclysmic effects, and we underestimate the extent to which material progress has enabled us to temper those effects.[3]

The effort to have it all is futile because attempts to eliminate risk are both tremendously expensive and, quite often, self-defeating in unexpected ways. "Playing it safe, doing nothing, means reducing possible opportunities to benefit from chances taken, and can hurt people."[4] Prometheus, the god of technology, brought fire—a fearful and very risky new technology. However, these new risks—of burns and asphyxiation, for instance—produced far fewer casualties than had the earlier risks of exposure to the elements, vulnerability to wild animals, and starvation. Thus, the introduction of fire compares favorably to the contemporary approval process for pharmaceutical drugs, which requires manufacturers to spend years of expensive research and studies to prove that a the new drug will be "safe and effective." The possibility that the new drug, though dangerous, might be less dangerous than the remedies now extant—which may be none at all—receives little consideration. The resulting "drug lag" has made the United States a far more dangerous place.[5]

Once society demands the elimination of risk, government gains a vast advantage over private risk management. Only government would even purport to pursue the utopian goal of eliminating risk; only government has the power and the resources to make such a claim remotely credible. Only the political process makes it possible to compensate losers—with no regard for their own coresponsibility—by raising revenues from less visible and less powerful sources. Only politicians promise "free" health care, "zero" pollution, and "zero" risk.

The desire for zero risk dovetails with a general distrust of markets and corporations. The underlying notion is that the profit motive encourages businesses to cut corners and sacrifice safety and the environment for profits. This notion either presupposes that neither consumers nor their "middlemen" (such as insurers, rating agencies, or purchasers somewhere along a product's distribution chain) can adequately assess the riskiness of a product or service; or else, it presupposes that most private actors are "one-time players" who are indifferent to the prospect of obtaining repeat business.[6] One cannot otherwise explain how the knowing endangerment of one's customers could be a profit-maximizing strategy.

Of course, private parties make mistakes. Pipes leak, containment dikes give way, and control or treatment technologies fail unexpectedly. Private systems are not immune from sabotage or error either. For those who are predisposed to distrust markets, oil spills and drug poisonings come to signify the inevitability and catastrophic consequences of environmental failures in free and unregulated markets. It appears, therefore, that individuals cannot be trusted to concern themselves adequately with the risks created by their activities.

However, *all* private transactions pose a risk of market failure in the (nontechnical) sense that they may produce, individually or in the aggregate, social results that are widely considered undesirable. Private transactions may perpetuate social inequality; competition destroys once-flourishing businesses. Still, we have, on the whole, become rather skeptical of attempts to remedy such ills by replacing private arrangements with grandiose regulatory schemes. It is only when it comes to the protection of health, safety, and the environment that alleged market failures are considered irrefutable evidence of the need for drastic government intervention. Government regulation seems singularly compelling in the environmental area.

In part, this is the case because many private activities do produce environmental *externalities*—that is, costs that are not reflected in the price of a product or service. Factories and cars do pollute the air, and as long as the air they use is "free," there will be too much air pollution.

Appealing as the market failure argument may seem, though, it is too facile. The fact that markets are imperfect does not, in itself, demonstrate the superiority of political strategies; rather, it calls for a balanced comparison of the respective ability of private and political institutions to advance the public good.

More fundamentally, the market failure argument proves far too much. If the mere existence of externalities were a sufficient basis for government control, political intervention would be appropriate in virtually every economic decision: Practically every private transaction has *some* effect on outside parties or resources. In the end, externalities are limited solely by our ability to detect and measure them.

This threat of boundless externalities, every one of them requiring political intervention, is not imaginary. Until not so long ago, the EPA regulated only a handful of bulk pollutants emitted from a few major sources—for example, large factories belching smoke and urban sewerage flowing untreated into the sea; now, environmental statutes mandate the control of substances at concentration levels that could not even be detected a decade ago. The EPA is rapidly gaining central planning authority over the entire U.S. economy. Six years ago, Richard B. Stewart, a law professor and member of the Board of the Environmental Defense Fund who, under the Bush administration, became Assistant Attorney General for Environment and Natural Resources, observed that environmental regulations and statutes had "created an elaborate system of Soviet-style centralized planning for the production of a clean environment."[7] Stewart's observation predates the 1986 Superfund Amendments, the 1987 Amendments to the Clean Water Act, the 1990 Clean Air Act Amendments, and various other enactments that vastly expanded the existing centralized planning schemes. In contrast to the Soviets, who at least had the wisdom to declare victory with the failure of each five-year plan, we seem to use defeat as a springboard for intensified folly.

Unless we want to march mindlessly down the road mapped out by the market failure paradigm and pave the road to serfdom with green bricks, we must begin to take the task of environmental reform seriously. In the remainder of this conclusion, I will argue that managerial and regulatory reforms may play a useful role in this endeavor. In the end, however, meaningful reform depends on our ability to recognize that the failures of environmental regulation are rooted not in markets but in their *absence*.

BETTER MANAGEMENT OR INSTITUTIONAL REFORM?

The increasingly widespread recognition of the failures and follies of environmental policy has prompted increasingly urgent calls for reforms of the EPA's decision-making processes. Once confined to a narrow circle of economists, the chorus for reform has been joined by political scientists, policy analysts, and, recently, by the EPA itself.[8] The reform agenda encompasses proposals such as improved scientific and risk assessment procedures, increased public participation in the agency's decision-making process, and government-sponsored public education on risk and environmental matters.

While these and other proposals merit consideration, they are ultimately unlikely to address the serious failures of environmental regulation. Those failures do not occur randomly or, for that matter, as a result of bad management (although this may occasionally be the case). Rather, they stem from deep-rooted institutional and political incentives that systematically bias the EPA's decisions. Better science and risk assessment procedures, public participation, and civic education, in and of themselves, do little to counteract these biases, and may exacerbate them.

Science will not automatically inform the policy debate. Scientific findings reach decision-makers only through the distorting prism of political power, and they are used in a political context. The examples of the political use and abuse of science are legion. A recent and particularly dramatic instance, briefly discussed by Jonathan H. Adler in his contribution to this volume, is the fate of the National Acid Precipitation Assessment Project (NAPAP), a massive 10-year study of the effects of acid rain. The study, which was released in early 1990, failed to confirm earlier suggestions that acid rain might be creating major damage to lakes and forests throughout America. By that stage the Bush administration and congressional leaders had already committed themselves to an extravagantly expensive acid rain program. The NAPAP study was shelved by the EPA and never received a full hearing in Congress. It is safe to say that the NAPAP study would have received quite a different treatment if it had confirmed the worst fears about acid rain and, thus, lent credibility to the legislation then under consideration. In short, the extent to which science informs policy depends largely on its political acceptability and usefulness.

Enhanced public participation, another item on the reform agenda, is similarly incapable of counteracting the incentives that bias political risk management. Almost invariably, participation is not "public" but highly selective. For the public at large, the costs of obtaining sufficient information and setting aside sufficient time to participate in a meaningful way are prohibitive. The likely participants are either business interests, who can easily bear the cost of the attorneys and lobbyists that the regulation game entails, or the leaders and attorneys of ideological public interest groups, who systematically favor comprehensive government intervention and whose views have consistently been found to be highly unrepresentative even of the membership of those groups, never mind the public at large.[9] In effect, then, public participation shifts power from the uninvolved majority to intensely concerned interests, and it increases the likelihood of political over private resolution of environmental issues. As a result, public participation has a tendency to exacerbate an already existing bias against the new and for the old; for entrenched interests and against the as-yet unidentified producers and consumers of improved products.

This is also the case with civic education, a proposal that has been advanced by both policy analysts and by the EPA. It is unquestionably true that the public is often inadequately informed or positively misinformed about the nature of environmental risk. (This very chapter calls for a radical revision of the way in which we as a society think about risk—a civic education project of monumental proportions.) However, civic education is an undertaking fraught with perils, especially when it is done by government.

In a very real sense, ignorance may not only be bliss but may also be rational: It serves as a filter that tends to screen out remote and exotic risks, thus leading individuals to occupy themselves with more substantial ones. It may seem desirable that individuals be made aware of *all* environmental dangers, including those posed by minute trace amounts of carcinogens. Realistically, though, people have no way of comparing these risks to anything in the real world; they become subject to information overload and scare campaigns.

To be sure, scare campaigns would be staged with or without government-sponsored civic education, and there might be a real role for the EPA in countering shrill but false fire alarms and calling attention to genuine risks. However, experience shows that we cannot trust government to correct public misperceptions. The line between education and propaganda is not always very clear, and it is crossed with particular ease when the issues are highly uncertain, as they typically are in the environmental context, and when a political agency has an incentive to emphasize risks that fall within its jurisdiction, as does the EPA. As Marc K. Landy has shown in his coauthored contribution to this volume and at greater length elsewhere, the enactment of Superfund was accompanied by an intense EPA public relations campaign aimed at persuading the public that the agency's public health programs were necessary to abate immediate and mortal risks.[10] The campaign was plainly motivated by a desire to build political support for an expansion of the agency's mandate and budget.

The purpose of these admittedly sketchy deliberations is not so much to question the usefulness of better science, public participation, and civic education in general and under all circumstances but, rather, to show that the usefulness of these policies and practices depends on the political and institutional context within which they are utilized. It is that *context*, which produces biased and misguided decisions, that needs reform. While this is not the place to outline a master plan for reform, we can state the general principle that any reform should satisfy and provide a few examples of promising proposals.

The general principle is to introduce reforms that simulate and institutionalize the competing and conflicting considerations that should inform the management of environmental risk. Currently, some of these considerations enter into the EPA's decisions only in a highly distorted form; others are ignored altogether. Decisions are made centrally and far away from those who incur their costs and benefits, thus practically ensuring that they will be influenced more by considerations of regulatory feasibility—and by national lobbies—than by the concerns of those who have to live with the results. The costs of regulation enter the decision-making process largely in a conceptual form: The agency may consider costs, but it does not bear them. Moreover, the EPA's mandate to preserve the environment and to protect the public naturally incline it toward regulation and against technological innovation, as does the fact that the potential beneficiaries of products and processes that are yet to be introduced and invented are unrepresented in the decision-making process. Institutional and procedural reforms should counteract these and other incentives that create a regulatory fantasy land.

To an extent, such reforms can be accomplished within the existing regulatory structure. The EPA has, on occasion, experimented with regional, decentralized risk management and encouraged participation by those directly affected by regulatory decisions. For example, the EPA effectively suspended the imposition of a clean air technology standard that would have shut down a copper smelter in Tacoma, Washington, and held local meetings with the goal of having local residents determine the appropriate level of pollution control and to make the trade-off between jobs and clean air. (The smelter closed for unrelated reasons before the experiment was concluded.)

The Superfund reform scheme proposed by Marc K. Landy and Mary Hague in their contribution is a variation on this theme of decentralization and greater local control. Their proposal would allocate a fixed sum to each state for Superfund cleanup. Each state would then face the decisions now made by the EPA, such as the selection of sites and cleanup options. This proposal would bring the decision closer to those concerned; it has the added and considerable advantage of introducing real-world concerns of economic scarcity and of destroying the illusion that toxic site cleanup is free. As Landy and Hague show, it is this illusion—which is carefully nurtured by Superfund's beneficiaries and by their congressional patrons—that has made Superfund an ineffective and wasteful program.

In order to counter the EPA's institutional and political bias against innovation, jurisdiction over industries and technologies that have not yet clearly been assigned to an agency (for example, biotechnology) should be conferred on agencies having both a regulatory and promotional policy role, or at least should be designed to strengthen the role of promotional agencies in the interagency regulatory review. Biotechnology regulation would much better be managed by the U.S. Department of Agriculture than by the EPA or, for that matter, the FDA. Since the Agriculture Department is charged both with protecting food safety *and* with improving agricultural productivity, it is far more likely to weigh the benefits of bovine growth hormone as well as its potential risks than is the EPA, which has no promotional role.

This jurisdictional solution is not a serious option with respect to regulatory responsibilities that have already been clearly established; the EPA is highly unlikely to relinquish its powers. Accordingly, we should consider establishing an Office of the Technology Advocate—a sort of devil's advocate agency which would be charged with making the most compelling case possible *against* regulatory impositions in the environmental risk area.[11] The Technology Advocate's Office would receive a fixed percentage of the EPA's budget, which would protect the office against political pressures, and it would obtain access to all agency data. In addition, the office might be permitted to pocket, for its own operations, some percentage of the projected cost savings of its activities. The office would provide an access point for—and might actually seek to mobilize—constituencies that are currently frozen out of the regulatory process or that are unlikely to participate but likely to bear the costs of regulation, such as small businesses, nonunionized workers, and economically disadvantaged groups that suffer disproportionately from particular regulations.

As part of its duties, the office might conduct a "postregulatory approval audit," estimating the public health and economic costs accrued to the delay of approval for such products as pesticides and other agricultural products. Sam Kazman has proposed such an audit for the FDA which, like the EPA, is highly biased against the risks of innovation and largely indifferent to the risks of stagnation and delay. Kazman's proposal would have the FDA (or possibly a third party) prepare detailed estimates of the public health costs of the "drug lag"—that is, delays in the drug approval process.[12] A requirement for public, official acknowledgments of risks that are now largely ignored in the regulatory process would eventually encourage a more balanced decision-making process. It would begin to simulate, albeit crudely, real life for agency decision-makers.

MARKET-BASED REGULATION

As the inefficiencies of command and control regulation and central-ized ecological planning have become more evident, proposals have proliferated to replace planning with more flexible, market-based ap-proaches, such as pollution taxes and tradable emission rights.[13] Such schemes seek to replicate the efficiency of normal markets by introducing pollution costs as a factor in private investment and production decisions. Proponents see such devices as means of internalizing the external costs of pollution and, thus, of encouraging more ecologically sensitive behavior.

In principle, such market-based schemes do offer several advantages. They reduce the regulators' need for information and technical expertise. Regulators need determine only the overall price or quantity of pollution; the pollution sources themselves then decide which firms would clean up to what degree. Since these sources know more about their respective cost structures and technology options, they are more likely to identify least-cost compliance methods. Market-based schemes also offer greater flexibility; productive (though polluting) activities are not banned out-right, but instead can continue where they are most valuable. Moreover, in contrast to mandated technology approaches, market-based schemes improve the visibility of pollution control costs, which may encourage greater attention to the costs and benefits of each particular pollution control program or, at least, reduce the tendency to view environmental protection as a "free" good. Finally, if the charges or financial burdens of emission rights schemes are imposed directly on polluters and in proportion to their actual pollution output, they will tend to produce long-term improvements in the availability and selection of pollution-re-ducing technologies and operating policies.

Still, market-based schemes have serious flaws, which stem from the fact that all such schemes embody the fundamental assumption that the socially desirable level of pollution must be determined politically.[14]

Even so-called pollution rights are *not* private property but solely a function of politically predetermined goals. Thus, the initial allocation of pollution entitlements or taxation levels will be subject to the very same political influences and systemic biases that now distort government decisions on risk. This is true, for instance, of the acid rain "emissions-trading" program in the 1990 Clean Air Act Amendments, which has been widely hailed as an efficient and innovative program.[15] Surely the real tax code—in many ways, a compendium of special interest provisions—inspires no confidence that a pollution tax code would be designed in accordance with objective environmental criteria as opposed to being determined by political clout. Moreover, the predetermined goals and, hence, the "rights" remain subject to political intervention and revision. Some groups will always find current standards too permissive, and firms may find themselves stripped of legitimately acquired emission rights. The desire to maximize revenue may soon drive out attempts to impose financial burdens in proportion to the actual externalities produced by each polluter. Highway user fees have taken this route: Trucks with very heavy axle loadings pay far less than warranted by the road damage they cause, while cars driving during off-peak hours are heavily overcharged.

Further, while incentive-based schemes may make regulation more efficient in a technical sense, but they may also make it *easier*. For example, EPA and Congress shun plant closures; for that reason, they seek to impose the toughest requirements on solvent firms while going easy on firms facing economic difficulties. Such strategies—which bear no relation to the actual amount of pollution output but take "from each according to their ability"—are difficult to implement through technology-based standards (although the EPA has managed to accomplish the feat); they become much easier via taxing schemes, which can be set at a level just low enough to persuade the firm to continue operations.[16]

Finally, and most seriously, taxes and emission rights emphasize means rather than ends. However, as noted earlier, EPA's primary problem is its inability to set well-defined, environmentally sound priorities. Focusing on implementation, rather than goals, would thus address the wrong first question.

In the end, market-based regulatory schemes are not genuine markets but market knockoffs. They are the ecological equivalent of the Eastern European experiments with market socialism during the 1970s and 1980s, which also sought to attain politically determined objectives by means of incentives and without establishing private property rights. The markets that resulted from these experiments were mere caricatures of real markets. Prices were artificial constructs and failed to provide the information and incentives needed to equilibrate supply and demand. Market socialism failed to invigorate innovation and productivity; eventually, it proved only marginally more efficient than Soviet-style command economies.

Command and control regulation is an attempt to produce environmental goods in the way in which the Soviet Union produced (or failed to produce) shoes. Market-based environmental regulation is an effort to produce environmental goods in the way in which Hungary produced shoes two decades ago. This is a small step forward. We can, however, do better: Just as some Eastern European countries are moving aggressively to privatize their economies, we can begin to reacquaint ourselves with producing environmental goods through property rights and private, voluntary arrangements.

PRIVATE RISK MANAGEMENT

We have become so used to the idea that the socially acceptable levels of environmental risk and pollution must be determined politically that we find it hard to even contemplate the alternative. The very concept of "free-market environmentalism" seems oxymoronic.

However, we have this reaction only when it comes to *environmental* risk. We do not normally believe that the government should determine and enforce socially acceptable levels of private activities—even if these activities create substantial risks and negative externalities for third parties.[17] The most instructive example is economic competition, which entails the risk, and often the reality, of business failures, job losses, and, sometimes, the ruin of entire cities or regions. It is true, of course, that the political landscape is littered with laws and regulations aimed at sheltering particular firms and economic sectors against the forces of competition and that the antitrust laws are intended to guard against unusual breakdowns in the competitive process. But such protectionist measures and government guarantees have lost much of their intellectual respectability, as well as a large measure of public support; we have come to understand that they help special interests but hurt the public at large. Nobody would maintain that the United States government should, as a general matter and for reasons of public welfare, determine and enforce a socially acceptable level of competition.

There are two reasons why we generally tolerate the externalities of competition. First, we understand that economic competition is a process of creative destruction, and that we cannot prevent the externality of destruction without losing the benefits of creativity and innovation.

Second, and perhaps more important, we understand that the alternative to centralized political management is not anarchy; it is private, decentralized risk management. We all seek to regulate our behavior—to anticipate the consequences of our actions and to act accordingly. In fact,

[Centralized political] planning owes its popularity largely to the fact that everybody desires, of course, that we should handle our common problems as rationally as possible and that, in so doing we should use as much foresight as we can command. In this sense, everybody who is not a complete fatalist is a planner, every political act is (or ought to be) an act of planning, and there can be differences only between good and bad, between wise and foresighted and foolish and shortsighted planning. . . . But it is not in this sense that our enthusiasts for a planned society now employ this term. . . . The dispute between the modern planners and their opponents is, therefore, *not* a dispute on whether we ought to choose intelligently between the various possible organizations of society; it is not a dispute on whether we ought to employ foresight and systematic thinking in planning our common affairs. It is a dispute about what is the best way of so doing.[18]

The question, in other words, is not whether risks should be managed, but who should manage them.

Private and political risk managers face many of the same problems: They must review the data, assess the level and nature of the risks involved, and determine the appropriate response. The case for *private* risk management rests on the proposition that the information on which such decisions should be based is far too dispersed and fragmentary to permit central planning. The political authority must make decisions for millions of individuals; since the "optimal" level of risk is largely a function of private, idiosyncratic preferences, the political risk manager would have to aggregate those preferences and, ideally, weigh them in some proportion to their intensity and their proximity to any given risk—a task for which even the wisest official is thoroughly ill-equipped. Moreover, even if he could somehow achieve this incredible feat, the political risk manager would still face the even more daunting task of motivating millions of people to act in accordance with his decrees.

One might argue that the accurate aggregation of private preferences is too demanding a standard to require of the political decision-maker. The point, though, is that *private risk management allows us to approximate that standard*: Myriads of voluntary transactions register private risk preferences and tolerances far more accurately than even the most informed and open political process.

Consider the risks associated with transporting waste materials across private property. Under a private system, the shipper would require the approval of the property owner to transit the property and would likely agree to pay a fee for that privilege. The parties would reach an agreement on the procedures to be followed in the event of an accident. Both would seek ways to shift their residual risks, and private insurance firms would evolve to meet that demand. Specialized risk managers might well be trained by one or all the parties to the transaction. The exact agreements would differ depending on the perceived riskiness of the transportation activity, the nature of the cargo, the extent to which the property would be harmed in the event of an accident, the property owner's attitude toward risk, and other considerations. Private arrangements, in other words, would take full account of the parties' concerns (but *only* the parties' concerns: Third parties might comment on private arrangements, but they would have no power to modify or influence them).

Although, of course, some parties will "get it wrong" and underestimate the risks involved in such a transaction, one can expect the private actor to generally outperform the political actor on a one-to-one basis. However, the proper comparison is not between the political risk manager and the average private actor but between the politician and the one marginal private actor who, among millions of others, gets it right: His decision will soon dominate the market.

A political risk management regime, on the other hand, will produce outcomes different from those that would be agreed on by private parties; that, indeed, is the purpose of the exercise. Negotiations of transit rights over politically controlled rights of way will involve public hearings which, as we have seen, selectively empower groups with an intense economic or ideological stake in the decision. Established economic firms may well use the occasion to restrict competition; for example, barge operators will lobby for high transit fees for truckers and railroads so as to raise their rivals' costs. Environmental groups, none of them with a genuine interest in the controversy other than an ideological one, may oppose transit rights on any conditions. In the end, the outcome may reflect *no one's* risk preferences.

Finally, private risk managers are far more likely than political institutions to consider risks in an unbiased fashion. Risks are ubiquitous; any decision will increase some risks and reduce others. The question is whether any given decision will raise or lower overall risk. Consider the question of whether a new technological process or product should be approved: The risks of innovation are heavily weighed by both private and political agencies. Change is dangerous, and no private or political actor wishes to assume the liabilities associated with approving a harmful innovation. On the other hand, stagnation and doing nothing are also dangerous. If only for competitive reasons, a private firm will take the risk of stagnation seriously. Few political risk managers, in contrast, experience any pain by delaying or even blocking change. The victims of inaction are statistical artifacts of a healthier and safer world that might have been; rarely do they weigh significantly in the political process.

MARKET FAILURES RECONSIDERED

Admittedly, the preceding section was based on somewhat idealized assumptions. Notably, it did not deal with instances in which private parties can impose external costs on society and avoid paying.

While such situations are common, they are not caused by the existence of markets but by their *absence*. Market failures might, therefore, best be addressed by extending market arrangements to the widest possible array of environmental resources. As the economist Ludwig von Mises stated:

It is true that where a considerable part of the costs incurred are external costs from the point of view of the acting individuals or firms, the economic calculation established by them is manifestly defective and their results deceptive. But this is not the outcome of alleged deficiencies inherent in the system of private ownership of the means of production. It is on the contrary a consequence of loopholes left in the system. It could be removed by a reform of the laws concerning liability for damages inflicted and by rescinding the institutional barriers preventing the full operation of private ownership.19

Rather than viewing the world in terms of market failure, we should view the problem of externalities as a *failure to permit markets* and create markets where they do not yet—or no longer—exist.

As a practical matter, we may wish to begin by experimenting with private risk management solutions in limited areas where the case for them seems especially compelling. Current American law, for example, prohibits ownership of endangered species. This is the environmental equivalent of prohibiting the adoption of orphaned and abandoned children. A procedure whereby environmental organizations or even for-profit enterprises were allowed to adopt endangered species would appear to be a plausible alternative to the current practice of prohibiting the development of areas that are designated as endangered species habitat. Private organizations such as Ducks Unlimited, the Nature Conservancy, and the Audubon Society acting in a private ownership capacity have proven far better stewards of natural resources than the government, and they have proven willing and able to arrive at agreements with private parties to permit limited economic development in environmentally sensitive areas. Such mutually beneficial arrangements have proven difficult to attain in the political sector.[20]

Although the project of creating markets may seem similar to market-based regulation, the differences are substantial—and all-important: A genuine market based on property rights privatizes not only the *how* of risk control but also the *what* and the *how much*.

A comparison with the ordinary risk of trespass illustrates the significance of this difference. We do not have a Federal Bureau of Trespass charged with defining the socially optimal level of trespass (certainly not one charged with *eliminating* trespass). The decision as to whether a trespass has occurred is left to private property owners, who also determine whether the benefits of punishing any given incident of trespass are worth the costs. Casual transit is likely to be ignored by all but the misanthrope, as will the occasional windblown litter and the smoke from the neighbor's fireplace; more serious events will trigger more serious responses. Pollution is no different in principle. (In fact, many landmark legal cases that defined the law of tort and trespass involved pollution.)

It is often objected that private arrangements are infeasible for practical or technical reasons. Emissions may be too small to constitute trespass, but, in the aggregate, they may do a lot of harm. Moreover, private property requires proof of trespass, and in many cases, the nature of the pollutant and the distances involved make such proofs difficult.

These problems are real, but they require closer analysis. To begin with, tossing them into the political sector does not make them any less difficult; it simply changes the range of possible solutions—and possible error. Since the optimal level of pollution is not *no* pollution, it is possible to err in both directions. Under a private regime, proof problems and the like will sometimes cause a failure to abate pollution. The political manager, in contrast, can limit pollution even without proof of damage (although, as we have noted, politically preferred polluters may still escape controls). But this apparent strength of government is also a great danger: In the absence of identifiable harm to someone or something in particular, the costs and benefits of risk control become highly conjectural. Moreover, precisely *because* no showing of harm is required to justify regulatory intervention, the purpose of pollution control is eventually disconnected from *any* harm; the productive activity that generates externalities itself becomes the harm. This, precisely, is the logic of the Clean Air and the Clean Water Acts.

There is a second, equally fundamental point. The facile comparison between the private and the political ignores the innovative capacity of the market and the stifling nature of government risk management. The private market's response to enforcement problems is not paralysis; it is innovation. The invention of fencing technologies—such as the development of barbed wire that permitted the fencing of vast areas in the West—is one common response to the problems of enforcing property rights, as was the earlier creation of cooperative joint venture arrangements to protect grazing lands from roaming cattle. But innovation *depends* on property rights. A world without private property might never, or only belatedly, have developed locks, burglar alarms, finger-printing, and other tools to protect property. Moreover, the great variety in people's sensitivities to pollution and other externalities suggests that a range of innovative solutions will be explored far in advance of the dramatic events that are typically needed to trigger political responses.

The fact that these technologies *were* developed shows that markets are not rigid, frozen arrangements unable to address emerging concerns. Private environmental risk management would create demand for monitoring and chemical fingerprinting, which could identify the culprits responsible for oil spills and toxic dumping. Environmental regulators, in contrast, have no incentive to promote or use such technologies and may even view them as a threat to their authority.

One can concede that there are genuinely difficult issues for which private, voluntary solutions are difficult to imagine; global warming and ozone depletion come to mind. But one must suspect that these problems rank so high on the political agenda precisely *because* they seem to illustrate the failures of markets, *because* they seem to defy private solution, and *because* they seem to require comprehensive government interventions. In any event, it is one thing to observe that there are difficult and seemingly intractable environmental problems; it is quite a different thing to conceptualize *all* environmental issues from the perspective of those problems or to presume that a political approach will easily overcome these difficulties. The former is a useful observation; the latter, a dangerous mistake that forecloses innovative and effective private risk management options even where they are feasible and sorely needed.

CONCLUSION

A politically owned resource is a resource at risk, and a politically managed risk is a risk that is on the verge of unmanageability. These two precepts do much to explain the current state of EPA regulation.

They do not explain everything. EPA suffers from the usual panoply of bureaucratic failures: an urge to be seen as "doing something," a hankering for the dramatic, an inability to reject trendy pseudo-crises, and a disregard for the costs that it imposes on private parties. But no other agency shares EPA's ability to create and chase indeterminate and indeterminable hazards. No other agency operates with such a total lack, not only of performance criteria, but of even the *prospect* of performance criteria.

A move toward private ownership would mean little unless such ownership encompassed the rights to use and transfer one's property. Regrettably, the rights of property and contract have been seriously eroded by legislatures and by the courts. Contractual arrangements have been replaced with tort law which, in turn, has been almost completely socialized. Today, courts often award compensation to parties who have suffered no demonstrable damages while imposing liability on parties who have caused no harm.[21] In fact, modern tort law has become an even more ambitious and misguided effort to redress environmental harms than regulation; government regulators, at least, are subject to budgetary and political constraints that establish some minimal threshold of regulatory concern.[22] Civil liability is constrained by little other than the ingenuity of lawyers.

Nonetheless, reforming environmental policy is not a hopeless task—certainly not in comparison with the tasks expected of the EPA which, rather than simply being extraordinarily ambitious, are existentially impossible to accomplish. Our knowledge of how political entities operate is growing rapidly, and if we focus on EPA as an agency, rather than on its substantive goals, our task may become simpler. We should view political risk managers as risky in their own right. We should concentrate less on the problems of political risk management, and more on the nature of political risk.

Like disease, political risk is not a necessary element of life. Like disease, political risk can be managed, treated, and cured. We seem to be getting better at it, and both old and new disciplines, ranging from economics and history to public choice theory, offer a wide variety of tools for dealing with it. Life is inherently risky, but it need not be inherently political. A world without risk may be impossible, but one without political risk is not. A world with less political risk is now being created abroad. Why not here?

NOTES

1. Harvey M. Sapolsky, ed., *Consuming Fears: The Politics of Product Risks* (New York: Basic Books, 1986), ix.

2. Aaron Wildavsky, *Searching for Safety* (New Brunswick, N.J.: Transaction Books, 1988).

3. Mary Douglas and Aaron Wildavsky, *Risk and Culture: An Essay on the Selection of Technical and Environmental Dangers* (Berkeley, Calif.: University of California Press, 1982) have noted that values determine what people choose to fear. Individuals focus on risks that validate and reinforce their values. Modern intellectuals, who distrust free enterprise, focus on the risks of economic and technological change and weigh natural risks much less heavily. For example, environmentalists give little attention to the massive quantities of chlorine, particulates, and acidic material spewed forth by volcanoes, while attaching great significance to the CFC residues from aerosol containers.

4. Wildavsky, *Searching for Safety*, 2.

5. See Sam Peltzman, *Regulation of Pharmaceutical Innovation: The 1962 Amendments* (Washington, D.C.: American Enterprise Institute, 1972).

6. The fact that "external" environmental costs are not always fully reflected in the price of a product or service, thus permitting the producer to ignore those social costs, is discussed below.

7. Richard B. Stewart, "Economics, Environment, and the Limits of Legal Control," *Harvard Environmental Law Review* 9 (1985): 10.

8. See Science Advisory Board, Environmental Protection Agency, *Reducing Risk: Setting Priorities and Strategies for Environmental Protection* (Washington, D.C.: EPA, 1990). This report, which contains the results of an extensive study conducted by the EPA's Science Advisory Board, has been favorably received by the EPA leadership. Perhaps the best discussion of "managerial" and institutional reforms of the EPA is Marc K. Landy, Marc J. Roberts, and Stephen R. Thomas, *The Environmental Protection Agency: Asking the Wrong Questions* (New York: Oxford University Press, 1989).

9. See Robert Lichter and Stanley Rothman, "What Interests the Public and What Interests the Public Interest?" *Public Opinion* 6 (April/May 1983): 44-48.

10. Landy, Roberts, and Thomas, *Asking the Wrong Questions*.

11. Its explicitly "partial" role and mission distinguish the Office of the Technology Advocate from existing institutions that examine the impact of EPA regulations, such as the Office of Management and Budget and the Office of Technology Assessment.

12. Sam Kazman, "Deadly Overcaution: FDA's Drug Approval Process," *Journal of Regulation and Social Cost* 1 (September 1990): 35-54.

13. There is a vast literature on this topic. See, for example, T. H. Tietenberg, *Emission Trading: An Exercise in Reforming Pollution Policy* (Washington, D.C.: Resources for the Future, 1985). Recent applied efforts have paid more attention to the nuances of these ideas and have sought to relate them to specific policy goals. See, for example, Robert Stavins, "Clean Profits: Using Economic Incentives to Protect the Environment," *Policy Review* (Spring 1989): 58-63. See also my response to that article, Fred

Smith, "Let's Pretend Markets," *Policy Review* (Summer 1989): 94–95; and Stavin's reply in that same issue, 95–96.

14. The basic arguments for and against market socialism were exchanged in the 1930s between F. A. Hayek and Oscar Lange. See F. A. Hayek, *Collectivist Economic Planning: Critical Studies on the Possibilities of Socialism* (London: Routledge Press, 1935); and F. A. Hayek, *Individualism and Economic Order* (Chicago: University of Chicago Press, 1948). See further, Donald Lavoie, *National Economic Planning: What Is Left?* (Cambridge, Mass.: Ballinger Publishing Company, 1985).

15. See Francis S. Blake, "Tilting the Marketplace," *Regulation* 13 (Summer 1990): 5.

16. Robert A. Leone, Richard Startz, and Mark Farber, "The Economic Impact of the Federal Water Pollution Control Act Amendments of 1972 on the Paper and Pulp Industry," National Bureau of Economic Research, Inc., report prepared for the National Commission on Water Quality, 15 June 1975.

17. The exceptions, of course, are force and fraud, which are *criminal* activities.

18. F. A. Hayek, "The New Confusion about Planning," in Hayek, *New Studies in Philosophy, Politics, Economics, and the History of Ideas* (Chicago: University of Chicago Press, 1978), 234.

19. Ludwig von Mises, *Human Action: A Treatise on Economics*, 3rd rev. ed. (Chicago: Henry Regnery Co., 1966), 657–658.

20. Obviously, this is not the place to develop a full agenda for the creation of markets to protect the environment. A comprehensive treatment of the subject is Terry L. Anderson and Donald L. Leal, *Free Market Environmentalism* (San Francisco: Pacific Research Institute; Boulder, Colo.: Westview Press, 1991).

21. See Peter W. Huber, *Liability: The Legal Revolution and Its Consequences* (New York: Basic Books, 1988).

22. George L. Priest, "The New Legal Structure of Risk Control," *Daedalus* (Fall 1990): 208.

SELECTED BIBLIOGRAPHY

Ackerman, Bruce A., and William T. Hassler. *Clean Coal, Dirty Air*. New Haven, Conn.: Yale University Press, 1981.

Anderson, Terry L., and Donald L. Leal. *Free Market Environmentalism*. San Francisco: Pacific Research Institute; Boulder, Colo.; Westview Press, 1991.

Benedick, Richard E. *Ozone Diplomacy: New Directions in Safeguarding the Planet*. Cambridge, Mass.: Harvard University Press, 1991.

Buchanan, James M., and Robert D. Tollison, eds. *The Theory of Public Choice-II*. Ann Arbor: University of Michigan Press, 1984.

Clarkson, Kenneth, and Timothy Muris, eds. *The Federal Trade Commission since 1970*. Cambridge: Cambridge University Press, 1981.

Crandall, Robert. *Controlling Industrial Pollution: The Economics and Politics of Clean Air*. Washington, D.C.: Brookings Institution, 1983.

Dotto, Lydia, and Harold Schiff. *The Ozone War*. Garden City, N.Y.: Doubleday, 1978.

Douglas, Mary, and Aaron Wildavsky. *Risk and Culture: An Essay on the Selection of Technical and Environmental Dangers*. Berkeley, Calif.: University of California Press, 1982.

Environmental Protection Agency, Science Advisory Board. *Reducing Risk: Setting Priorities and Strategies for Environmental Protection*. Washington, D.C: EPA, 1990.

Gaedeke, Ralph, and Warren Etcheson. *Consumerism: Viewpoints from Business, Government and the Public*. San Francisco: Canfield Press, 1972.

Harris, Richard A., and Sidney M. Milkis. *The Politics of Regulatory Change: A Tale of Two Agencies*. New York: Oxford University Press, 1989.

Hayek, F. A. *Collectivist Economic Planning: Critical Studies on the Possibilities of Socialism*. London: Routledge Press, 1935.

———. *Individualism and Economic Order*. Chicago: University of Chicago Press, 1948.

———. *New Studies in Philosophy, Politics, Economics, and the History of Ideas*. Chicago: Unversity of Chicago Press, 1978, p. 234.

Huber, Peter W. *Liability: The Legal Revolution and Its Consequences*. New York: Basic Books, 1988.

Landy, Marc K., Marc J. Roberts, and Stephen R. Thomas. *The Environmental Protection Agency: Asking the Wrong Questions*. Oxford, England: Oxford University Press, 1989.

Lavoie, Donald. *National Economic Planning: What Is Left?* Cambridge, Mass.: Ballinger Publishing, 1985.

Leone, Robert A. *Who Profits: Winners, Losers and Government Regulation*. New York: Basic Books, 1986.

Meiners, Roger E., and Bruce Yandle, eds. *Regulation and the Reagan Era*. New York: Holmes and Meier, 1989.

Melnick, R. Shep. *Regulation and the Courts*. Washington, D.C.: Brookings Institution, 1984.

Molnar, Joseph J., and Henry Kunnucan. *Biotechnology and the New Agricultural Revolution*. Boulder, Colo.: Westview Press, 1989.

Noll, Roger, and Bruce M. Owen. *The Political Economy of Deregulation*. Washington, D.C.: American Enterprise Institute, 1983.

Norris, Ruth, A. Karim Ahmed, S. Jacob Scherr, and Robert Richter. *Pills, Pesticides and Profits*. Croton-on-Hudson, N.Y.: North River Press, 1982.

Ornstein, Norman J., ed. *Congress in Change: Evolution and Reform*. New York: Praeger, 1975.

Ostrom, Elinor. *Governing the Commons: The Evolution of Institutions for Collective Action*. Cambridge: Cambridge University Press, 1990.

Peltzman, Sam. *Regulation of Pharmaceutical Innovation: The 1962 Amendments*. Washington, D.C.: The American Enterprise Institute, 1972.

Rosenbaum, Walter. *The Politics of Environmental Concern*. New York: Praeger, 1973.

Sapolsky, Harvey M., ed. *Consuming Fears: The Politics of Product Risks*. New York: Basic Books, 1986.

Singer, S. Fred. *Global Climate Change: Human and Natural Influences*. New York: Paragon House, 1989.

Vig, Norman, and Michael Kraft, eds. *Environmental Policy in the 1980's: Reagan's New Agenda*. Washington, D.C.: CQ Press, 1984.

Vogel, David. *Fluctuating Fortunes*. New York: Basic Books, 1989.

Von Mises, Ludwig. *Human Action: A Treatise on Economics*. 3rd rev. ed. Chicago: Henry Regnery Co., 1966.

Wildavsky, Aaron. *Searching for Safety*. New Brunswick, N.J.: Transaction Books, 1988.

Yandle, Bruce. *The Political Limits of Environmental Regulation*. New York: Quorum Books, 1989.

INDEX

ABOUT THE EDITORS AND CONTRIBUTORS

MICHAEL S. GREVE is a founder and Executive Director of the Center for Individual Rights, a public interest law firm. He received his Ph.D. in government from Cornell University in 1987 and has taught political science at Hunter College and John Jay College in New York City. His articles on environmental policy and administrative and constitutional law have appeared in the *Tulane Law Review*, the *Cornell International Law Journal*, the *Journal of Law and Politics*, and other publications.

FRED L. SMITH, JR., is the founder and President of the Competitive Enterprise Institute in Washington, D.C. He previously served as a Senior Policy Analyst at the Environmental Protection Agency and a Senior Research Economist at the Association of American Railroads. His numerous articles on public policy issues have appeared in such publications as the *Wall Street Journal*, *New York Times*, *Washington Post*, and *Regulation*.

JONATHAN H. ADLER is an environmental policy analyst at the Competitive Enterprise Institute. His articles on environmental issues have appeared in such publications as the *Los Angeles Times*, *Detroit News*, and *Christian Science Monitor*.

CHRISTOPHER L. CULP is an adjunct policy analyst at the Competitive Enterprise Institute. He is pursuing a Ph.D. in corporation finance and industrial organization at the University of Chicago, Graduate School of Business.

MARY HAGUE is a doctoral candidate in political science at Boston College.

MARC K. LANDY is an associate professor of political science at Boston College and a senior research fellow at the Gordon Center for Public Policy. He is the author, with Marc Roberts and Stephen Thomas, of *The Environmental Protection Agency: Asking the Wrong Questions*.

DANIEL F. McINNIS is a law student at Georgetown University Law Center and a former environmental policy analyst with the Competitive Enterprise Institute.

R. SHEP MELNICK is an associate professor of politics at Brandeis University and the codirector of the Program on Constitutional Government at Harvard University. He is the author of *Regulation and the Courts: The Case of the Clean Air Act*.

DAVID VOGEL is a professor of business and public policy at the University of California at Berkeley. He is the author of numerous books and articles on business regulation including, most recently, *Fluctuating Fortunes: The Political Power of Business in America*.